How to
RAISE an
Indigo Child

How to
RAISE an
Indigo Child

10 Keys for Cultivating a Child's Natural Brilliance

by
Barbara Condron
D.M. D.D. B.J.

published by the
School of Metaphysics
Windyville, Missouri 65783

© December 2003

Library of Congress Control Number 2003113186

Library of Congress Cataloging in Publication Data
Condron, Barbara G
      How to Raise an Indigo Child
      10 Keys for Cultivating Your Child's Natural Brilliance

      Summary: The evolution of the talented and gifted child produces new paradigms for parents and society to meet the needs of these multidimensional children.

ISBN: 0-944386-29-6
October 2002 by the School of Metaphysics No. 100175
Photographs by Daniel Condron, Paul Blosser, Barbara Condron, Paul Madar

PRINTED IN THE UNITED STATES OF AMERICA

If you desire to learn more about the research and teachings in this book, write to School of Metaphysics World Headquarters, Windyville, Missouri 65783. Or call us at 417-345-8411.

Visit us on the Internet at www.som.org

Who are the *Indigo* Children?

The reality of these exceptional children, who are coming into our world in increasing numbers, was first noted by Nancy Ann Tappe who coined the descriptive term in her 1982 book *Understanding Your Life through Color*. Almost two decades later national lecturers Lee Carroll and Jan Tober brought the characteristics, needs, and experience of these children to life through first person accounts in their 1999 book, *The Indigo Children*. It is my hope that this book will add to the pioneering efforts of their works.

TABLE of CONTENTS

The child must know that he is a miracle,
a miracle that since the beginning of the world
there hasn't been, and until the end of the world
there will not be another child like him.

–Pablo Casals

Most mornings Ki and I spend together, greeting the new day,
talking and learning. We may read a chapter from Abe
Lincoln's biography or clean the aquarium or do a mudra and
sing a song. On this particular morning, Kiah was waiting for
Carrie, one of his teachers, to arrive at 10:30 a.m. Needing to
ask me about a flyer for Dr. Laurel Clark's new book *Karmic
Healing*, it was Paul Blosser who came upstairs.

     Paul had been away, and when Ki saw him he decided
he wanted to be with him. Hezekiah was five years old at the
time. When he had his head set on something you could
reason with him, but when his heart was set, reason would not
sway him. His heart was set on being with Paul.

     Ki was generous about it. "I can play with Paul *and*
Carrie!" His bright smile reflected his pleasure in figuring this
out.

     Paul said, "Can we play a little later?"

     Living in the eternal now, Ki said adamantly, "No,
now!"

     Many thoughts flooded my mind – calming Ki, wanting
him to be interested in what others do thus grow compassion,
the need to respond so Paul would be more at ease, also the
desire to resolve the reaction before Carrie came. "First," I
said, "Carrie is probably on her way right now. She's planning
to play with you. Paul told you he will play later."

     Ki wasn't budging.

     "Hezekiah, Paul came up to show mommy something."

     He could stretch to realize the truth of this. "Okay," he
replied in that Indigo royal tone. "Half an hour." I had to
smile because this was a new development.

     The idea of physical time was relatively new to
Hezekiah. I had been very conscious about how I thought
about time and how I taught it to Ki. I had learned early that
he only respected the present. For him there was no yesterday
or tomorrow, only now. I relished the reality of that be-here-
now consciousness, refining my own ability to experience its
depth with each experience we shared.

T
I
M
E

The richness of being fully present connected us in ways I had experienced with students of all ages many times. The dimension Ki added for me was the immediate awareness of when my mind would wander. Every time I found myself out of time and space, more often thinking about things I wanted to do - books to write, sessions to plan, classes to teach, conversations to have - than things that had already happened, Ki would reflect it back to me. Sometimes through constant questioning, at others through insistence, often through emotional displays of frustration or anger.

Over time I sifted through my every reaction from "I should be able to soothe my child" to "You're making my head hurt" to "Others will think I'm a bad mother" and everything in between. Past all the busy mindedness of a brain full of television plots and very old memories, both fodder for an overactive imagination, I found the reward of countless practices in concentration: the still mind. When my mind was fully in the present, Ki and I had a great time exploring what was at hand. Whether reading, singing, investigating a rotten log or building a tunnel, doors opened to learning for Ki and me as long as Mommy was present.

My understanding of the separation of past, present, and future was multiplied. And what I would now consciously, intentionally teach this child would be very different because of it. I was now in less of a rush to teach him to wait, to put things off until another time. I could see why insistence of this kind is often met with resistance from any child. Why? Because it denies the natural movement of consciousness. It interrupts the complete expression of thought. That's why Hezekiah, and me and just about every young child I have ever seen, rejects the out-of-sync ideas adults advocate. Adults live in a fragmented world of separation. This counters the workings of the inner mind. It is unnatural.

Scattered attention is taught and reinforced throughout our lives. We continue to do what we have seen and learned from others throughout our lives. We try to think of three, four, five things at the same time, even value and boast of our ability to do so, until we wake up!

In large part undivided attention is the experience of the Indigo child. Their concentration powers far exceed most of the adults in their world. Their laser attention is so quick, so incisive, so pure, that a scattered mind can only reach it by altering it. The means to alter is often mind-controlling drugs. No one likes to think about this, much less talk about it, but ignoring it, being unconscious about it, does not change the truth.

We must learn new ways of responding to these children, our own children and grandchildren, better ways than putting them to sleep.

I want to be an awake parent. I want to help all children remain awake, using every day to become more Self aware. I want to aid others to do the same. This is why I teach adults the principles of Universal Law and how to apply these principles through life. This is why I have written this book, to share the experiences of teachers of metaphysics for the enrichment of your own experience.

It is our hope that what we are learning and how we are responding to the children around us will prove valuable for you and the children in your life.

–Barbara Condron
August, 2002

E
S
S
E
N
T
I
A
L

L
I
F
E

S
K
I
L
L
S

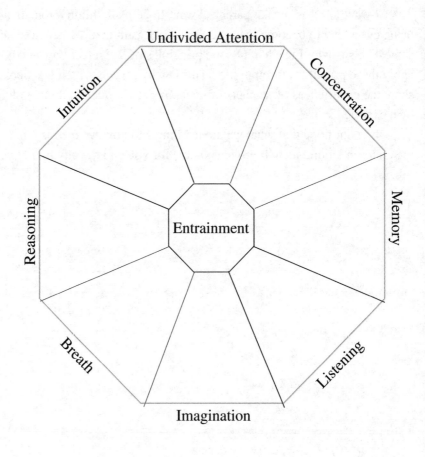

The Self Respect Bagua
created and being developed by the author

Indigos are predecessors to children of Light – what we at the School of Metaphysics call intuitive, Spiritual Man.

The 20th century began with the genius of Sigmund Freud. Freud brought awareness into a new light. Through his way of thinking and the work it spawned, consciousness became the individual's domain. Self analysis was easily borne from psycho-analysis and great keys for Self discovery were found.

Primary among these was symbolic language, the language spoken by great minds throughout history and until now heard by few. By the end of the 1900's, technology connected humanity globally. We had the opportunity to move our thinking from me to family to community to country to planet. More people want the freedom to learn. This opens the door for the Indigo who wants to be responsible for learning; who wants to teach.

In the mid-1950's, Americans taught their children to identify life by segmented, fragmented desires for physical things. This is more than materialism, although certainly as the world's largest consumers the people of the United States can claim this label. I was raised in the household of an evangelical preacher. Spiritual matters were ever-present, from praying before every meal to Bible reading to miraculous faith healings. I learned spirit from the time I was born.

I learned materialism at school.

"What do you want to be when you grow up?" takes on new meaning in the 21st century. The answers move beyond doctor, lawyer, fireman, chief. Indigos have values that differ from their parents. *What* is less important to them than *who*.

When I was a teenager, facing the need to choose what I would do with my life, my desires changed daily. It was years before I understood my inner desire for leadership was the seed of the outward claim that I wanted to be the first female president of the U.S. From entertainer to U.N. interpreter to Olympic skater, they were all activities I wanted to pursue. I wanted it all. So do Indigos.

As the years passed, I fought the idea that I would have to choose one thing that I would do the rest of my life. I could not fathom it. I realized even at fifteen how boring, limiting, frustrating such a life would be. By 17, I was poised to go to college, the great American dream of my parent's generation. I felt pressured to choose a field. I knew to do well, to use all resources to their fullest (time, money, scholarships, etc.), I had to choose a single area of concentration, an area where I could get my degree. My major, journalism, was my second choice. Psychology was my first.

I wanted to understand people. I wanted to understand myself. I wanted to understand why we think as we do, why sometimes we agree and other times we don't. I thought psychology was an avenue to find those answers. Erroneously or not, I believed it would take eight years and more money than I had to become a psychiatrist. This restriction became part of my greatest fortune for it meant I pursued psychology as a sideline, a minor area of study. It also meant I had to go further in my thinking because I still had to determine a major.

Upon further reflection I figured out that what I wanted was not a "what", it was a "how." I wanted to continue learning, to continue meeting new people. I believed journalism could satisfy that. So, I might never be president, but I could meet one, or two, or a hundred. I could interview a U.N. interpreter, a teacher, an astronaut, a Nobel prize winner, the butcher, the baker, the candlestick maker – for a while sharing their lives, their perspectives. I could live a creative life.

At the time I didn't realize the construction of my thinking was mystical. Classical Indigos need more than desire to unite, to understand Self and others and the connection between the two. This need would, in time, be the driving force in me that would get me to the School of Metaphysics. The study of consciousness was not so much a conscious desire, as a subconscious edict.

I had to know.

I had to change.

I had to learn how to become that change.

I was here to build a bridge, and to build it I needed to learn how. *Being alive* was always more than what I wanted to be when I grew up. It has always been about how I can be everything I am to be. Now.

So it is with Indigos. They live fully in the present. They resist being physicalized with rules of order that defy creative thought. They are here to bring something to the world. They may not know what that is, but there is no denying the willful presence that ties them to their ethereal, spiritual destiny.

Indigos are predecessors to full spectrum children. For this reason, Indigos, like the talented and gifted who preceded them, desire to function as a whole Self. They do not settle for remaining unconscious and so as infants they are not prone to sleep, and when they do they talk and walk and emote as if awake.

I remember asking an endless chain of "whys?" – that to this day continue – only to be thwarted by loving but frustrated parents and grandparents who cared enough to want me to get what they believed was a good education. I pleased them with my grades and scholarships and proofs of appreciation, but what I found was that existing public education fed my brain while frustrating my soul. Through my young years, I also drew to me some exceptional teachers who fed my starving soul, often outside of the confines of the 8-4 p.m. curriculum. I learned from an early age, life is about people, about souls, about whole Selves.

We all enter this life as mystical children. We are all full spectrum beings. We begin physical life knowing we are all the same, alike. Some of us never let go of this awareness, even when life's lessons are tough. Indigos are like this. The awareness is always present. Omnipresence. You and I must find ways to foster and empower that awareness to reach its full potential.

This book is about the Essential Life Skills that every soul wants to learn. It is told by people who are dedicated to living and teaching the how's of human consciousness so our souls can flourish and prosper.

R
E
S
P
E
C
T

Hezekiah & Dr. Pam discovering
their reflections in the pond

The New Teacher

At six, Hezekiah knew he had boundaries. He was not to go into the woods about a hundred yards east of the campus greeting center unless daddy or mommy were with him. The teachers knew this, then came the day when a new teacher arrived.

One evening Ki told me about some of the guys killing a snake. He told how he had seen it in the big rocks which I knew lay inside the woods some distance down the tree line.

"Was Daddy there?" I asked.

"No," he replied, listing those who were in attendence.

"Who were you with?"

"Paulina," he replied with that knowing smile on his lips.

"Hezekiah, you took advantage of her."

"How?" his favorite word could mean why, or what do you mean, or I don't understand. This time he wanted to understand.

I knew Paulina wanted Hezekiah to have what he wanted, and she wanted to be worthy of the trust Daniel and I placed in her. I also knew Ki loved the woods and he was smart enough to figure out that since Paulina was new, she might go with him. This was more than some kid manipulation, this was a Self-respect lesson for Hezekiah in the responsibility knowledge brings. So to him I said, "Hezekiah, Paulina didn't know you were not to go into the woods unless Mommy or Daddy are with you. *You* knew."

A bit begrudgingly he acknowledged the truth.

"Kiah," I said pulling him on my lap, "all your life there will be things you will know that others won't." I was speaking from my heart, with the authority that comes with experience, and he was listening. "That's a good thing. It means you must be more responsible."

He thought about this, "What does it mean, responsible?"

"It means loving others enough to teach, to take care of them when they don't know."

He thought about that for days. And he did not ask anyone to come with him into the woods again.

Respect is the powerful ability to use reasoning for soul growth. A far cry from the normal confusion with fear – as in respect/fear authority – respect is the product of owning our own experiences. Respect is believing that grew up!

The prefix *re* means both again and anew. From the Latin *respectus* meaning look at. When we respect something we are willing to see it from another viewpoint. Sometimes this means standing in someone else's shoes. Respect given in this way is the great equalizer that builds compassion.

Sometimes respect means stepping outside who we are at the moment so we can see ourselves as others do. Given this way, respect becomes a motivator for productive change. Sometimes it means being willing to think about how we will view the situation ten years from now, or at least tomorrow. Respect now becomes the doorway to reasoning, will power, intuition, and wisdom. Sometimes it means realizing we aren't two or five or twenty years old any longer. In this light respect frees us into our own growth so we can claim our own authority.

Sometimes respect is loving someone just because they are, not because they love us or we want them to stay or they like the same things we do or we think we owe it, have to, or should. Loving others just because they are lets go of any ideas of separation – "they" talk, walk, eat, pray, believe....strangely, wrongly, etc. – while inviting us to see the similarities, the likenesses, the relationship between Self and others. This respect practices the Golden Rule of *love ye one another* which is taught in some form by every religion on our planet.

This is respect that changes the world.

Respect is what the Indigo is here to learn, and to teach.

The Self Aware Parent & Schooling

I met Terri Pope in 1992. We had talked on the phone several times, and we became fast friends. Terri's connection with the School of Metaphysics was through our Intuitive Reports, particularly the Intuitive Health Analyses she regularly requested for herself and her family.

Terri is one of those rare people who have an incredible acumen for understanding humanity. In Multiple Intelligences she would be an interpersonal type, yet that limits her. Terri can possess laser accuracy in understanding and responding to people. That's part of her success in the hair design business and more importantly as a mother.

Several years before I actually met Terri and before Daniel and I were married, Terri requested an Intuitive Analysis on her son, Beau. The following story is from conversations Terri and I had about her experiences and why she appreciates the Intuitive Reports so much. Through the years we have had numerous conversations about the depth and breadth of wisdom gleaned from the Akashic Records. Terri can readily connect the information given in a Family Profile, for instance, to the dynamics of the people today. In fact, how she did this with one of her own Family Profiles, which centered on the women in her family, is recorded in the book *Work of the Soul*.

I wanted to share Terri's experiences with you in this book because I have learned so much by watching how Terri's mind works, through her fierce loyalty and love for her son and husband, and how that all translates into one family's living the American dream. The way Terri puts together the information from a health analysis which is mental, emotional, and physical information, and the physical facts and impressions she has from knowing the person, is an example of just how far intuitively-accessed information can take you. Through our conversations, she gives accounts of doing just this with herself, her son, and her marriage.

We started talking about a health analysis that was done for Beau on October 3, 1989.

"Beau was just 6 years and one month," Terri began. "By now he knew about the (intuitive) reports and he was listening. He wanted to know what happened to him.

"When I read about him having difficulty in distinguishing *'this one's own self identity from the identity of people around this one'* I just explained that he was a unique individual and no one else was like him and that's what made him special. That all of us were special because we are all unique and individual and there is not another person on this planet like us. I believe at the same time I was having similar issues with that. Explaining what the report said helped me to clarify my thoughts.

"I began working with him on taking in information and listening to the full instructions before starting to do something. I believed he would half listen, and I thought what was going on at school and what was going on at home were two different things. He had some conflicting information going between the two.

"At Montessori school they taught that when you take something out and play with it, you put it back up and that is follow through. If another child leaves something out, it's not for you to pick up. It's for them to pick up. You want to ideally begin a project, get to the middle point, finish it, put it away. It's one of the great things about Montessori.

"This is fine when you are at school, but when you are in the household, we all work together. There are household chores like dishes that have to be done. When you finish, put your dishes up. Help out with things. This was a concept that was beginning to be introduced to him that he had problems with because he felt "'I didn't do it, so I don't need to pick it up.' "

Terri's willingness to know what Beau's school life was like was an enormous help in understanding her son then and has been a contributing factor to his healthy growth throughout the years. It also made it easier for her to understand some of the information in his health analysis. For instance, about halfway into the mental part of the reading this report said Beau *disdains weakness.* It referred to a type of self-hate that I found troubling and I asked Terri about it. This is what was described in Beau's report.

This one wants to be able to handle things but feels inadequate and we see that this one does not like to consider these things for he sees it as weakness and this one disdains weakness. We see that there is almost a type of self hate because of this and we see that there is great difficulty in this one refusing to admit who this one is, where this one has come from, and where this one wants to go. (10389BGO)

Six is very early for such strong attitudes and I wondered if this attitude was brewing from what Terri had told me about Beau getting in kindergarten too early. I knew from my own schooling experience that kids go to school and bring home a host of thoughts and attitudes, some of which are unhealthy.

Terri answered, "I chose a Montessori School because I believed it moves at the child's pace. This is not what occurred for Beau. The teacher moved him up into kindergarten with the rest of his 'peers' and one boy was a year and a half older than Beau. At that age six months makes such a difference. The cut off date is September 1 which means if you are a certain age by September 1st then you move on into kindergarten. His birthday was August 30th and so the teacher moved him in. He was more of a four year old than a five year old."

Hearing her own assessment, Terri began thinking about Beau's situation on a new level. "It could have been brewing," she paused and I could hear the wheels turning as the images came up one by one from her memory. "My gut feeling is it had a lot to do with it because it was a major ordeal (having him wait). We had to really talk with him about it because he took it as he wasn't smart enough. I explained to him that it had nothing to do with whether or not he was smart. He is not of age yet, that six months at his age made a huge difference in your development and that in the long term I wanted him to be ready."

Terri's depth of respect for her son is clear in her willingness to assert her parental rights. Indigos need loving, disciplined adults who know their own minds and who will go to bat for them when the time comes. Terri is one of these.

In addition to Terri's clear headedness and foresight, she had a great deal of heart-centered hindsight in the way she communicated with her son. "I knew what it could be like because what happened with me was I was put into school as one of the youngest. Usually seventh grade is when it (the difference in ages) hits and at seventh grade for me I had problems. And not that Beau would or wouldn't, that was part of my thinking and I shared that with him."

Separating your experience and memories from your child's current experience is a milestone for effective parenting. It is one of the mental skills parents of Indigos have the opportunity to learn. The quicker study we are, the easier and more rewarding our interactions. Terri has a great ability to discern emotions. The way she put it, "The bottom line was, Beau showed signs of a child that was stressed. He was urinating in the trash can on the playground. It's a classic symptom of being 'POed.'

"I had no idea, the school did not tell me this. After two weeks, I met with the teacher because Beau had become a problem; I mean very difficult to deal with. She said, 'Well, now that he is in kindergarten...'

"I said, 'Wait a minute, he's in kindergarten! He's not ready for kindergarten. Do you think this might have something to do with it? Why don't we try moving him back.' And she told me her reasons for putting him there is he deserved to be with his peers. And I didn't challenge her on it, but one of the things I felt real strong about was I didn't care about if he deserved to be with his peers or not. What he deserved to be was in a situation appropriate for his age which he was not at that point."

Beau's health analysis substantiated this very clearly and Terri saw it. "The report states, *underneath this facade is the actuality of what this one lives in in his own thinking. And we see that in this regard this one does not want to take things seriously but does. This one wants to be able to handle things but feels inadequate, and we see that this one does not like to consider these things for he sees it as weakness and this one disdains weakness.*

"At this point Beau is six. He is well into kindergarten and he is trying to act older, bigger, than he is in the only way he knows how. He's not a bully so his stress shows in other ways and the teacher didn't know why or how to help. Her blindness to pushing Beau beyond his capabilities became apparent in more than the socialization field, it also manifested in what and how he was learning.

"At this particular time Beau would memorize books and when the kids would read, the teacher realized Beau couldn't read. He wasn't reading, he was memorizing. He tested on a fourth grade level for environmental and below his age group for reading and writing and math." Something more and more common for Indigos. The old educational structures and their testing methods are inadequate. "So we go into this. They are on me after this point for him to get testing, that there is something 'not right with him.' He has got a 'learning disability'."

The effect of all this on Beau shows very clearly in what his health analysis said about his emotional system.

We see the emotions for the most part to be ignored. We see that this one has a particular set emotional pattern that this one allows the self to indulge in and this one, although experiencing other emotions, does not admit them. Therefore, these are suppressed and we see that they do cause difficulties in the body at times. Would suggest that this one become more honest with the emotions as well and begin to realize that admitting what exists is not having to admit weakness. It is not a matter of whether this one is weak or strong.

"Well Beau had a great pattern to emulate because at that point Bob (Terri's husband) only had one way – I don't think he was aware of emotions or what they were. And of course, I was just perfect with everything," Terri said in her tongue-in-cheek manner. The comment reflects her willingness to see herself honestly and from the self awareness to open a door for change. The report went on:

It is a matter of this one's willingness to admit what exists and to face facts and to learn how to use facts productively. Would suggest that this is part of the ability of a reasoner and that as long as this one is not doing this, this one is not reasoning but is relying very heavily upon habitual, compulsive patterns and emotional reactions. In this way this one is being weak, being what this one most does not want. (10389BGO)

Terri and Bob now had a window into their son's mental and emotional state which validated their influence as parents and empowered them by understanding the cause of his situation. Far from being slow or disabled, Beau had a phenomenal memory that was being taken for granted and dismissed. No one expects someone the first time they touch piano keys to play like Mozart, nor palm a ball like Jordan, nor sing like Streisand. In time, with practice, such genius can come to maturation.

So it is with Indigos. One of their strongest abilities is the potential for photographic memory. When the adults surrounding the child value the mental faculty of recall, wielding it themselves, they provide both example and the greater experience the Indigo seeks. For above all the Indigo wants to learn. Now. Completely. Through experience.

"When I first received this report, I was confused. I really didn't understand. This is one of the reasons I point out to parents if there is information in a report you don't understand, talk to an alternative health care practitioner. Ask them what they know. If they don't know, find somebody else who does.

"What I didn't understand is *'some difficulty in the heart and circulatory system...arrhythmia... and the need to relax.'* When you are putting on a facade at school that you can read when you can't..."

Terri was doing one of the most important things a parent can ever do. She was putting herself in her son's position, seeing the world through his eyes. In the ten essential living skills this is number one: respect.

Respect is such a powerful attitude. It is the ability to see again. Sometimes this is recalling a long past experience, or imagining a future outcome, or standing in someone else's shoes. The result is an opening of the mind, a warming of the heart, a sparking of the will, and a connectedness with others. Through respect, Terri was bringing understanding into her consciousness. "You know something is wrong with you," she explained, "but you don't know what it is."

"The difficulty in the liver was also puzzling. Chemical residue? Beau was having stomach pains at that time period and the report spoke of light ulcerations there. When it was asked, *What would be the cause of these ulcerations?* The response was: *Once again the type of self-hatred that has been described, this is where it manifests and is in a worry that this one is going to be caught.* It made so much sense to me. This was Beau's fear of being found out. He was fearing he was going to get caught.

"So there is difficulty in the colon, respiratory, also when the respiratory, the colon and the stomach were all toxic, toxins would attempt to rid itself through the skin glands of waste and to a certain extent the kidneys. Beau had little bitty bumps on his skin, and now I knew why."

What the report said about Beau grinding his teeth when he would sleep helped put all of this together for Terri and Bob. When asked the cause, the reporter replied, *We see that this is a hold over of the attention into the day. The suggestion for relaxation mentally and emotionally would aid this one greatly.*

"We started reading with him, just to relax. Actually at first the reading wasn't relaxing to him, probably because it was a tense situation for him. We started doing tapes, like the healing waterfall and guided imagery tapes, which even today if he's not feeling his best he'll listen to those tapes.

Or he'll listen to them at night to go to sleep." Terri and Bob were learning about undivided attention as well as Beau.

When it came to the final suggestions for the parents, the report had timeless wisdom that is useful to every parent at any age:

Would suggest that these ones become much more invested in discovering who this one is, in stimulating this one to think and encouraging the expression of his ideas rather than attempting to mold this one in a certain way which is not this one's way, which is not in alignment with what this one thinks. We see that in the ways that these ones express many times there is the judgmentalness of right or wrong which this one has learned to take into the self and misuse in the ways that have already been described. Would suggest that rather than right or wrong, punishment or reward, this one be taught responsibility. This is all. (10389BGO)

Candidly, Terri said, "I do believe at that point we were telling Beau who he was supposed to be, what he was supposed to be, even though he was supposed to be special. He's supposed to be special in a certain way. We were definitely into what's right, wrong, punishment, reward, and responsibility. I can't think of an example of punishment or reward right off the top of my head but I'm sure we were dealing with that. Oh yes, Beau was biting kids at school and at that age they don't usually do that, and I bribed him with M&Ms. It worked."

Patterns are challenging. I think of my own experience with Hezekiah biting. We each figure out how to respond. Energy always seeks the least line of resistance. Like a river moving to the sea, in time its course can change. Or sometimes an earthquake comes and carves a new channel for that energy to flow through. Indigos are like those earthquakes.

Self Portrait
in the style of Pablo Picasso
by Elizabeth Vaughn, 13

*"We often lose our geniuses and our visionaries
because we don't see that they have,
in some sense an evolutionary mind,
a mind that perceives the next stage – a visionary mind.
So many of the great geniuses of the past
would have been utterly trashed in our society.
Saint Francis, one of the most disorganized human
beings who ever lived, would never have made it, you
know. Theresa of Avila, a nut by contemporary standards
would have been kept on Ritalin!"*

*– author and sociologist Jean Houston
in New Dimensions magazine Spring, 1994*

Indigos
The Evolution of the Gifted Child

When I was young I read books and saw television shows based upon the lives of famous people. Even as a young child, I saw the paradoxes. One person makes a global success out of meager beginnings while another squanders a fortune in reputation as well as money. I wondered why. Is it fate or luck that determines success? Is it predestination or windfall that determines a well-lived life?

The cause had to be more than when and where you were born and to whom, because many times this just didn't seem to matter. In each case, the individual did matter. Think of da Vinci, Einstein, Curie, Churchill, Plato, Confucius, Lincoln, Lao Tsu. Who each of these people became depended upon who they were as individuals.

If who we are, what we are made of, determines our success in life, each of us must be in control of our destiny. The inquisitive among us wonders what about the opportunities missed or passed by, the roads not taken. To the degree we can respond to opportunity, can we expect to produce happiness, peace, and security? I wanted to know the answers. I was led to believe that school would provide me with what I needed to find them.

Public school gave me a great deal. It introduced me to many wonderful people, living and dead, who would serve as role models, ideals. At one point or another I wanted to be just about everything, a lawyer, an interviewer, an actress, a pilot, a playwright, an architect, an interpreter at the United Nations. By high school my interest in helping people was steering me toward psychology. Our school didn't have psych courses, so I talked with teachers. I read about it. I educated myself and found not enough financial security in psychology and too much medical study and upfront expense in psychiatry. I settled on journalism, partly because I would be able to learn the rest of my life and partly because my scholarship to the University of Missouri helped financially.

What I learned came from the experiences I had in school and college more than the book learning. So six months after graduating I found myself wondering what I was going to do with my life. I was so depressed – with no goal, the breakup of an engagement, yet not wanting to return to my parents' home – I began thinking of how to get out, how to end it all. I'd visited mental institutions as a college student and knew I didn't belong there.

Therapy was a bit too expensive and I knew the basics there anyway. Religion was not an option because I had so many prejudices about it. So I fell into escaping through will busters for a while; alcohol, drugs, excessive sleep. I didn't want to face a hopeless life, so I ran from it.

Since then I have found a lot of other people follow this same pattern. Sooner or later you have to wonder, is this all there is? Like most middle class people I grew up believing that if I had a skill in life, a career, a niche, which are all products of schooling, then I could expect to find happiness and security the rest of my life. I'd played by the rules. Where was my reward for being good? The distance between my thoughts and my physical reality was oppressive.

Running never set well with me however. I had too much self respect. Just like the Indigos.

One day I asked the right question, "What causes my pain?" The usual suspects flashed before my mental eye, some, like my parents, were miles away having no direct impact on my life; others, like the ex-fiance, weren't even in my life anymore. I had to admit the answer was me.

Within a month of this life-changing, consciousness-raising realization I began studying mental law at the School of Metaphysics. Having been roused from the sleep of victimhood, I quickly realized this was the school I had been looking for all my life. Here I could learn the answers to the really important questions in my life and everyone else's. Who am I? Where did I come from? Why am I here? Where am I going? I wondered why I hadn't been taught how to find these answers earlier in life.

Less than a year into my study I learned something that helped me to understand.

In 1976, students and faculty of the School of Metaphysics were invested in educating the soul from birth. Many of us were parents or taught those who were raising children. The lessons we taught, the heart of the School, were then as they remain today for adults. We wanted to do something for the kids. Clean Up America (CUA) was our first answer.

The first year, CUA covered one state. It expanded to over a dozen in a few years. Clean Up America's mission was two-fold in nature. First, we demonstrated personal responsibility by cleaning trash along state highways. Such citizen initiative was unheard of in those days. People, citizens, did not go out and pick up trash! Governments hired people to do this or used prison labor, so John Q. Citizen did not have to go out and pick up trash left by Paul Z. Citizen.

Many Americans had become elitists. We could throw our debris out our car windows anytime; afterall, we paid taxes so somebody else would do the cleaning. It was time for a change in consciousness, and those changes always begin with individuals.

We began with ourselves, our friends and families, our associates. We became examples of respect by respecting ourselves and our environments. The School of Metaphysics has a strong reputation of visionary leadership toward expansive consciousness, and elevating our collective sense of environmental responsibility with CUA is a good example.

Interestingly, we had the hardest time convincing some local and state governments to *let* us clean the highways. For instance in Iowa we had to lobby the state legislature in order to get permission to pick up litter on state roads. We were not allowed on the interstate highways there. You would think the government would positively respond to citizens volunteering to do the job since such efforts saved some states thousands of dollars.

The momentary challenges we faced then produced big returns, causing a wave of citizen initiative everywhere. Our experiences paved the way for the "Adopt-a-Highway" programs available throughout the United States today.

It was the secondary purpose of Clean Up America that opened our eyes to the connection between the education the School of Metaphysics offers and the talented and gifted child. Knowing the value of the under-standings each individual possesses, we wanted to support the talented and gifted, so we decided to give one hundred percent of the money collected for the project to schools for talented and gifted children. It seemed like such an easy and joyful task! What we encountered was mind opening.

In a nation that affords all of its youth a basic education, you would believe we would also respond to the accelerated needs of the future leaders, inventors, visionaries, and explorers. We learned that in the United States of the 1970's much attention was being drawn to the handicapped or disabled child with almost none toward the meeting the needs of the exceptional child. In fact, "exceptional" child often referred to the "underprivileged". We felt very strongly that the talented and gifted children were natural leaders, children whose innate faculty for learning, reasoning, organizing, and initiat-ing made them outstanding. Fellow students, and teachers, often did not understand their needs. Peers saw them as bossy or different or loners. Teachers expected them to take care of themselves, and often other students as well.

The first year of the project it was difficult to find a school solely devoted to the gifted. Schools for quick learners were rare and programs often consisted of only one hour a week of studies different from the regular curriculum. Even in subsequent years, the funds were given to programs in existing schools or specialized programs statewide. We were not discouraged, we knew the work we were doing would make a difference in so many lives — the children, their parents, and ultimately all of us because these children would grow to become the leaders of tomorrow.

This is now true with the mystic children of today, the Indigos.

As the years of Clean Up America continued, awareness of the needs of the talented and gifted grew for us and for many others. Through contacts with teachers and parents we learned amazing lessons which we then passed on through lectures and radio-tv-newspaper interviews. I learned a great deal about myself, my upbringing, the root of my successes and failures in school, by interacting with the talented and gifted teachers and schools. In many cases the attributes of the gifted child are mirrored in what is now called the Indigo child. Compare the following:

Intellectual traits

Gifted child: Possesses keen observation abilities with an excellent memory. Their great curiosity fuels interest in a variety of subjects and they often possess skills beyond their years. Enjoys intellectual challenges, organizes thoughts well, displays good judgment.

Indigo child: Possesses keen observation abilities with an excellent memory. Desire to know is a requirement. Creative, unifies elements in what appears diverse, uses power of mental visualization. Organizes and catalogues information with great speed, makes connections mentally. Natural philosophers.

Academic Skills

Gifted: Excellent command of language speaking fluently with a wide vocabulary. Enjoys writing stories, poems, plays. Learns quickly, therefore, progresses rapidly. Knows and understands scientific information beyond physical age, keeps up with world issues. Can use advanced mathematic process and excels in problem solving.

Indigo: Draws connections quickly between subject areas. Technologically adept. Multi-media, multi-dimensional learning and application. Learning is based upon cause and effect relationships. Old educational model is left behind. Has preferred ways of learning, integrates broad range of information in innovative, creative ways. Use oriented, if there is a way to do it, they want to experience it, not talk about it.

Interests

Gifted: Persistence in exploring ideas, wants to know everything. Many interests and aptitudes, including art, music, dance, drama, graphic arts. High standard of achievement, perfectionist. Enjoys searching for information relating to interests. Keeps records, journals, diaries. Well organized collection of various things: stamps, coins, rocks, shells, insects.

Indigo: Everything. Already knows and has big ideas. Very interested in your thought processes, the whys. They probe other's experience to help them understand their own. Must be interested for something to hold their attention, when it does they are voracious. Inexhaustible energy when engaged.

Social/Individual Characteristics

Gifted: Independent, individualist, self-sufficient, stubborn. Bored by routine. Good sense of humor. Easily occupies own time without stimulation from others. Likes to be with and converse with adults and older children. Impatient with no challenge. Considered different by other children. Generally thoughtful, assuming leadership easily. Good sense of justice, dependable and responsible. Developing thinking.

Indigo: High self esteem, strong integrity, honest, direct, highly sensitive. Has a sense of mission and exhibits it early. Will not be dissuaded once head/heart is set. Demands choices and right to make them. Excessive energy leads to quick shifts in attention. Bores easily. Needs emotionally stable adults, constant loving. Innate healing abilities. Drawn to group thought when need arises, will not be isolated. Developing being.

The relativity of the Gifted child to the Indigo when cast in this light speaks to an evolution of thought and consciousness in human beings. Could the brilliance of the Gifted exist to offer guidance to the Indigo? To serve as a bridge for evolutionary progression? I believe this to be true.

A disturbing truth related to this came to light during our search for the talented and gifted in 1970's America. There were teachers for the Gifted, but you had to dig to find them. I could dismiss the absence in the small midwestern town where I had been schooled, but programs were equally hard to come by in metropolitan areas like Chicago and Tulsa and Kansas City. It became alarmingly clear that few people knew enough about *how to learn* to adequately teach these young minds. Left unrecognized and unstimulated, these children fell into daydreaming in an effort to escape boredom or into laziness because their half-hearted effort often set the class grade so why put out any more effort than needed? Or they became elitists, because they knew they were gifted even if others did not. Most gifted kids were growing up settling for a lot less and, as a result, their talents were being wasted.

In those early days, having my own children was not in my mind; helping those who did was. As I learned about the gifted child, I realized I was one. I had grown up. And I was still looking for a way to learn how to understand and use the gifts I had. Mental disciplines like concentration, meditation, and visualization learned at SOM gave me a scientific way to develop my abilities and measure them over time. The thought often crossed my mind, "I wonder who I would be, what I would be doing now if I had been taught these skills earlier in life?" That question which will never find an answer in me became a motivating mantra for me to teach the parents of the children who can.

Learning about others' lives, genius, contributions is available in schools around the United States, and in much of the world. This is valuable. It can be a profound stimulus for those with supernormal abilities who already have the imagination to invent a better mousetrap or the discipline to research a cure for a disease or the memory to deliver stirring speeches in a dozen languages. What about the rest of us? Is it possible to understand the workings of those creative minds? Can we be taught how to think like Leonardo da Vinci or William Shakespeare or Mohandas K. Gandhi or Marie Curie?

How does one become a mental gymnast, fluid in thought and expression? Can intelligence be developed? Can intuition be taught? Is mystical experience everyone's future?

An urgent need to know these answers is present in the minds of increasing numbers of people. People are waking up, realizing that maturity, wisdom, and self mastery are worthy goals in life. They are redefining life experience beyond the cars they drive, the money they make, and the people they know. In greater numbers they are viewing life as a spiritual journey for Self mastery.

This is where your willingness to excel begins. Indigo energy brings an incredible opportunity for reuniting the soul. With guidance from those who are already doing so they can excel. The energies are present for all of us to use. How we interpret our experiences, like the 9/11/01 tragedy in New York City, dictates individual progression. The degree to which we accelerate our own growth in awareness is the degree to which we can expect global change.

We may doubt our individual importance. Indigos never do. They have an inner link that connects them with the whole. They have a strong inner sense that goes beyond the fears that may have held you and me back.

And, free of mind control drugs, they will continue to embrace experience completely, moving beyond the polarizing world of light/dark, good/bad, right/wrong inherent in those who think with the brain instead of the mind.

The School of Metaphysics teaches the structure of the mind which makes understanding polarity easier. The ability for the mind to separate, identify, and admit its place in the scheme of creation can be taught and it can be learned. This produces respect for self and others. Attention, the sense of the mind, can be unified. Like a light focused into a laser, undivided attention enables us to completely absorb and give, mentally and emotionally, for greatest learning. Concentration can be taught as an art and as a science through the daily development of the individual will.

Memory, listening, imagination, breathing, reasoning, and intuition round out the essential life skills that every school can and should be teaching. For the parent, these are essential tools for raising an Indigo child. As we know how to raise the consciousness of ourselves, we know what guidance to offer the Indigo soul.

Living with people who understand the basic essential living skills and who practice them daily establishes thought patterns in a child's growing mind. Seven-year-old Hezekiah's length of meditation lasts three minutes. That's more than the fifteen-second, close my eyes and breathe deeply, of two years ago. Progress is easy to see with children.

Ki is around many adults who meditate daily, who perform life force exercises, and project healing energies to those in need. I am so grateful for this because I know what happens in the first seven years of our lives lays the foundation, the pattern, for an entire lifetime. These patterns are repeated throughout the life over and over; the strengths as well as the weaknesses. The strengths shine through the gifts and talents that come so naturally and are given so freely. The weaknesses highlight areas where the true lessons of a lifetime, the learning for the soul, are recognized.

Applying metaphysical principles and practices in your own life prepares you for parenting. I now know it from direct experience as well as observation. When you know what causes the mind to function, you can teach this to a child. When you understand the basics of disciplining the mind, you can teach these to a child. Concentration, remembering, listening, imagining, reasoning and intuitive skills are basic essential living skills. Your demonstration of these abilities gives your child an example of living ideals. Teaching them the skills gives them the best start in life because it sustains connection with the Soul, and this is the single most important factor in bringing balance and success into your life.

Self respect, the first essential life skill, brings personal responsibility, integrity, wisdom, and a love for Truth.   Imagine what you might be able to accomplish throughout an entire lifetime when spiritual principles are learned and practiced from a very young age! Imagine what kind of world we will create.

Experiencing God

God has many descriptions

His form is that of a tree, green and glorious.

He smells like that of a rose, sweet and vibrant.

He feels like a satin pillow you'll never forget to take on a trip.

He tastes like cookies that your best friend would bake for you.

He sounds like the faintest flapping wings of a butterfly.

I'm thankful for teachers.

– Briana Padilla, age 12

Kiah's First recipe

It is a custom at the College of Metaphysics that when the anniversary of a student's birth comes around they receive the dinner they envision. Whether hummus and pita bread with Greek Salad or meatloaf and potatoes or Seafood Gumbo and crabcakes, students delight in having all their favorite foods and enjoying those of their fellow students.

On this day, we were preparing a special dessert for one of the student's birthdays. Ki wanted to help. Flour, sugar, eggs, and the like were everywhere! We'd recently been reading a magazine that featured a recipe in one of the stories.

Indigos typically do something creative, different, new, and original, rather than follow the "tried and true". This showed itself through Ki. It is common for kids to make kitchen messes whenever allowed access, this is part of growth and learning how to hold tools, feel the softness of flour, and wield the math of measurement.

In Indigo fashion it occurred to Hezekiah that he needed to *invent* a recipe himself. He dictated just as it appears here. "This is for...

Coconut Whipped Cream

1st 1 inch of coconut into a container
then 1 tsp. of sugar
then 1 container of honey, 2" x 1" x 1/2"
then 4 tsp. of whipped cream

We tried it that night and it was actually quite good, although we couldn't get Ki to even taste it.

Respect
The Steps of Compassion

Respect is the essence of compassion. It is all the steps of compassion rolled into one beautiful lotus blossom. Acceptance, admitting, adjusting, affirming, allowing, aligning all hold their place in being a compassionate, loving human being.

In order to respect Hezekiah in his learning experience, I had to learn a lesson in Self Respect first.

First the thoughts of *oh, you're going to make such a mess!* My reasoning mind said, *of course he's going to make a mess, this is the first time he's been around flour in large quantities.* So where did this thought, this prejudicial idea come from? I made the connection quickly. The thought went straight to my mother.

The predominant memories of the two of us in the kitchen were not pleasant ones. This was one of the reasons I relished living in my own apartment in college. One of my first purchases was a cookbook so I could begin learning and experimenting with something I felt I had been deprived of. What I remembered about all my years living with my parents was mom's voice saying, "No, honey, don't do that, you'll make a mess!"

When I was ten years old I didn't know that every time you cook, you dirty dishes and spoons and mixers and pots and pans. Years later I would realize this was the mess my mom was talking about. The few times I remember making a mess in her kitchen, when I cleaned it up, it didn't suit her. She would rather have had her perfectly groomed kitchen than the birthday cake or seafood gumbo I made.

So I grew up with a great desire to cook. I also grew up holding onto an old, increasingly outdated thought that cooking meant making a mess. The positive side of this was when I would create a culinary masterpiece, I would strive to clean as I went thus leaving a beautiful kitchen even mom would approve of.

These thoughts in the forefront of my mind, right out there where I could take a good look at them, told me I had passed the first test of **acceptance**. This thought of making a mess was mine, not my son's. He didn't want to make a mess.

He wanted to learn.

Just like me!

Acceptance opened the door for my second lesson: **admitting**. Just intellectually diagnosing what was going on did not change the cringes I felt seeing Hezekiah dig into the huge bowl of flour with both hands. These cringes had to be identified for my head and heart to be in alignment. At this moment they weren't. There were a lot of lower heart things, a lot of unresolved emotions, being stirred up. One of these was irritation. In teaching Ki how to use the spoon, he'd flip it sending showers of flour dust everywhere.

Now I was really getting into those old memories that needed resolve. Here was the reality of the "mess" my mother dealt with, or more accurately never dealt with. Her thoughts loomed in my mind. They wanted to direct my thinking about myself and my son. Psychologically it's called projection. Physically it's a brain pathway, a habitual way of thinking practiced hundreds of times and now automatic. I could see how easy it was for me to think the old thoughts connected with my mom, and I could see these thoughts are not in alignment with my ideal of teaching/parenting.

Admittance brought me to a fork in the road. There were two paths available. Was I going to be like my mother, "No, you'll make too big a mess" and banish Ki from the kitchen? Or was I going to begin a new pattern of thought *in my mind?*

I wanted the new thought, and I was willing to create it. This moved me into deeper levels of admitting. I wanted Hezekiah to be able to learn anytime, anywhere, with anyone. I wanted him to be able to use his mind in ever increasing ways. I wanted to empower him not stifle him, guide him not limit him. To do this I would need to achieve a higher level of emotional equilibrium than I was exhibiting in the moment.

I had to admit that what my mother had sometimes called my "lack of maturity" was not really mine at all. When the thought crossed my mind that I was upset with Hezekiah's lack of emotional maturity, I knew this thought wasn't mine. It is not the way I think, but I had to admit it was the way I was behaving. *I* was the one in need of emotional maturity.

My need for **adjustment** became clear. How did I intend to grow up a bit here? The big thought I uncovered from the recesses of my conscious thinking was a resentment toward cleaning up someone else's mess. It may sound silly to you, but this was a major key in my learning. I can best describe it like this. I had absorbed my mother's attitudes about perfection. This went way beyond cleaning up the kitchen, perfection – at least the appearance of perfection – permeated her whole existence.

Looking back, I can see how mother was very concerned with how things looked. Her sense of self worth and respectability were tied to what others thought about her own appearance. Dress, shoes, and accessories always matched, and people usually did notice. When I was growing up I directly experienced it in the apartment we lived in. Everything had a place and was in it, including me. Mom was one of those women who would pick white lint off of your navy blue suit in front of everybody. She dusted lampshades. Her house was not overly expensive but it was sparkling, and she expected me to follow her example.

Decades after living on my own, when mom opened the door of her new apartment and I saw white carpets, I immediately took off my shoes. Partly from respect, partly from fear. I remembered how carpet stains could send Mom into a panic. I remember feeling these thoughts, even this same kind of panic, when Daniel and I brought Ki to visit in the days of toddling and knocking over and occasional upchucks. I remember moments of being consumed with ideas of doing something that would displease her – with worry that something would happen that I couldn't make all right, or with fear that she would find out Ki's marker had accidentally gone off the paper and blanket onto her carpet!

These were not the thoughts of a 43-year-old woman, they were the feelings of an eight-year-old girl, left as they were first received and reinforced again and again for 30-something years. Applying the essential life skills I describe in this book and that we teach in the School of Metaphysics are what enabled me to become aware of these thoughts and have the power to change them.

With the power of Self Respect and undivided attention in the present, seeing Mom and Ki interacting was a blessing. Mom's reactions to what Ki would say or do were not at all how I remembered them to be! She was playful, and forgiving, and helpful, and loving. By *accepting* the reality of my mom, I was free to *admit* how she had changed. Rather than hold the past against her and between us, I found a breathing space that cleared my mind and emotions. Now I could place my own memories where they belonged. I began *adjusting* my attitude in the present. Just like upgrading a computer program, I left the 8-year-old stuff in the past, by accepting my mom in the present. The new perspectives brought ease and joy to our adult interactions. To me, this is the reality of Self respect. Self respect naturally produces respecting others. Some people call this process forgiving, and certainly respect gives us the reason and impetus to give.

These experiences with my mom predated the kitchen experience with

Hezekiah by about two years. Just the thought of making a mess brought these memories forward. I realized I had more updating to do. If I really understood this lesson, the emotional cringing wouldn't be present. The thought entered my mind: *It's your mess, you clean it up.* Suddenly the new perspective I wanted surfaced. I was being led to affirm a simple truth: *thought is cause.* I realized my early training had been centered more on how things looked than how they came to be. That's how I could ace so many tests, even take a course in Russian history, yet retain so little from all those years of public schooling. I had been taught how to play the game, how to score the points, how to do what it takes to make it look good to others. And my sense of self worth had struggled because of it for years.

Now, as a parent, this physical thinking of how things look eroded my potential joy in shared experiences with my husband and our son. Thought is cause. Ki's thoughts are very simple. He wants to learn about anything and everything in his world. His physical world is smaller than mine. Fewer experiences, less freedom for experience, a fraction of the memories of experience. He is voracious. His appetite for learning is limitless.

I had to ask myself, "What limits do I want to put on my son?"

I've learned how we answer this question is the affirmation of the soul who is your child. I'll describe it like this. Along about this time I just happened to be traveling alone which gave me a rare opportunity to listen to talk radio. Being late in the afternoon, I settled on *Dr. Laura (Schlesinger)* a well-known counselor with high integrity and a strong faith in our ability to do the right thing. On this day she read a letter from a listener. It was one of those folksy, conversational anecdotes often passed on through email because they embody universal sentiments. This anonymous story cited four keys to parenting that resonated with my parental ideals.

These points have served as a backbone for me to learn more about and teach respect every day, to adults as well as children. They come in the form of questions to ask yourself in any situation where thoughtfulness is needed. These questions open the door to the power of your conscious mind, which is reasoning. The questions are:

> *1) Is it safe?*
> *2) Is it moral?*
> *3) Is it legal?*

Being a metaphysician, I added: *4) Does it make sense?*

I usually ask number four first. So in the kitchen with Ki, I ask myself, "Does it make sense to include him when he asks?"

I affirmed, "Absolutely!" For years I have told people the only prerequisite to studying metaphysics is a desire to change. Teaching the youngest souls has revealed this to me in a new light: *when the student is ready to learn is the time you can teach him the most.* And Ki was eager to experience.

I proceeded with my mental checklist. Would Ki be safe? Yes, with supervision and no sharp knives, as long as we learned a healthy respect for the heat of the oven which mom would handle until he gets tall enough to reach the upper cabinets, we could pass this test.

Is kitchen play moral? What I was learning all by itself supported this point. The newly found interpretations of my old thoughts gave me the truth in this real life morality play.

And legal? Absolutely, we would be learning about laws far beyond man's invention! We would be learning about the Universal Laws of Proper Perspective, Creation, Cause and Effect, Relativity, and more.

With this checklist I can **affirm** the learning in any situation for myself and often for others. Right there in the kitchen, on this springtime Wednesday afternoon, I was moving far beyond appearances, old thoughts of how things look holding such a lofty place in my sense of well being, which had driven my initial reaction of "What a mess!" I was becoming free of my own limitations and my son would be a beneficiary of that. By **allowing** myself the freedom to learn, to respond differently, I could give the same allowing to him.

My heart swelled with love. I had put myself in Ki's shoes and learned a new application of Self respect. I was no longer standing in my mom's shoes, or my own eight-year-old ones, now I could see the situation in another way. By revisiting and updating my own youthful experience I freed myself to see the experience for the first time, like Hezekiah was seeing it. This **aligned** me with my son, allowing me to respect him, his desires and learning. This is what people call compassion – the ability to experience in honesty from another's point of view.

We had a great time that day in the kitchen. Our time was filled with love and joy and discovery. Ki created a dessert masterpiece while I accomplished a quantum leap in Self awareness. When we were done Ki even helped clean up. Mom would have been proud.

U
N
D
I
V
I
D
E
D

ATTENTION

Hezekiah, age 2, counting and sorting

This Child Came to Me for a Reason

"I'm Del North." The anxious voice on the other end of the phone introduced herself. "Rick Menendez gave me your name because he thought you might be able to help me."

"I'll be happy to try," I replied.

"I have a seven-year-old son and they've told me he can't go back to school unless I put him on Ritalin. I've had him see two doctors and he's been tested and he's a genius but in class he daydreams, and his second grade teacher says she won't let him back into class until he's treated. He did fine in first grade, but this teacher doesn't like him. The doctors won't put him on drugs and I don't know what to do." Her voice was thin, almost breaking.

"Okay," I said collecting my thoughts as I reassured her, "breathe a bit. First you must know this is a blessing – that the two doctors don't want to drug your child."

"I know it is, but what am I supposed to do? They won't let him in school!" She was still a bit panicked.

"Think about how much you love him. That's what's most important." I could feel her relax at the other end of the phone. She told me more of the story, more details about the school situation and her working status.

"You need to decide how important your son is to you," I counseled. The truth is always simple. "It may seem like a strange request but this is where you decide what you're willing to do to give your son what you think he should have."

She answered that he was important.

"Then you may need to be willing to change your life." I said with gentle firmness. I went on to paint the options. "You may need to homeschool.....What about the father?" Absent since the age of two and now in the process of divorce.

I knew this woman needed help from someone closer. Fortunately, she lives in St. Louis, a city where we have a School of Metaphysics. I gave her the name of our field representative there who had been researching exceptional schools and whose daughter is schooled at the College of Metaphysics. In this way she would find the counsel, help, encouragement and education she would need for the months and years ahead.

Del was learning, as have all parents of Indigos, they enter our lives as much to stimulate our learning and soul growth as to fulfill their own.

Attention is the sense of the mind. The body has five senses for experiencing: seeing, hearing, tasting, smelling, and touching. It is the mind that can link them together. This is accomplished by mind thought, a single point of focus.

Indigos have keen attention. When Hezekiah was less than a year old, I would be holding him and he would cup my cheek with his little hand and literally turn my face to him. At first I laughed about it, thinking he had real potential as an osteopath. Then I saw him do this with others. The turning of the face would be followed by Ki pointing in a direction or saying simple words. Seeing this happen with others made it easy to understand. This was a way Ki could get the adult's attention! When he wanted something and the person carrying him was talking or listening to someone else, otherwise occupied, Ki would first get their attention by physically moving their head. It was an amazing thing to watch, and foolproof. It worked every time.

To master the mind, we must first master the attention. When your attention is undivided the entire mind is still, focused on one thing. The brain is fully functioning, the mind awakened to the truth of the experience.

Some years ago, Oxford researchers including C. Maxwell Cade wanted to discover what happens in the brains of healers, mystics, and yogi masters. Were their brains different from the average person? What they found, they called the awakened brain. All brain waves – beta, alpha, theta, delta – were present when the healers heal, the mystics teach, and the yogi meditate. This means full consciousness, from awake to reverie to sleeping, is experienced thus lighting up the whole brain!

Undivided attention is a taste of this state of consciousness, an enlightened state we can all attain.

When ADD Doesn't Add Up

by Damian Nordmann

It is crucial that parents know their child's needs in order to serve the learning of the soul. Often parents have a difficult enough time identifying their own needs for learning and the changes that will produce fulfillment, let alone setting up the conditions for the optimum growth the child desires.

We all have a universal urge that gives us the security, tools, and foundation that encourages us to reach our full potential. Concentration, love, self expression, discipline, honesty, affection, directed imagination, and emulation are some of the qualities, skills, and needs we require to experience the greatest joy and fulfillment in life. Sometimes parenting can seem an overwhelming task - one of the greatest you'll ever choose and the one you want to give your best to. Intuitive Health Analyses can give remarkable insight into your child and your parenting.

In one Intuitive Health Analysis a mother who was feeling pressured stated that she thought her seven-year-old son did not want to learn from her. Here is the response:

This is not accurate. In actuality what is occurring is the one of the child wants more of the mother's attention and, therefore, he purposefully causes her to put out more effort. It is in part because the one of the son needs love greatly, particularly the kind the mother can give and it is in part that he feels in some way he has not received this because of other factors in the life. Would suggest therefore, that the mother be more acutely aware of this and then learn to be very demonstrative in her love and affection, to come to terms with her own grievances or fears or doubts concerning her own choices and her own conditions and how they have affected this one then there will be greater rapport established. It is not that this one does not want to learn, this one learns much from the one of the mother. (31498BGC4)

This boy had been diagnosed with Attention Deficit Disorder (ADD). In this case he was not the one who was attention deficit, rather it was his parents, as is often the case with children stigmatized by the ADD label.

Each soul chooses the parents for the qualities the parents have to give when they are at their best. This boy wants more of his mother's attention, more of her love and the essence of what she has to offer him. It can be easy for adults to look at the things children do and see them as strange or contrary to the kind of conduct that should be displayed. Perhaps we can better learn from our children the kind of behavior and experimentation that can produce greater understanding.

This boy's mother asked a question concerning the "compulsive behavior" of her son and how she can help him manage it. The answer to the question shows how impulsively the soul always acts to produce learning.

We see this is temporary and this one should not be concerned about it. These are the experimentations with the emotions, the emoting and then seeing what happens. It is another formation for this one in learning cause and effect. Would suggest for those around this one for them to recognize it as so and therefore direct or channel this one toward a more cognizant experimentation with (emotion) rather than it being an unconscious fashion and therefore seen as compulsive or improper.(31498BGC4)

Children are like sponges, soaking in everything from their environment. The younger a child is, the more true. The child has not yet developed the filters of reasoning and discrimination characteristic of the conscious mind as we understand it. This is good in the sense of openness for learning because the child has no limitations in the early years. The only limitations the child acquires are the ones learned from the parents or limitations of society that the parents allow the child to perpetuate. Over a period of time any restricting ways of thinking (diseased attitudes of the parents) will have an affect on the mental, emotional, and physical health of the child.

Parents of a two-and-a-half-year-old girl asked what they could do to aid in the healing of their daughter's lung infection. The answer showed them how critical it was for them to change their thinking and the way they express their thoughts and emotions.

The most important change is for these ones to be clear in what they communicate; that is, there is a need for these ones to speak words that match their thoughts and to speak words that match the emotions. Much of this one's difficulty is that this one receives very mixed messages particularly emotionally. When this one feels emotion from these ones that is not communicated, this one absorbs this and has difficulty releasing it.

These ones (parents) deny their emotions. Both of these ones in different ways desire to maintain a particular posture, a particular image, that is not based upon truth. Therefore, when these ones are angry and are not pleased with this, they deny it. When these ones are feeling guilty these ones do not want to admit this because it would mean failure in some way. Therefore, there is an attempt to cover this up. (111996LJC2)

The parents' denial was being felt by their daughter. She was confused mentally and emotionally and, therefore, didn't know how to express or understand emotions, particularly anger. The pent up emotions caused a restriction and breakdown of the immune system resulting in the infection in her lungs.

The parents were used to stuffing their emotions and creating a facade that did not match their true thoughts. Their daughter needed a means to understand how the inner and the outer should match. This was pointed out in another question they asked about why their daughter would hurt her newborn little sister.

This one is experimenting with her own expression and her own means of communication. This one's intention is not to hurt. This one is simply attempting to cause there to be an outer manifestation. We see that because this other who is younger is new and is very open, there is a direct match between what this one does and the effect it produces, and this one is curious about this. (111996LJC2)

It was a relief to these parents to learn that their daughter was not ill-intended in any way and that a change in her behavior could be so easily forthcoming as they would be more truthful. The souls that inhabit the small bodies of children will go to what may seem to our worldly wise minds extreme lengths to further their learning. This is because young children are still connected and aware of their reason or purpose for incarning which is to gain permanent understandings.

The most crucial formative years for a child are between the time of birth and about the age of seven. Learning from the example of their parents and people they look up to in their environment continues on into the pre-adolescent and teenage years. One mother asked during a Health Analysis how she could aid her twelve year old daughter to fulfill her soul's purpose - her "assignment" - for this lifetime.

To recognize that this one's concept of what her assignment is is not neces-sarily true. To first become open within herself to develop a capacity to communicate and to perceive what exists within the child, rather than what this one wants the child to become. These are different. We see that this one of the mother needs to become much more invested in her own development and growth so that this one will have the skills to influence the other in this regard. At the present time period, this one lacks the skills to do so.

Would suggest to these ones of the parents that there could be a great change for this one were they to become more aware of their own ways of thinking. We see that in many ways the interaction with this one is attempting to teach them this, but they are reacting to it rather than learning from it. Therefore, avenues which would enable these ones to become more enlightened in regards to the cause and effect of their own thinking would aid in causing there to be some hope and expectation that is in some way unconscious, but in other ways not, that they need to fight in order to get what they want.

This one of the child senses this and does not want to fight. She wants to give up, she does not want the conflict, and therefore, she will go to extreme lengths to try to please those in her environment to avoid conflict. In that way, this one's construction of thinking is very much the product of what she has been taught to this point in her life. If what she is taught is to change, the parents will need to change. (31498BGC3)

As souls all we desire is to learn and grow, to become compatible with the Creator who brought us into existence. As each individual becomes aware of this truth and lives this truth each day, we will find it much easier to understand our children and serve their needs. This is because the learning of adults and the learning of children are really the same. We all want to develop reasoning, concentration, imagination, will power, compassion, integrity, determination, intuition, and peace. When we understand these universals as part of everything life offers, then education in our world will finally match its true meaning which is to draw forth, to draw out the best that is within us all.•

Damian Nordmann is a teacher and director at the School of Metaphysics. Originally from Louisville, Kentucky, Damian began directing the Oklahoma City branch of the school after graduating from the College of Metaphysics in Windyville, Missouri.

Establishing Order in an Individual's Universe

The incredible resource of Intuitive Health Analysis has advanced the art and science of psiology light years ahead of commonly-accepted modalities. Here we find the truth of thought as cause in action in the lives of men, women, and children of all ages, backgrounds, nationalities.

These analyses describe what is occurring within the individual's psi, his inner mind. They reveal how specific patterns of thinking cause specific patterns of illness through mind and in the body. They also relate what will reestablish order within the individual's universe. From vibrations sounded mentally that will interrupt seizures and stabilize brain function to attitude adjustments which free mind and body from long-standing, stagnation-producing concepts to the mental and emotional state of the comatose, the research is astounding and deserves to be noted, explored, and utilized more widely.

Analyses on children are particularly insightful for the parents and loved ones, and to all of us in a universal sense for they reflect societal, mass consciousness.

The following health analysis was performed on a seven-year-old boy upon his mother's request. A divorcee with four other children, "Bradley" is "Rachel's" youngest and the only child who lives with her. Recently school officials said her son would not be able to return to public school unless he saw a psychiatrist/medical doctor. Upon doing so, the doctor wanted to put her son on Ritalin, a drug widely prescribed for prepubescents diagnosed as being hyperactive. This was an option Rachel did not want but felt "trapped" into taking.

Bradley's health analysis reveals the importance of parental environment in shaping a child and what can be changed to improve that influence. In so doing, it also addresses the current trend to place "disruptive" young boys on a drug that mimics the effects of amphetamines (speed, in slang) in adults. The analysis begins:

We see within this one there is an extreme degree of confusion. We see that this one is very quick in the thinking and that there are many stimuli around this one that barrage this one much of the time. We see that this one has very little control of the attention and reacts very quickly to whatever stimulus is the most apparent, the most strong to this one. We see that, therefore, this one has very little understanding, of the self, of the environment, of what is stable, or truthful.

The first time I met Bradley he was attending a family camping week-end at the College of Metaphysics with his mother. He acted shy, as is common for four year olds, hiding behind his mom who alternately fed the attachment and ridiculed him for it. This tendency to one moment soothe her son and the next minute encourage him to be adventurous could have been a nurturing action in the hands of a self-aware mother.

At times this was true for Rachel, but just as often the soothing came from her own need for love rather than a response to him; the encouragement was from her desire to be free of his voracity for her attention and an obvious reaction to what she believed someone in her environment expected from her. The result was Bradley never knew how his mom would respond or if she would. He was beginning to learn ways, not all productive ones, to get her attention. Even hearing "Stop it! I told you not to do that!" was better in Bradley's eyes than being ignored or abandoned particularly since he lived apart from the rest of his family.

This analysis followed almost three years later and by now the patterns are well-established. The constant shifting, the unreliability of the most profound influence in his young life - his mother- has shaped Bradley's consciousness into what it now is. He is confused with little stability in his thinking. This leads to displays of temper and fearfulness that school officials don't know how to respond to. Rachel, the strongest influence, can "control him" but nobody else can. They don't know how to reach him because he does not know how to reach himself. This is the source of Bradley's problem.

The answer comes in methods for gaining self awareness and self control:

Would suggest to this one that there is a need for some solid source of security, for some point of focus for the attention. There is a need for this one to develop the will and the will power. Would suggest concentration exercises. Would suggest that this one extend effort to direct the attention and to hold it for given periods of time. For this one to have some kind of structure or boundaries for this one to use as parameters for not only this one's mental attention but also for this one's physical body.

The source of security for Bradley could come in many forms. As is true with every child, being certain of his home life is essential to well-being. Simple representations of security: who he lives with and the place he calls home are especially important to Bradley now. These can be given to him when his mother and father resolve any differences they may have. When Rachel is more secure, she will provide stable energy for Bradley be it in the form of regular meals, bedtime stories and hugs, or weekly religious communion.

Bradley is a testament to the fact that these parents have not always put their children first. If they want the best for him, if they want him to change, then they must be willing to lead the way, to demonstrate how. This will go farther in aiding Bradley to develop will than any words. Example is a most powerful teaching tool.

Concentration exercises will give Bradley a sense of self control he has not yet experienced in his young life. It is universally true that when you can make your thoughts do what you want them to do rather than feeling like a victim of them (something Bradley has imitated that his mother does) your security immediately grows. Within is where the real security lies.

The suggestion for "structures" can be met in any of various forms of athletic disciplines where mental attention is paired with physical strength and development. This could be in martial arts, a favorite of many young boys, any Olympic sport, or in hatha yoga or dance. The choice should be Bradley's for this will insure motivation from his interest.

This one does not even have a strong concept of this one's own strength, this one's own ability. The use of martial arts would be of great benefit in aiding this one to learn how to direct the energy mentally, emotionally, and physically. And to learn how to wield this one's own power mentally, emotionally, and physically. This one needs a teacher. This one needs some kind of strong image or influence to imitate and to give this one guidance and direction.

If Bradley agrees, the martial art suggestion will be the most compatible for his development. One of the reasons martial arts is effective for boys is the presence of a strong, directed older male in a parental position of authority. The relationship of teacher to student is one of trust, obedience, strength, and love - all the qualities every child deserves and needs for wholistic development. Since Bradley does not live with his father or any other male whom he can interact with and learn from, it is essential he receive this kind of attention from a male who is invested in his well-being. So essential to well-being is the balance of family structure - mother, father, and child - that I predict one day soon a study will link the absence of the father and/or mother from the home to ADHD diagnosed children.

We see within the emotional system, this one is extremely angry much of the time.

Confusion, a lack of understanding, breeds anger in anyone. Bradley's anger has been learned, as we will see, and is the result of the unhappiness in those to whom he is entrusted.

We see that this one is also fearful much of the time. We see that this is a result of the confusion that has been described. This one has very little concept of parameters or truth. We see, therefore, that this one allows the emotions to rule this one much of the time. And much of this is what this one has learned through imitation.

As those who care for Bradley are willing to look at themselves, becoming cognizant of their influence, they are much more equipped to make changes that will in turn affect Bradley. When a child is diagnosed with attention deficit hyperactive disorder, the parents' egos immediately motivate them into action. One parent may wear it as a badge, "My son has ADHD", as if that explains most things and excuses the rest. Another parent is ashamed, wanting to deny that there is anything wrong or hide what is. Both foster the willingness to say "yes" to the quick fix of drugging their own child.

As Rachel said, "What am I supposed to do? They won't let him back in school unless he goes on Ritalin." Not one to accept the closed doors of limitations, I suggested alternatives: private school or home schooling. Rachel's tendency to box herself in, to feel forced into action, affects Bradley as well as herself. I later learned what she had been told was not a true statement. In this state school, officials cannot force a child to be on drugs, nor can they refuse to teach one who isn't. Rachel was fed a line that she heard through the filter of her own ego, her own badge. If her son went on the drugs, it would solve her problem.

Truth is, it doesn't, and the drug can have life altering side-effects. After Bradley developed a couple of these, his mom took the first step in controlling her ego and her emotions by saying no to the drugs.

It would benefit this one to direct the emotions in a loving manner, in an affectionate manner. It would benefit this one to have a plant or a garden that this one could tend in order for this one to give love, in order for this one to use the sense of touch, in order for this one to have the means of learning cause and effect in a direct manner, in which this one could give and receive directly.

My first impression of Bradley is a revealing mental image. The adults were talking and Bradley's mom was somewhere else, leaving him to his own devices. Bradley entertained himself by using his foot to push on Sir, the College of Metaphysics collie/Australian sheepdog, who was resting on the ground quietly. Sir was very good-natured about the whole thing but I could tell the boy was, with each push, becoming more intent on sparking a reaction.

I pulled my chair next to his and bending down to stroke Sir, said, "Sir likes it better when you pet him with your hands instead of your feet." I didn't think Sir would hurt the boy, but I didn't know what might happen if the boy hurt the dog. It was apparent Bradley was a bundle of emotions, wondering where his mom was and how long she would be gone, feeling a bit at a loss among many people he didn't know, and Sir was the recipient of all this energy.

I offered Bradley a way to direct that energy saying, "Did you know that energy is received and given through the palms of your hands?" I showed him by having our palms face each other without touching. By expanding my electromagnetic field Bradley could feel my energy pressing, then mingling, with his. His eyes lit up.

Years before this suggestion was given in his analysis, the truth of it was very real in Bradley's life. He was highly affectionate then, just as his mother could be. Throughout the weekend I remember seeing them several times cuddling and hugging. Bradley always had a big smile on his face. Then there were the times his face would distort into anger because he wasn't getting what he wanted or he would be trying to hide tears of frustration when he wasn't being understood. It seemed the times Bradley needed love and affection the most, both were missing, a common occurrence when one parent is absent.

We see within the physical system there is a great degree of imbalance that occurs within this body. We see that the nervous system is extremely taxed.

We see that much of this is from the barrage of stimuli without direction that this one experiences. The concentration exercises that have been related will be of great benefit.

When the attention is allowed to scatter, there is little identification or intelligence in its use. Attention is the muscle of the mind, the precursor of will power. It controls accuracy in memory and freedom in imagination. You are where your attention is is a universal truth. If you are preoccupied about a job interview next week, you will miss part of the conversation now or maybe run a red light. Likewise, if you are consumed by a sense of loss from the parting last week of a loved one, you will forget to stop at the store for needed supplies or lack motivation to get out of bed in the morning. Living in the future or the past, keeps you from the present, the time when you can effectively learn and grow.

Adults who understand the nature and control of attention are examples for children. They teach concentration in the way they communicate with the child and with others, in the way they approach work and play. Concentration is the developed skill of focusing your attention on one point, at will, for whatever period of time you desire. It can be practiced and is important to the development of the human nervous system at any age, particularly during the first seven years of life when the brain is receiving the foundation of information that will shape all the years to come.

We see that there is a lack of oxygen to the brain and that this one needs to breathe fresh air out of doors daily. This one needs daily exposure to sun-light. The use of picnogenol from pine bark would be of benefit.

The incidence of asthma in young children has skyrocketed in the past decade. This is the result of two factors: first, demands are being placed on children at younger and younger ages to mature, to separate from their parents, to leave their homes, to act in certain ways far beyond their years. In some children this creates a web of restrictive thinking that inhibits expression, the productive part as well as the unacceptable. "Feeling like you can't breathe" describes an attitude, a frame of mind that is taught. When it becomes your own, the body eventually responds with respiratory difficulties.

The second factor is the type of lives we live including big city pollutants and poor diet from processed foods that weaken the child's growing system rather than support it. Parents must be willing to examine their own expectations, fulfilling their own desires rather than expecting their children to do so. Parents must also be willing to make life changes that will produce health in their children - spiritually, mentally, and emotionally as well as physically. Often this is more than moving to a smaller town or the country, it is moving the self, changing our level of self-awareness and self-discipline.

We see that there is inadequate nutrition for this one. There is a need for B vitamins, protein, all trace minerals. Would suggest that this one eat whole foods rather than processed foods or chemicals. Fresh vegetables, whole grains, and a variety of protein sources are needed by this body.

It has been only in the past decade that I have come to know and understand the nature of Western diet. Built around processed foods, the nutrients we expect and that our bodies need are often absent. Processed foods are not just candy bars, boxed cakes, and flavored cereals, they include white flour and sugar and most of the foods you find on supermarket shelves. Often the food in restaurants comes from large cans instead of fresh ingredients, cans filled with chemicals that preserve the ingredients for months and years. Heat and pressure often used in sterilizing and preserving rob the food of nutrients. So do pesticides and herbicides used in producing the food, or hormones given to animals. All of these are to some degree passed on to man, the consumer of the food.

Again I predict connections will be verified between these realities and the rise in liver disorders in American society and between added hormones and early juvenile puberty.

Physically, the answer is supply the nutrients, by supplements when necessary, needed by a building body. Know what's in your food. Eat the best food possible, organic, natural, grow your own when you can. Receiving from all the earlier life forms - gas, mineral, plant, animal - is essential for a strong human body. Be willing to give your child the fresh air, trace minerals, fruits and vegetables, and red organ meats needed for building his or her body.

There is a need for this one to drink water when thirsty rather than other kinds of beverages....

For four and a half years, our son has lived without knowledge of soda pop. It can be done. (Since the time of writing this, Ki has learned of soda pop, mostly from relatives, and having tried it prefers water, juice, smoothies, or an occasional Olvatine). Once started, the amount of sugar and caffeine carbonated beverages supply can be an addiction hard to beat at any age. For instance, twenty years ago soda vending machines in public schools did not exist, now they are commonplace.

No matter what, do not give your child fake sweeteners. You will find when you drink water, your child will want to be like you. Keep up the good example.

There is a need for this one to eliminate sugar from the diet.

What, no sugar!? If your child is eating canned or boxed food he or she is eating sugar. Not long ago a popular brand of juice advertised as all natural was exposed for containing significant amounts of corn syrup. To eliminate sugar first means refraining from putting the white stuff in food you make. When your child won't eat it unless it's sweet, try stevia, an herb that tastes just like the white cane sugar he's used to without the same effects on the body.

Would suggest that this one listen to certain types of music to aid this one in directing the attention as well as soothing the emotions, and calming the body. Particularly types of classical music would be especially helpful. This would also aid to some extent in synchronizing to some extent the nervous system and the brain. This is all. (122298LJC5)

The influence of Mozart's music upon temperament and intelligence is becoming widely known. Science has entered the realm of why certain melodies endure over time and cultures thus earning the title "classic". Every style of music from jazz to marches, from waltzes to heavy metal, produce vibrational patterns that affect the energy of anything the sound touches, including people. That's why certain music makes you happy or sad or peaceful or angry. There are universal principles behind these conclusions. The science of resonance is one of the most startling.

In recent decades research has been conducted throughout the world regarding musical patterns that promote learning. The entire concept called "superlearning" is one of the best. For Bradley and all children with growing bodies, the best learning music is baroque melodies with distinct, metered rhythms. The largo movements from Bach's *Concerto in G Minor*, Handel's

Twelve Concerti Gross, Opus 6, or Vivaldi's Winter from *The Four Seasons* are excellent choices.

Each Intuitive Health Analysis is unique to the individual receiving it therefore the suggestions for Bradley may or may not be the best for another child. A personal analysis offers the greatest benefit for anyone desiring wholistic health. When used as a tool of intuitive research, analyses do however offer insights into the cause and effect relationship of the mind and body, parent and child, health and illness.

By drawing upon intuitive knowledge, psiologists seek to understand the wholistic nature of the human being and his connectedness with all of Creation. They understand the health of each part is essential to the health of the whole, be it the cells that make up the human body or the individuals that make up humanity. In time we will come to God knowledge, understanding it all.

–written by the author and first published in the Wholistic Health & Healing Guide Vol. 8, No 2. Copyright 1998, School of Metaphysics.

Dr. Pam Blosser is a wonderful woman, an insightful teacher, and a good friend. She and her husband Paul live on campus and are very much a part of the everyday community life. Pam is the person who directs our annual summer camps for youngsters. With a background that includes Montessori training, watching Pam interact with the children has been a source of inspiration, instruction, and sometimes comfort for me. She brings the fresh viewpoint only a nonparent can, with the spiritual love of a sister.

With encouragement, Pam has begun writing about her experiences and ideas. Here is one of her pieces that is a perfect illustration of undivided attention, the second essential living skill every soul needs to learn.

Attention

by Dr. Pamela Blosser

Three children are given a math problem to do in their heads. One gets the answer in less than a minute while the other two are still grappling with the figures. All three children are very smart, so what is the difference?

The first child upon receiving the problem becomes still. Her gaze is fixed to a point of focus in front of her. As her body and eyes remain still you can almost see the internal work going on inside her head. Her determination is strong until she completes her calculation.

The second child begins, has already made up her mind, thinking this problem will be hard, she doesn't "know math", and people will think she's stupid. Maybe she really is stupid. By now she's forgotten what the numbers are and has to ask for them to be given again.

The third child begins his mental calculation even before receiving the problem to be solved. His mind is not disciplined enough to still his thoughts and complete his mental calculations. He looks over at the other two wonder-

ing how they're coming along with figuring out the problem. Then he looks at the clock wondering how long it's been when the first child gives the answer.

All three children are bright. The one who excels and gets the answer knows how to still her mind, focus her attention, and concentrate until she achieves the desired result.

Being able to focus and hold the attention is the key to improved memory, faster learning, better grades in school, and more efficient use of time. When you're using undivided attention you can be in the middle of one experience or train of thought, remove your attention to take care of something else and return to your first task right where you left off. Do you lose your train of thought in the middle of a conversation? Walk into a room and forget what you came there to do? Forget where you leave things and have to spend time searching for them? Get distracted from tasks so you spend a long time completing them or don't finish them at all? Do you remember facts for a test but forget them afterwards? These are all signs of the need to strengthen your undivided attention.

In our society we are taught to scatter our attention, thinking of many ideas at once. Trying to hold a number of thoughts in your consciousness at the same time is inefficient and tiring.

Attention comes from the Latin word, attendere. A (or ad) means toward and tendere means to stretch. So the original meaning of attention is to stretch toward. With attention you direct your consciousness, you reach or extend your awareness toward a desired destination whether that be towards another person, an experience, a physical object or a train of thought.

The words attention and attend come from this same Latin root word. Attend is to follow, listen, or serve. Attend and attention are closely related because when you attend to something you care for it or you are ready to listen and follow instructions. What you give your attention to is what you care about. When you give your attention to something you attend to it by listening, heeding and following, or giving and aiding it in some way.

Undivided means only one object, idea, or experience at a time. Undivided attention is the focusing power of the mind.

There are several exercises you can do to strengthen the power of your undivided attention. You can turn these exercises into games with your children.

One exercise is to give your attention through one sense. For example spend the day focusing on hearing. How many enjoyable and lovely sounds do you miss throughout the day because your attention is scattered or you're worrying about what people think about you or some other trivial thought? Try focusing on the sense of smell for one day. How many smells are there in one shopping mall: the smell of leather in the shoe store, perfumes in the cosmetic store, popcorn popping or chocolate chip cookies being baked, the paper smell in the bookstore, the aroma of potpourri in the housewares, and the sweet scent of soaps. Focusing your attention through one of the senses provides a daily adventure in expanded physical awareness, greater appreciation of your world leading to heightened physical and mental experiences.

Another exercise is to choose a word and see how many words you can find that are related to it. For example, how many words can you discover related to the word horse? Mare, mane, carriage, bridle, animal, stable, hay, Kentucky Derby, foal, hoof, races, jockey, etc. How many other words can you think of?

Doing brain teasers or math problems in your head, saying the alphabet backwards are all ways to exercise your attention as well as other mental skills.

Undivided attention is used to explore an idea fully, to complete a train of thought, to accomplish tasks, fulfill desires, learn and grow quickly, and be successful at whatever you endeavor to do. And undivided attention is essential in building a closer relationship with God and reaching enlightenment.

Begin now exploring how you and the children around you use attention. Is it scattered or focused? Do you get distracted easily when you are challenged; do you want to give up or rise to the challenge? Are you able to complete tasks quickly or does it take you a long time? How is your memory? Evaluate your present use of attention. Teach yourself and your children to slow thinking down and focus attention so you may excel and fulfill your potential.•

Dr. Pam Blosser has been teaching metaphysics to adults for twenty years and to children for ten. As director of Camp Niangua, she interacts with Indigos 10-15 years of age each summer, introducing them to the Essential Life Skills.

The Garden
by Dr. Sheila Benjamin

Hezekiah and I made our way out to the College of Metaphysics garden after dinner. This was the first day of Camp Niangua (for children ten to fifteen) and Hezekiah was excited to be with the campers. He made an announcement at the table that he was going outside to begin the evening activities of watering.

We arrived at the garden to find the water barrels only a quarter full. Assessing the situation, we got the garden hoses and connected them. Hezekiah very purposefully placed the hose in the barrel which was the fullest.

Since he had more experience in this task, I followed his lead. He very graciously gave me the watering can with the nicest handle. Then he let me know that this was the can that was all of the college students' favorite. I was grateful for this seven-year-old wanting to make this a pleasant experience.

When the college students came out to help they were focused on the completion of the activity and disrespectful to Hezekiah and me having been here first. Mari, one of the students, took the hose out of the barrel that Hezekiah had placed it in and put it in the very last barrel which was going to be used. Hezekiah, having placed the hose in the middle barrel, dropped his watering can near the middle barrel, saying in dismay, "I can't help water."

When I asked him why he told me it was because "I can't reach the water when it is so far down the barrel."

Seeing that he was right, I went up to Mari and asked her if she had realized that without asking she moved the water hose. I then passed on to her what Hezekiah had told me about the need to have the barrels full so he could help.

This lesson was filled with the first essential life skill, as well as undivided attention, in the sense there was something happening before all the college students and campers came out to help. There was the lesson of concentration in the sense of follow through and insuring that the area would be ready for the next person or the next day's watering.

It was very important to Hezekiah that he achieve the goal he set out to accomplish by making sure at least one barrel became completely full before it was used.

The next day I went out to check, and all the barrels were full. The college students had learned their lesson.•

A wonderful healing presence, Dr. Sheila Benjamin is known by Hezekiah as Aunt Sheila. She is one of those people in his life who come and go with regularity, teaching him the respect that comes with trust and the love that is timeless transversing space.

C
O
N
C
E
N
T
R
A
T
I
O
N

Andisa creating a da Vinci creature during 2001 Camp Niangua

The Girl at the Health Food Store

It had been some time since we'd visited the health food store in Springfield. Before going in, I told Daniel, "They've expanded!" You could see through the window they had doubled their size. When we entered the proprietor apologized because they were still clearing and moving products.

A pretty blond girl of 6 or 7 with a green feather duster was whisking bottles on the shelf. I smiled thinking how proud her parents must be and said, "You're quite a helper!"

I expected a smile of pride or perhaps a blush of embarrassment. What I got set me back. Flashing eyes stared me down, daring me to say anything else. I'd seen the look before on Ki's face and knew I had met a strong-willed Indigo just like him. As I walked past her I caught her mother's eye. She smiled a bit chagrined, a bit grateful. I made eye contact with the girl again and said, "Your mom and dad must be proud of you."

She almost growled at me!

I thought about the girl as I went around the store.

A while later, Hezekiah met a younger blond probably 3 or so whose speech was slurred and difficult to understand. Ki told her his name and she said she wasn't supposed to talk to strangers. Then she proceeded to follow him, eventually dancing with him, something new for him!

There was no mistaking, this was the younger sister of the first girl. Where the first girl had separated herself, not wanting contact, this girl was forward, reaching for Ki. He was enthralled by her feminine charms.

I continued shopping, keeping the dancing pair in the reach of my attention. I rounded the corner just in time to hear the older girl harshly say, "Get back in your cage" to the younger girl who was on the floor under a wire rack. The words shocked me less than what came next. The older girl then kicked her younger sister.

When the elder looked around to see if anyone had seen her, my questions about her intentions were answered. She knew what she was doing. She knew it was wrong in some way.

The girl saw me looking back.

I stood there holding a level gaze on the girl. I was shocked by what I had seen, and saddened, knowing I must respond. Quickly thoughts about interference, "it's none of your business", and "what right do you have" filtered through my mind. These were the thoughts that had so often kept me from doing what I believe and know from experience is the right thing. These are the kind of thoughts that we have all been taught, somewhere by someone probably with good intention. These are the kind of thoughts that may have been true at one time yet now stand as a mountain between us and our power to make a difference in the present.

Concentration freed me from these distracting thoughts, freeing me to reason in the moment and respond. I came near the girls and offering my hand to the small one I looked the older one in the eyes and said, "You want to be good to your sister. Kindness comes back to you and you may need her help someday." Then I went on to look for Ki, who gratefully had not witnessed this.

I purposefully kept my attention on the girls as I walked around the corner. I was able to see over the display counter and when she thought I was gone the older child started to do it again. Before kicking she looked around, and stopped this time.

I used the time I had left in the store to think of what action I should take. Should I say something to the parents? Both were close by in the store and could be aware of what was happening in the same manner I had learned. It was obvious this was not new behavior on either girl's part. Remembering the way some strangers had influenced my life when I was young, I decided upon the direct approach.

As Daniel, Ki, and I walked out of the store we passed the girl standing next to a frozen food freezer. She watched, but I walked on by. Then over my shoulder I whispered loud enough for her ears, "Bye sweetie, remember someone's always watching." Then we were gone.

Concentration is the ability to hold your undivided attention upon one subject or thing for as long as you will it. In the physical part of mind, concentration is the beginning of stillness, the condition of receptivity. In Zen teachings it might be described as "no thought". It is expectant rather than blank.

Concentration is used in every act of creation. It is essential for hearing what some- one else is saying. Carrying a train of thought requires a concentrated mind. Adding a column of figures, developing compassion, giving a good speech, praying, and Self control all require concentration. I drew upon my skill in concentra- tion in this experience. I listened to them, and to my inner Self, my own better judgement.

In that moment with the girls, I might have turned away. I might have denied I ever saw anything, forcing it from my conscious memory. I might have condemned the children or their parents falling into gossip. There were many options to choose from.

This I was certain of: when the outer mind is concentrated – still – it opens to the inner mind where the soul's treasure chest of wisdom is stored. A still mind can hear that inner voice. It can also hear the voice of others.

After the initial emotional reaction, this experience was bringing insights to me because I continued to hold my mind still. The cycle of archetypal warring sisters was revealed and the clairvoyant images of what "might be" unfolded before my mental eye. I wanted to help both girls to possibly have a different life.

In the moment I wanted to spare the younger physical harm which meant making an impression upon the elder.

Karma is life's inherent teacher. It is set into motion by our intention behind our acts. I wanted to give the older girl a new intention, separate from the one that motivated her to kick and dominate her sister. The developed skill of concentration frees us to identify our thoughts, the intents that motivate us.

I was very clear about my intention in that moment. I might never see these children again. They and I were here at this place at this time in this situation for a reason. I understood that I was being asked by the Universe to respond to the drama revealing itself before me.

Love serves as a foundation for discovering your own wisdom. Love draws to you and you to love. People tend to become uncomfortable with their own expression of love very early, just as this young girl had. Love is the one incentive capable of transforming animal man into spiritual man. The ideas planted in fertile young minds can free the soul for a lifetime to express openly and honestly.

I know the girl heard my words. I know I consciously planted a seed in her mind that day in the health food store. It was a seed of kindness, of mutual need, of the connection of all life. I hope the seed found fertile soil and the nurturing attention needed for it to flourish.

The Hyperactive Mom climbs out of the Box

Terri Pope's father was a pharmacist. He spoke with people all the time about health, so early on she says she realized that doctors weren't gods. They are human and they make mistakes. Personal experiences verified this as she grew older.

At 26 she received her first Intuitive Health Analysis from the School of Metaphysics. She was having symptoms that looked like hypoglycemia and "I didn't want to go through the glucose tolerance test. These symptoms I was having were pretty severe. I would have moments of being paranoid, anxiety, my mind would race and I would shake uncontrollably. And you can't cut hair (Terri owned her own salon in Houston) when you do that.

"The first part of the reading talked about what was going on in the mental system which was the lack of self love. In the physical body there was hypoglycemia, borderline diabetes, and at that point the report recommended chiropractic care.

"Everything that was related in that report hit home with me and so I didn't really want to like that reading. I didn't want to believe what it said was any good. So I got a chiropractor (my mother's) to x-ray my spine. All the vertebrae causing problems that were noted in the report were confirmed by the x-ray. So in other words the health analysis that I had from ya'll had been confirmed by a third party who didn't even know. At that point I went out and got my book on learning to love myself."

Thus began a longstanding relationship between Terri, me and the School of Metaphysics. When her four-year-old son complained about his stomach hurting, headaches, and earaches, it was a natural response for Terri to contact the School.

The doctors were suggesting tubes in his ears and she knew there had to be an alternative, a better way to restore her son to health. "The report told me what I needed to know. It described the spinal misalignments. It got into imbalances of fluid levels in the inner ear that produced some difficulty in the maintaining of balance and coordination. With the stomach problems — basically he was having constipation and also he wasn't absorbing the nutrients from the substances that were taken into the system."

When she received the report, Terri focused first on the physical system because she wanted to alleviate Beau's symptoms. "My first impression was realizing that Beau was starting to limit his foods: *we see that this one is quite capable of handling many varieties of food substance but is defining or beginning to establish a pattern that limits the willingness to take in food substances.* First impression, it ticked me off because it was such an irritating point between Bob and I at the time.

"Beau had always been real open to any type of food that I gave him. The only thing that he would not eat was sushi. He would eat anything. Bob and I had different experiences with food growing up. He had opinions about children and food substances, what they could and could not take. He believed that children only could take sweet or salty, and he began to cook for him, like French fries and fish sticks. I was totally against it. However, he was the house husband so to speak and I was the working person. So he did the majority of the cooking at that time and I did not. I was too busy rushing about. So I believe that that also had something to do with Beau's problems in the colon area.

"What's funny is that Bob's health analysis had the same thing with the colon; my report had the same thing with the colon."

"All three of us also had respiratory problems. During that time we also took the carpets that were in our house out. Old duct work got cleaned which helped. But what we learned in those health analyses, knowing what was going on in the mental and the emotional parts of each of us, was invaluable."

After combing the descriptions of the physical body, Terri's attention was captured by the last question asked. *Are there any further suggestions for the mother of this one?* The intuitive reporter answered in this way:

Would suggest that there is a racing in this one's thoughts when there is communication with this one. We see that because of that there is inconsistency in the expectations and inconsistency on the willingness to follow through. Because of this there is insecurity that is fostered in this one by the ones around the self. Therefore, it is when there will be the consistency, the full attention when there is communication and the willingness to follow through upon what is seen to be correct which would aid both of these ones. This is all. (6-2-87-GBM-a)

"*Racing in this one's thoughts.* This echoed reports I'd had three years prior which I had tried to change. Beau's reading, however, told me there was a greater degree to master. I started looking at all the stuff that was going in the mental system and the emotional system. I didn't really know what to think about it all. But with your advice, I began experimenting, doing new things.

"One thing I started to do differently at that point — when I talked with Beau — was to kneel down and look him in the eye and give him my attention when he spoke to me and when I spoke to him. I began to make an effort to do so. At first, I believe it was surprising to him. It would startle him when I would get down like that and just kind of focus all of my attention on him. What I do know is that within two weeks of doing this combined with a couple visits to a chiropractor, Beau was off antibiotics (for the ear infection) for good.

"Also during that time period he had a tendency to stutter. When he would talk he would kind of 'ummmm,' you know thinking about what he wanted to say, and he would repeat the same sentence over and over before he would finally get it out." Terry was describing a mental stutter quite common in Indigos who have received stimuli from so many sources that they find it difficult to isolate one at a time as they age, accumulating more experiences.

"When he would start repeating himself, I would kneel down, eye-to-eye with him, and I'd say, 'Beau, I want you to slow down for a second and I want you to think about what you want to say and then say it.' I believe that that was what occurred in that situation of me slowing down and giving him my attention. I don't believe at that time it was full attention. I don't think I knew what full attention was. But that's how he responded."

When going over this report with Terri I asked her about a line describing Beau's mental state: *Because there is not the consistency in this one's environment, this one becomes either temperamental, or very withdrawn or very secretive.* She said she couldn't identify it at the time but she knew there wasn't a consistency. Terri said, "I believe that this reading brought to my attention that when I asked Beau to do something or started to direct his attention to do something, that I needed to stay with him on it until it was completed. Or mean what I say and just stay with it.

"At that point too, Barbara, my life was crazy. I was running a salon with six hair dressers and pretty manipulative and pretty temperamental in my own way as well. In a lot of ways, Beau's health analysis is such a blend of what Bob and I were going through. In my health reading, that was at the very same time, I had a lot of impatience and intolerance. I wasn't communicating well or wasn't communicating, period. Nor was I consistent in action progressively. With Bob, he was anxious most of the time. I don't think he even knew.

"I would say Beau was around a lot of harshness, a lot of criticalness, manipulativeness, restrictiveness with both parents not being able to express emotionally. I think at that point I was living life the way I thought that I was supposed to and real frustrated with it; — having a certain amount of knowledge beyond the box about things but not being able to put it together, in wanting to help but not knowing how to help.

"Getting this report made a big difference in our lives."

Terri's life could be any typical American mother's. She's working, her husband's working, the children are going into school. There is less and less time spent in the home. The American way of life has become the driver, the focal point, and the high ideals of what can be are getting lost in the shuffle. Sustaining those high ideals while participating in activities requires concentration. Good, sustaining, fulfilling marriages and relationships require concentration. Creative, productive, philanthropic work requires concentration. The ability to carry a train of thought gives us the freedom to exit that box.

Once outside, anything we imagine can happen.

A Primer for Optimum Learning Ability

In 1991, Terri Pope's son Beau was seven years old, 10 months.

Terri's story continues with another story that will empower the parents of every Indigo. If you'll remember from Section 2, Beau was speeded up into a kindergarten class without Terri's knowledge. She found out when Beau started having "behavior problems". The teacher who speeded him up then began talking about learning disability. She and the school wanted Terri to have Beau tested.

This testing in the public school system can easily be replaced by teachers who understand and utilize Dr. Harold Gardner's multiple intelligence system. This was not happening yet in 1990's Houston.

Terri began, "I didn't get all the testing that the kindergarten teacher wanted me to get done because it would have cost me anywhere from $10,000 to $20,000. At least that was the estimates I had gotten from parents who had done this with their children. I could have had it done for $800, but what they put children through to do that, I didn't want to put that on Beau.

"I talked with different people, principals, people in the educational system who came into my salon to get their hair done. I talked to a pediatrician and at that point it was decided that I would wait until Beau had gone through first grade to make a decision on what I was going to do with him. And you can see this was in the summer of '91, Beau had completed first grade.

"So I went to his first grade teacher and I said, 'Miss Jones, I want to ask you something. How do you feel Beau is as a student? Do you feel like he has learning disabilities?'

"She looked at me and she said, 'Terry, I strongly suspect Beau's dyslexic. I went to my mother who is also a teacher of many years beyond mine and I told her about Beau and what my mother told me is teach him differently.'

"I had learned this with Beau already when the kindergarten teacher couldn't teach him how to subtract. At home, I took ten teddy bears out and put them on his bed. I said, 'There's ten teddy bears. You know, you've got five fingers here and five fingers here, that makes ten fingers. Now if I take two teddy bears away, how many teddy bears are left?' "

"Beau said, 'Eight.' "

"I said, 'That's subtraction, Beau!' Well we're still trying to wean him off his fingers but it worked. So what his first grade teacher said made sense to me.

"I got an Intuitive Health Analysis *(7991LJF)* for Beau for my own peace of mind and to find out if there were problems or learning disabilities. The first question we asked is: Do you find any learning disabilities with the visual perception? The report says,

We see that the difficulty with the visual perception is related to the misalign-ment in the skull plates and also to some extent the atlas and axis. We see that this does cause there to be difficulty in this one receiving clearly through the visual system. We do not see this to be a learning disability however.

To correct the problem the report suggested chiropractic attention for the physical difficulty and gave the following mental suggestions:

Would suggest that this one practice exercises which would strengthen this one's ability to concentrate and to understand what the attention is and how to direct and use the attention by giving the attention along with the use of the eyesight.

Armed with the information that Beau had potential rather than a brain disorder, Terri and Bob immediately responded by looking for a chiropractor. "In response to this, we first took Beau to a local chiropractor. I did not give the doctor the information on the intuitive reports. I just asked him to look at Beau and tell me what he saw, what he thought was going on with him. Through kinesiology, he discerned a misalignment of Beau's skull plates which was putting pressure on the optic nerve. This was what Beau's report said.

"The chiropractor quoted me a price of about $1,200 a month to work with Beau for an extended period of time. That's when I consulted with Lucille (a chiropractor and friend from Minneapolis). I told Lucille that my gut feeling was that Beau didn't need that, and she agreed. So we ended up traveling to Minneapolis to get Beau the treatment he needed.

"From there we went to a nutritionist and let her do her thing with Beau. She said that his liver wasn't fully functioning because of a chemical residue. This had appeared in a previous report also. The first question the nutritionist asked us was, 'Do you give him antihistamines?' And what mother this day and age, who doesn't know better, *doesn't* give her child antihistamines? You know, it's just over the counter. Got a runny nose, take this. Don't worry about the colon or whatever else that is associated to it. The nutritionist explained that the reason there was such an increase in prostate cancer was the use of over-the-counter antihistamines.

"This report said:

We do see...there is a difficulty within the area of the liver in processing and removing toxins from the body. We see that there is a kind of toxic condition that is occurring and we see that this does have other effects. We see that there are times when this one does experience headaches. We see that there are times when this one does experience a great sluggishness in this one's energy.

So we were on to it with this.

"Coming back from Minneapolis, Beau started to read the signs on the side of the road and license plates. It was the first time he ever really read and that was the first summer he ever rode a bike."

Terri and Bob's willingness to stick by their son, to find the truth and the ways that support it, returned to them many fold. When the right combinations were present, the results were immediate. Terri's determination for her son to have the best is reflected in her way of responding to him, his teachers and health practitioners, and most importantly, herself.

"There was a lot that was going on around Beau at this point. There was a situation in mine and Bob's relationship that since we didn't have full and complete communication we had started living totally different lives and I was like doing the silent rebellion into dance. One thing led to another and I was real close to having an affair and Bob was in his own way not knowing, and he was also in massage therapy school at the time. When I realized this, I went to Mexico with my friend Melanie. Part of this trip was to get away from everything and try to make some decisions. When I was there I read your book *Going in Circles: Our Search for a Satisfying Relationship* and in doing that I made some decisions to make the relationship work and stay committed to it. We went to a marriage counselor who wanted us to spend $800 to $1,000 in therapy a month and Bob and I agreed that was enough to cause a divorce. We went for intuitive counseling through Past Life Profiles and Past Life Crossings every three to four months. If we needed to, we would go to a Unity Church minister and work with them.

"So in Beau's mental and emotional state we are seeing a lot of what was going on in mine and Bob's relationship. The opening lines of his report says it all: *We see within this one there is a great deal of secrecy that this one practices.* He had secrecy in his environment but also he was practicing it himself."

Children learn what they live. There's a beautiful poem expressing the thought quite eloquently. When children live with love they learn to love. When children live with truth, they learn truth. When children live with discipline, they learn to be disciplined. When children live with creativity, they learn to create. When children live with reason, they learn how to reason. And it applies to the less desirable traits as well.

The point of greatest friction, conflict, for Beau was living with secrecy and he was learning it. The first paragraph of his report described how.

We see that therefore when this one does experience thoughts or perceptions or attitudes that are not in alignment with this image that this one is creating that this one does attempt to hide these from others. We see that in the process of hiding these from others that this one has also developed a kind of insecurity in that this one does hide from the self the awareness of what this one's thoughts truly are. Would suggest to this one that in order for this one to be at ease with the self that there is a need for this one to practice honesty.

Terri describes it this way, "If full communication was going on and if Beau had the mental skills, the reasoning and attention, he would have been able to put the things together. He would have known something wasn't right and communicate it to us. Or we would have been able to perceive it in him. We had to a degree, but at this point we were still living life with our eyes closed. It describes it well in Beau's report, *in the process of hiding these from others, this one developed a kind of insecurity* and in many ways I was hiding a lot of who I was and what I thought from Bob. Honesty was not really part of our vocabulary. In fact, I was actually practicing dishonesty until I realized the value of complete communication."

When I asked what caused the change, Terri said, "A reading." This is why the intuitive reports provided through the School of Metaphysics, are invaluable to parents. Each report is an insightful, very deep, comprehensive perspective of your child, giving you all the useful information to make intelligent choices as a parent. It also makes you closer to your child than you would have been otherwise, and I learned this through mothers like Terri before ever having a child.

"The health reports on children are invaluable," she would tell me. "A lot of times the child cannot tell you what's going on. They don't have the words. They don't have the experience. And it's a great tool for a parent to be able to understand and get greater understanding, not only for the child but for themself."

I remember remarking what peace of mind this must bring. "Yes, especially when you think your child is having seizures," Terri said.

Back then I could only imagine the peace of mind knowing the health of your child brings. Now I have experience.

Before we leave Terri, Bob, and Beau, I want to share with you the brilliant suggestions given in the description of Beau's mental system. Specific mental skills that would improve and enhance Beau's innate intelligence were revealed. Far from describing a youngster with a learning disability, these suggestions outlined a plan for bringing forth and developing Beau's potential. The list reads like a primer for every Indigo.

1) *Would suggest that this one practice some form of concentration in which this one is listening to this one's own thoughts.*

2) *Would suggest as well that this one practice communicating this one's thoughts in verbal form.*

3) *Would suggest that counseling could be beneficial.*

4) *Would suggest that writing could be beneficial.*

5) *Would suggest that even this one using another person to speak this one's thoughts to that this one does trust could be beneficial.... the goal (being) for this one to cause there to be an external expression of the thoughts that this one does have.*

When acted upon, these suggestions aid an Indigo by strengthening the reasoning power in the conscious mind during its most formative years. By determining which thoughts the child wants to practice, which thoughts s/he wants to change, which thoughts are being productive and which thoughts are being destructive the child learns cause and effect rather than punishment and reward. He becomes a versatile thinker capable of great insight. The key here is the precision in communication. Direct and straightforward lends itself to the honesty and clarity needed for pure reasoning. The greatest learning ability is reasoning.

Through the years I've found myself counseling teachers again and again to be open and honest with their students whether 4 or 44. *"Tell them what you want. Tell them how you feel!"* Mystic children of all ages respect this. Indigos *have* to know. They don't want imitations. Let us be grateful each time they give us an opportunity to reveal our Real Self.

The Three Fishermen of Windyville

My dad started it. When he visited at Christmas he talked to Ki about going fishing. I remembered from my own early years that dad would deep sea fish in the Gulf when we went on trips to New Orleans. It seemed like I remembered his dad having a tackle box with wire and hooks and wiggly worms.

I knew dad was reaching to have something in common with Ki. Something out of his own childhood. Something he had never been able to share with his not very interested daughter.

In February, dad's birthday card for Hezekiah had a photo of a little boy about Ki's age fishing. Dad's note said they would have to go fishing the next time he visited! That time came on dad's trip to California.

I had been preparing Ki since the birthday card, talking enthusiastically about fishing poles, trout, and bait whenever it seemed to fit into the flow of conversation or activity. This was my way of helping Grandpa Bill and Ki bond. Since turning six, Ki had showed more interest. Paul, one of his teachers here at the College, talked to him about fishing. Ki began to play with his toy fish and watch *PBS Nature* shows on octopuses and sea life. I trusted that a wonderful shared moment between grandpa and grandson would create a memory they'd treasure for years.

Shortly after Dad arrived, Ki brought up the fishing trip. He'd been looking forward to going down to the river all day. It was hot and sticky in the Missouri Ozarks this July summer day. Grandpa, Ki, Daniel and I drove a few miles to Bennett Springs, a state park well-known for its trout fishing. We walked around the grounds, even ate dinner, and all the while Ki remained focused. He wanted to fish.

I could begin to see that Grandpa's enthusiasm did not match his grandson's. I could see trouble coming, it echoed from my own past. I was suddenly afraid that Dad might hurt Ki by reneging on his deal. I didn't want him to knowingly or unknowingly set up his grandson. I reminded my dad that fishing was his idea, and that Ki had been looking forward to this since receiving Dad's card.

Finally Grandpa said we'd see if we could rent a fishing pole. The sight of my dad, Daniel and Hezekiah in the shop trying to figure out all the pieces they needed for fishing – pole, line, then bobber, then bait (Ki liked that part the best) – warmed my heart and brought a smile to my lips. It was the first time I had seen all the men in my life in this position and I savored the moment.

The guy behind the counter suggested string, and I almost laughed. When he asked if they knew how to cast, Dad seemed assured but we could tell he was bluffing. Daniel, honest and straight to the core, was the one who suggested the guy give a little refresher course which I encouraged Ki to watch.

The sight of the three walking across the road toward the river will be forever in my mind.

Ki held the pole for about five seconds, then he was off playing in the water. Grandpa Bill ended up sitting on a rock, with Daniel the only one fishing.

After an hour or so we returned the rented pole to the store. When we came out, Dad said, "Think that was worth it?"

Without hesitation Daniel said, "It was worth it for Ki to have the experience."

I smiled again. Truer words were never spoken. Twenty dollars bought Hezekiah a dream that would remain with him throughout his life.

Later Daniel told me he could see my dad starting to back out as he learned that every part of the fishing equipment was upping the ante. I immediately knew what he meant. Reneging was something Dad had done often when I was a child. In this moment, forty years or so later, I realized those kinds of experiences were where I learned not to get my hopes up too high because, after all, if your dad will disappoint you what will others do? This was the incomplete conclusion of a second grader, still lingering after all these years. A point that could now (forty years later), thanks to my husband, my son, and my dad, reach resolution.

Self awareness is exhilarating, yet what I appreciated the most was what Daniel said next, "If your dad had backed out, I was going to rent the equipment so Ki could fish. I knew Ki would probably only stay with it a little while, but he got to be there, and to see his dad fish."

Daniel was right.

Ki wasn't the only one who had learned a lesson. We all had.

M
E
M
O
R
Y

Hezekiah, age 3, and Daniel investigating word symbols

The Body Changers

After Ki was born my television viewing time went to less than an hour a day, quite a change for someone who prided herself on being in the know. Within three years, I was catching a bit of news here or there and taping a couple shows I enjoy for later viewing. For Ki the television set has become a means to view videos and even create them. What I call his Spielberg potential showed itself in the first three years.

At four, Hezekiah took an interest in *National Geographic* shows. A satellite channel was running the *Explorer* series every Friday, Saturday, and Sunday night, and one evening something caught Ki's attention as he moved through the Great Room of the College. Ki particularly liked the reptile segments, filled with sights and sounds from around the globe. We taped some of them for repeated viewing. Because of his keen interest, I began looking for other shows that might expand his realm of knowledge and give him valuable information for living among God's creatures in the Ozark Mountain countryside.

PBS's *Nature* series often contained shows fascinating to us and to Hezekiah. *"The Body Changers"* was one of these. It had more commentary than the other shows Ki had watched, including people as well as animals. The educational content was flawless with tidbits about the relationships between frogs, humans, and bacteria (!) all within the frame of change. Evolution. Growth. I hoped he would be ready for it. Turned out, he loved it, watching it a dozen times in a few weeks!

Then he didn't watch it for months.

One morning after Thanksgiving, Hezekiah was dancing up and down the hall in the fashion that was to become a trademark for expressing his creative genius. The dancing had begun when Ki was into his second year. He would dictate stories. He would recite the words and Dr. Pam, Dr. Laurel Clark (who you will hear more from soon) or whoever was with him would write them into a little book. Following this, either he or we would illustrate. This practice continues to evolve even now.

At this age, Ki would spend a good portion of his day walking back and forth (I call it pacing) talking out a story either from memory or of his own creation. This particular morning I thought he was creating. He was actually remembering. As I caught bits and pieces I realized it was from a science program of some kind. I asked him to repeat it, so I could enter it in his journal. He kindly obliged, and here is what I wrote:

> " 'In the beginning there is the fertilized egg. Its form couldn't be simpler, but this will change. Change doesn't stop with hatching or birth. Growing up is also a story of transformation. Some creatures do far more than simply grow up, they reinvent themselves. A fish can start life as a female but end up as a male! Polliwogs become frogs, caterpillars turn into butterflies and even weirder transformers live among us. Turn and face the strange.....The Body Changers!'*
>
> *Dictated by Hezekiah 11/27/2000 from Nature show intro. Delivered with enthusiasm and meaning, four times in a row! You are remarkable, your memory excellent.*"

Memory

What is received by the five senses of seeing, hearing, tasting, smelling, and touching is offered up to the pituitary gland for interpretation. The pituitary looks for similars – red looks like, red tastes like, red feels like, and so forth. How information has been previously interpreted (memory) in large part forms how we view ourselves and others.

All of this doesn't happen by magic. It happens as the result of our attention. The thinking part of us determines what stimuli we are around and what we will receive. We can enjoy the warm sun and cooling wind as it drifts off the ocean without ever noticing the sailboats nearby or the noisy beach party just down the beach or the aroma of fish frying at the cabana several yards away. *The real power of memory is not a physical one. It is a mental one.* The mind becomes a file clerk determining experience content and destination. When like goes with like, it is easier to remember.

When the attention is mastered, there is an even greater use for memory. The real power behind recall is the intelligence that chooses whether to be serious or humorous with the facts we have collected. Is it more intelligent to impress someone with what you know, or to give them a moment of joy and laughter? When do we do which? Memory plays an important part in the reasoning ability that will answer these, and other, questions throughout our lives.

Who Wants to be a Millionaire?

I was a techno kid myself. Of course technology when I was Ki's age consisted of new self-defrosting refrigerators, washer/dryers, and color television. So I watched a lot of TV.

I used to sit in bed, home from school with some half-concocted malady, a pen in hand and "play" *Jeopardy*. Looking back I realize I was getting as much, if not more, education watching the brainy game show than I would probably have received if I'd been in school that day. So it was natural that I would enjoy the phenomenon of *Who Wants to be a Millionaire*, a trivia show designed on the multiple choice modem.

When Ki was four I'd sometimes turn it on and he would show differing levels of interest. One night, when five, he knew the answer to two of the questions. One was about amphibians and the other about volcanoes, two areas of high interest to him.

Some time later, Dr. Laurel Clark was teaching Ki and Bri through a multiple choice game. Dr. Laurel asked, "Where did the first ink that was used for writing pens come from?"

The choices were: octopus ink, berry juice, graphite, or crushed loadstone.

Ki said, "Octopus ink." The right answer. That was a use of memory worth noting, being a piece of information he had learned from an *Eyewitness* video some months before. I knew the connection between attention, concentration, and memory, so this demonstration told me how developed Ki's skill was. I was learning the depth of this child's memory recall. Just short of photographic, Ki could remember faces and names, places and arrangements, who gave him gifts and when. Because I know memory is a function of giving your undivided attention and what you give your attention to is a function of your desire to give and need to learn, these displays of mental skill told me what I wanted to know about Hezekiah's growth and development.

What Ki came up with next, really left an impression on me.

Wanting to keep the game going, Ki took Laurel's lead and conceived his own question: "What land evolved in isolation from the rest of the world?" (Yes, the words were actually his. By watching *National Geographic Explorer*, he had become quite familiar with the question-multiple choice answer mode). The choices he gave were: Galapagos Islands, Madagascar, Greenland, Australia.

The answer came from an hour video on *Madagascar* he had received the Christmas before from adopted Grandma Beets. He had watched it, studied it, enough times to know the script by heart.

From birth, the mind is so hungry it soaks up every bit of information it comes into contact with. Indiscriminately. Whatever discrimination is present is provided by the parents or caregivers in the child's environment. What the child sees, hears, smells, tastes, and touches is what the environment provides. A mother's smile and a father's embrace impress the consciousness, leaving an imprint that will echo becoming more substantial with repeated experience.

The more complete the attention we give at any age, the keener the memory. Since young children are building conscious memory from the time their souls choose to enter this physical world, what we provide as stimuli becomes a significant contributing factor in the kind of person they will grow up to be. Nurture certainly has its impact, as does the absence of it. Nurture builds the brain connections for acceptance, kindness, and caring. It is an essential balancer to our head oriented, technologically virtual world.

Daniel and I are keenly aware of and attentive to the environmental stimuli Hezekiah receives. Many times he has said something that has prompted me to ask, "Who taught you that?" or "Where did you hear that word?" Being consciously aware of your own thoughts and words enables you to know your own influence and that of others. And knowing your own influence gives you security that you will draw on as your child matures.

Hezekiah's world is one of people he lives with and nature he lives in. Sacred geometry takes on the form of constructing monolithic domes. Science lives in kitchen chemistry, the organic garden, and in body kinetics. Language is developed from the thousand words hidden in each picture. Everywhere relationships are established, dissolved, and renewed, from the life cycle of a frog to the changing seasonal weather to the comings and goings of people. Memory gives us the ability to see the complete cycles in ourselves and in the world around us.

At the College of Metaphysics everyone teaches everyone else. Every day. Those who know more about a subject or skill, teach those who want to learn. Those who want to learn afford those who know the opportunity to figure out how they know what they know. It is a valuable system of community, a futuristic vision of human interaction evolving its spiritual identity. Some may call it utopian. We call it reality.

"Metamorphosis"

When Hezekiah was about two years old, Laurel would sing a song to him
that her 5th grade science teacher had taught her. The song was called
"*Metamorphosis.*" It had a catchy little tune that reminded me of a cross
between "Tiptoe through the Tulips" and some college fight song. The words
went like this:

> *What do we mean by metamorphosis?*
> *Metamorphosis, a kind of change is what it is.*
> *When it's a metamorphosis.*
>
> *There is an egg. The egg changes.*
> *Into an embryo, the embryo changes.*
> *Into a tadpole, the tadpole changes.*
> *Into a froglet. The froglet changes,*
> *And it's a frog a frog at last!*
> *There is an egg. The egg changes.*
> *Into a larva, the larva changes.*
> *Into a pupa. The pupa changes*
> *And it's a butterfly at last!*

Ki had Laurel sing this scientific ditty many times when he was three.
By four he was singing with her. At five, he might sing it to a butterfly or to
the bubbles in his bathtub.

Shortly after Hezekiah turned seven, we were working our way through
a science book for ages 6-8. We had recently illustrated a small book on the
growth cycle of a frog and I was trying to get him interested in the butterfly
book. The related memory was turned on and he broke out into the *Metamorphosis* song! It had been a while since he had sung it. All the words came
tumbling out like he'd rehearsed them.

Then Ki did something with the song that had never even occurred to
me. I had to laugh when I heard him sing:

There is a frog. The frog changes.
Into a froglet, the froglet changes.
Into a tadpole. The tadpole changes,
And it's an egg, an egg at last!

There is an butterfly. The butterfly changes.
into a pupa, the pupa changes.
Into a caterpillar. The caterpillar changes
And it's an egg, an egg at last!

Ki was purposefully mixing up the life cycle order! My ability to enjoy Hezekiah's humor did not always come naturally. In fact, it was a significant part of my learning that required some reorganization of memories.

I had made the mistake a couple years earlier of trying to correct Hezekiah when correction was the last thing on his mind. And he let me know it. One day he purposefully mixed up the names of the dinosaurs in a book we had read many times. Being a dutiful parent-teacher (and totally missing his joke) I said, "Hezekiah! The brontosaurus has the long neck and the stegosaurus has the pointy back."

He looked up at me with those big eyes, giggled and then a bit indignantly declared, "I know that Mommy!" Then he added, "They're both plant eaters." I was duly put in my place. He remembered more of what we had read about early Earth evolution than I.

To the ears of a former A student who had believed that earning the grades was the way to a happy life, I was most humbled by the little interchange. In college I began seeing the fallacy in the grade theory of life. John Taylor Gatto *(see page 182)* calls it class position which leads to social class position later in life. I wanted more from life and that had led me to study metaphysics. In the ensuing years I've learned the key to a happy life is developing Self awareness through meditation, pranayama, and visualization. With his dinosaur joke, Hezekiah was providing me with an opportunity to teach what I had learned while stimulating an update of old memory patterns no longer compatible with my current Self awareness.

This led to an associated memory. I recalled how irritating it was for me as a child when adults would try to tell me something I already knew. This irritation (or impatience) is a weakness in the talented/gifted/indigo character that is balanced by a strong heart, a healthy intuitive connection. Now as the adult, the parent, I was in a position to supply that balance. To do so, I would need to come to terms with some of my past.

I realized I had missed Ki's joke because I was attached to him having the right answer. Years of "here's the question, give us the right answer" programming surfaced and I realized how my natural joy and happiness had been buried under repeated demands of "prove to us you know the answer, and we'll give you something you want" (a grade, a reference letter, a job, a pay raise). I'd come a long way in freeing myself from this limitation, now I was facing a new level of awareness. My reaction told me that I needed to be as secure in Hezekiah's intelligence as I have come to be with my own. He would only learn programmed responses if I, or someone else, teach them to him.

At the bottom of my reaction, I found the remnants of caring more about what other people think than the truth I know. This was momentarily painful, since the love of truth is so strong within me. But I learned a long time ago that acceptance leads to freedom and denial to bondage.

A passage from the *Tao Te Ching* filtered through my mind:

> *"Most people fret about themselves and their status,*
> *but you don't have to do this.*
>
> *What is success and what is failure?*
>
> *If you have prestige and favour,*
> *all you worry about is that it'll get taken away.*
> *And if you have a lowly place,*
> *you are still basically afraid.*
>
> *So both, at the root, make for fear."*

My irritation with Ki not being serious, not giving the right answer, was rooted in what I had been taught about success. To be successful, you had to be smart. Others had to recognize that you were smart, then they would reward you and you would have what you want in life. That's a fair assessment of the train of thought that dominated my schooling.

I want something different for Hezekiah and all children, and with the help of others, equally invested, we can create something different for them. In the School of Metaphysics we teach success as a mathematical equation: ideal + purpose + activity = success. Purpose was what I learned to add, and purpose was what I was learning now with this Indigo child. The *Tao* describes it this way.

> *"What does it mean that success is a problem?*
> *It means people are too bound up in themselves.*
> *If they weren't so self-obsessed*
> *they'd have no need to be worried.*
>
> *If you can put yourself aside –*
> *then you can do things for the whole of the world.*
> *And if you love the world, like this*
> *then you are ready to serve it."*

Hezekiah's father and I have devoted our adult years to bringing this passage alive. Our energies are fully given in service to others. We strive to align our consciousness with the goodness for all, loving completely and freely, without condition. This has drawn to us (and us to them) thousands of people who have enriched our souls. It has also drawn to us a vital, brilliant soul who is, with our help, learning to live metaphysical principles from birth.

How do we teach our children to be in the world but not of it? Certainly, first by example. Next, by instruction. Then by expectation. When my mind rested on these truths, I could accept that I know Hezekiah is smart, and when you know something you no longer have anything to prove. You are free to breathe, to love, to move in the world performing your dharma, to give what you have to offer.

Two years after my initial smartening-up lesson,
when I heard Hezekiah's new rendition of "*Metamorphosis*", we both
laughed. He for the joke, and I in admiration of his skill. His intentional
mixing of the lyrics requires many essential life skills: undivided attention,
concentration, and memory to be certain. It also reflected an imaginative
flair that then leads to a bit of reasoning.

There was more to come this summer day. Later, I heard him singing
yet another rendition.

> *There was an egg. The egg changes.*
> *Into a caterpillar, the caterpillar changes.*
> *Into a frog, the frog changes*
> *Into a pupa, the pupa changes*
> *Into a froglet, the froglet changes*
> *Into a butterfly, the butterfly changes*
> *Into a tadpole, the tadpole changes.*
> *And it's an egg, an egg at last!*

He had integrated the life cycles of the frog and caterpillar into the tune of
the song.

This is the kind of mind you don't put in a box. You respect it. Encourage it, while developing the heart so its particular genius that it offers the
world can flourish with a sense that all people are kindred and our destinies
intrinsically linked to each other, to the planet, and to our Maker.

Hungry all the Time
Insatiable Appetites for Learning

When Ki turned seven I knew it was time to organize my thoughts so I could give guidance and a sense of mental structure to his learning. Seven was when the ancient Greeks began to school their boys. Seven was when youth were admitted into monasteries. If it seems like a magical number, it is. The physical world is based upon cycles of seven. For a newly incarned soul, this means the first seven years of life the child is using the body constructed for him or her primarily by the genetics of both parents and the thoughts of the pregnant mother.

During the nine months of gestation, her thought-energy goes into building the body that the new soul will claim around the time of physical birth. What she builds will continue to express its cycle, serving the soul throughout the next seven years. This dovetails as the soul's new conscious mind begins growing thus allowing the child to claim his responsibility for forming his own vehicle. This is one reason why children's mental and emotional disposition as well as physical appearance can during one stage pattern the father's, during another take after the mother, and in another manifest completely new expressions.

As a teacher of soul, I am concerned with *how* Hezekiah learns as well as what. My metaphysical practices spanning twenty five years have brought very rich experiences. The value of the ten essential life skills – the back-bone of School of Metaphysics teachings – increases every day of my life. Raising an Indigo child brought the need to translate these skills for the young.

Both Daniel and I have taught thousands of people the principles of Universal Law and how to harmonize consciousness for peace, security, and prosperity. I love teaching the metaphysics course because I learn how to make the teachings a part of myself. Teaching metaphysics in and out of the classroom, to people 14 to 70, is how I became a teacher. For me, teaching – the act of passing on to another what is most valuable in my experience – is as important as breathing. The ability to use your own influence to illuminate another's way is precious. It is the height of human relations for it fulfills an inner need while helping others increase in some way. Teaching another soul is the highest form of giving.

Until our son was born, the youngest person I had ever taught with any degree of regularity was a fourteen-year-old boy who wanted to be in the SOM classes so much he convinced his father to drive him and a fifteen-year-old friend to class each week. Their trek from Winfield, Kansas to Wichita, was sixty miles round trip. The young men had phenomenal success with the mental disciplines (they particularly enjoyed the ESP exercises) and devoured the concepts in the most brilliant manner, asking questions frequently, considering the response and asking a new question. The ability to assimilate constructs beyond the physical world is characteristic of Indigos.

Indigos "see" the world differently than most. Like the geniuses and masters in mankind's history, they are driven by a connection with an inner urge that must be satisfied. Experience has taught me that how our brains are programmed has a lot to do with the direction that genius takes. Our early exposure to the physical world shapes the conscious, waking mind. Since birth, Hezekiah's experiences have been in support of the Universal Principles his father and I live and teach. Living at the College of Metaphysics gives Ki an amazing wealth of experiences. He lives with people of all ages, colors, sizes, shapes, backgrounds, faiths, and from several countries. He is not learning them by neighborhood or nationality or class or grade. His experience is of people, living together, working together, laughing and crying together. Here the seeds are planted and nourished daily in Ki's mind for "loving one another" and "loving your neighbor as yourself."

Love is the ultimate human lesson. Everything in our existence substantiates this, from personal accounts of near-death experiences, to the thoughts and feelings that rise within the newborn's parent, to the teachings of every great master. Love is why Kiah's first seven years were spent with almost constant companionship. We have spent every night in the same house with the exception of four nights when his granddad needed Daniel's help. From even before Ki was born, our lives changed, willingly, to accommodate this new soul.

The physical stimulation is intentionally broad. In his first six months his father would walk him up and down the hall repeatedly reciting addition tables (1+1 is 2, 1+2 is 3, 1+3 is 4, etc.). It sounded like a sacred Indian ritual, with the steady pad of feet and chanting. The fruit of this effort would make itself known a few years later when at six Ki was doing mental math at a fourth grade level.

One of us is accessible to him twenty-four hours a day. As he is aging, he spends increasing amounts of time with others, enjoying the benefit of their experience and energy. These people are an important part of Ki's learning, feeding him attitudes and points of view with each answer to his endless stream of questions.

Like most Indigos his questions are probing ones. "How come your brother wanted a room of his own?" "Where did your daddy live if he didn't live with you and your mommy?" "How come she got her feelings hurt?" "What do you want to be when you grow up?" Since we live with a new group of people every six months (students come to study for a year at the College of Metaphysics each January and July), the answers are varied. Ki's socialization comes from people from four to eighty. This is a reality of multicultural education few have even dreamed of and it is a grand experiment in the making.

Hezekiah is learning global community from living it.

Multiple Intelligences

What does it mean to be Indigo or violet or red? Colors of the spectrum, the separating of light into differing rates of vibration, identify certain characteristics and potentials. The influence of color in our lives is best seen in nature. The blue of the domed sky and the cool ocean, the green of spring growth, the reddish brown of the fertile earth, the yellow of the warm sun, each lend an element to the whole of creation. So it is with people.

The Indigos are the result of physical evolution. What we will learn about their genetic characteristics in the years to come will astound us. These are wise souls who hunger not for the finite things of the material world. They are mystic children, who exist in more than one world. How well we respond to the Real Self, the inner souls of these children, can accelerate their spiritual evolution, and our own. How do we do this? What is the Real Self? Hindu scriptures, Taoist writings, and Buddhist texts are filled with such references.

The inner wisdom of the Real Self has been taught in secret schools of thought for centuries; in Buddhist and Christian monasteries, in Plato's Academy and in the Lyceum. The kind of education that promotes and encourages personal Enlightenment is what every soul craves. Expanded consciousness is what ultimately every soul will achieve. The School of Metaphysics exists as an open forum for teaching individuals how to live in harmony with the Universal Laws and Truths that govern creation. We teach the unfolding, understanding, and development of the whole Self – physically, emotionally, mentally, and spiritually – to adults.

Now we are responding to the needs of the incoming soul, extending the ideal of the SOM education to include the newly born so they may sustain awareness of their natural connections to the Creator. Love is an essential part of staying awake. It is the reward for the effort. If love is the ultimate lesson for human beings, equally important for the Real Self to flourish is respect, the ultimate lesson for reasoners.

When I began envisioning ways to describe education for these mystic children, I saw it as a kind of Venn diagram moving into infinity. A more accurate design might be the physical representation of Phi, the geometric principle known as the Golden Ratio found on all levels of existence, in trees and flowers, in the nautilus shell and even the bones of our body. I firmly believe that education can be rooted in ancient wisdom, in principles of the eternal creation that express through all living forms in our Universe. I know when attention is directed inwardly, access to the storehouse of knowledge in Universal Mind is yours.

The ten essential living skills we teach adults are reflected in this design. They reflect thought patterns, skills in thinking that have physical counterparts. They overlap because each builds on the next while feeding those that come later. Like a spiral they continue the action of giving and receiving, all from the foundation of Self respect.

Indigos demand respect. It has been said they come into the world with a feeling of royalty. To encounter this expectation free from fear in a toddler can be an enlightening experience. Four-year-old Iris commands a room of adults, easily directing them toward roles in a play, while five-year-old Hezekiah says to a room of two dozen people, "Excuse me! I have an announcement." The potential leadership in these children is awesome. It is inspiring. And it is in need of the maturity that only experience can give.

The maturing of this feeling of self importance is in our care, yours and mine. We can dispel this feeling by putting the Indigo "in their place" or by refusing to acknowledge their value with countless "time outs." This alienates them, they become thwarted, often bitter. And as we have seen in our world sometimes they lose contact with a conscience that respects life. In order to teach respect, we must first have a personal experience with it. From personal experience is born authority, and authority is the essence of respect. When you speak from your own authority, Indigos listen. They want to know how you think and feel. They are not impressed by the party line whether put out by politicians wanting to keep their jobs or by frustrated parents who are afraid of something they won't admit.

One of the greatest lessons I have learned thus far through my son is to be present. This has required me to be emotionally honest as well as mentally clear. Teaching is in my blood. I began passing on what I had learned to my dolls at the age of three and I have been teaching ever since. Teaching our son is natural, and he has taught me to be a better teacher.

One day I was trying to explain to him the value of reading. This child who has been read to for hours every day since he was born and who at two was dictating stories to adults who would listen and write them into little books, was showing little interest in learning the skill himself. I felt myself becoming panicked as the birthdays passed by, after all, weren't you supposed to be reading in preschool? What would Ki's aunts, public school teachers who had made their ideas of home schooling pretty clear, think? Was it something I was doing wrong? Did Ki need a "normal" education? As the thoughts flew, the emotions were stirred.

Having developed concentrative skill I could isolate the thoughts and learn from each when they were mine. I knew I was doing everything I could. I knew Ki was absorbing the information and my belief was one day it would all come together, as if by magic, and he would be voracious. I had heard this many times from many parents and teachers. I trusted them, and I believed in Ki. Still, I had emotions about it.

Sometimes the emotions would surface in our interchanges. The most provocative was when Hezekiah took to saying, "I can't read." I didn't know where it had come from. I still don't to this day. I tried reasoning with him, "You know your name and all the letters and this word or that". I tried affirmation, "You are a good reader!" I tried asking him why he would say such a thing. He had no answer. I backed off for quite a while being at a loss but certain that if I persisted he would become more and more polarized. I continued reading to him, and writing letters, and letting dad do all the direct teaching with letters and words.

Watching Daniel gave me the perspective I needed. It gave me the respect I needed. From this vantage point I could see Hezekiah, his dad, and me in a new light. Daniel was forever patient. Each morning for many months he would grab a plain white piece of paper about four inches square and write a word. Just one word, for that day. He would then tell Hezekiah what the word was and ask him to write it. If Ki needed help, Dan would offer it.

What I witnessed was so obvious. So simple. So universal. It was the building each day. The consistency of discipline which gave Hezekiah the experience he needed. My eagerness could so easily turn into impatience when Ki became uncooperative. It was too easy for me to let my feelings get hurt, to feel personally rejected and frustrated. I knew I did not want these emotions between my son and me, so *I was willing to change.*

I learned it is very easy to be patient when you only spend five minutes on something every day. It is a no-brainer for someone who already has the understanding. For those of us, like many of the Indigos, who want what we want when we want it, it is an epiphany for maturity. In my eagerness for Ki to learn I had been failing to apply truths I had learned through daily discipline of mind and body. Once I saw what I needed to do, I was free to do it.

Now at seven Ki and I read every day. Some days he reads one word, his favorite word is "and" which has become a joke between us. Some days he asks how to spell words he wants to write in a story or in a letter. The progress is there. I am no longer intimidated by book learning, nor is he.

As a parent, I have learned to respect book learning in a whole new light. Being a former trivia buff, I know the fun and self-competitiveness of mastering greater levels of information. Being a meditator, I know the thrill of aligning the outer self with the inner Source of all wisdom. I experience the difference between knowledge that feeds the brain, that enables me to function in the physical world with ease and competency, and wisdom that feeds the soul causing my heart and perception to open to all of creation. Seeing value in both, I hold this in mind when desiring to draw to me the people and experiences that will help me become a better student and teacher.

This is how the work of Dr. Howard Gardner came into my life. In the late 1980's, Dr. Gardner forged a new theory that has already begun transforming the traditional public schooling model. He called his theory Multiple Intelligences. Many resources exist on this topic and I encourage you to research them. I will try to summarize the concepts here, especially as they relate to what I am finding most helpful in educating the youngest of the College of Metaphysics residents.

Dr. Gardner began by asking, *What is intelligence?* The first concepts were based on three propositions:

1. **Intelligence is not unitary.**

2. **Intelligence is not fixed.**

3. **Intelligence is not fully measured by IQ.**

This process of elimination may seem like a long way around to find an answer, but bear with me. Gardner determined that how we define intelligence has a profound effect on what and how we teach. For instance it is intelligent for people living near water to learn to swim, whereas it might be deemed a waste of time for those living in the desert. Gardner asserted that intelligence allows us to survive, develop skills, communicate, create, perceive, know the world, and make wise decisions. In other words, whatever the soul needs for its growth and learning is made available through how we employ intelligence. Developing the overall, comprehensive picture of the Self is the work human beings are ready to undertake.

There are three objectives of Multiple Intelligences. The first is *matching* whose goal is to increase academic success. Second is *stretching*, the goal being increasing the development of all intelligences. The third is *celebrating* whose goal is increasing understanding of our own uniqueness and that of others.

The first objective (matching) centers on a principle I have learned by teaching adults in the School of Metaphysics. We describe it as keeping the individual's best interest in mind first. This means responding to the student's need for learning, a freeing concept for the talented and gifted of today. This is accomplished by becoming knowledgeable in the different ways intelligence expresses itself.

As a result of his research, Dr. Gardner brought forth a new definition of intelligence as sensitivity to and skill with certain kinds of stimuli. This is most exciting because it leaves open the possibility that educators may begin to value the sense of attention as readily as they do the five physical senses associated with the body. What we perceive with the mind through clairvoyance (clear seeing) for instance is of equal value to what we see with our eyes. Gardner's ideas are bringing a new respect to what makes us who we are, and expecting it to be honored and employed in educational settings.

To achieve the second goal of stretching, Gardner delineated eight intelligences found in human beings. These describe the ways we are sensitive to the world around us and within us. These are:

1. **Verbal/Linguisitic (word)**
2. **Logical/Mathematical (math)**
3. **Visual/Spatial (art)**
4. **Musical/Rhythmic (music)**
5. **Body/Kinesthetic (body)**

6. **Nature/Creation (science)**
7. **Interpersonal (people)**
8. **Intrapersonal (self)**

The most exciting aspect of Gardner's work here is his effort to distinguish how thinking occurs from the content of thought, from *what* we think about. It's like separating the scientist from his experiment, or in Zen terms the thinker from the thought, in Taoist, the knower from the known. This is the beginning of respecting the Real Self, and to think this is being introduced into some school systems in our country is so encouraging for our youth!

I have learned that by exploring these areas the ways to identify the talents and gifts – the understandings in the soul – become apparent. One child learns multiplication tables through the rap rhythm of a song, while another learns by counting beans. One child learns alone while another learns with peers. One child draws his ideas, while another acts them out or writes stories. The affinity for particular ways of expressing are open door-ways in the soul of the child. They are natural ways of experiencing. En-couraging these innate ways of experiencing and learning brings about the entrainment of the inner and outer minds of the child. The connections with the Real Self are realized and reinforced even when the teacher might be unaware of the magnitude of the endeavor!

Acting together these intelligences enable us to survive, to perceive information, to acquire knowledge and skills, to create solutions, to commu-nicate, and to make wise choices.

One of the first ways I incorporated Dr. Gardner's ideas into my thinking was through creating a Mind Map (*see diagram page 96*) of how I wanted to help Hezekiah develop his intelligences. Working with other metaphysics teachers we endeavor to bring out each intelligence each day in the children who live on campus. In order to teach it we must first be it, and so the entire community grows spiritually from the effort.

Depending upon the teacher's experience and understanding, the instruction can incorporate more than one intelligence. The ideal then becomes unifying the expression of each intelligence in experience. For instance, one day when five-year-old Ki was singing the *"Metamorphosis"* song (#4 music) over and over, the theme became life cycles. Everyone picked up the theme and carried it throughout the day. Hezekiah and Briana collected tadpoles and watched a rainstorm form and dissolve (#5 nature). They caught 57 tadpoles that day, returning 42 and keeping 15 (#2 math), then counting the subsets in the frog cycle: 23 froglets, 200+ eggs, the 57 tadpoles and a few pioneering full grown frogs. They read (#1 word) about the life cycle of a frog, watched the *Body Changers* video (#3 visual and #8 intrapersonal), then drew pictures of the metamorphosis (see Ki's illustration). All of this was accomplished with the assistance of five people (#7 interpersonal) who taught the youngsters throughout the day. By evening, Ki and Bri had experienced expressions of life cycles in each of the eight

The Life Cycle of the Frog
by Hezekiah Condron, age 5

Drawn in bright green marker, Hezekiah did this rendition completely on his own. The numbers were later added by his mother.

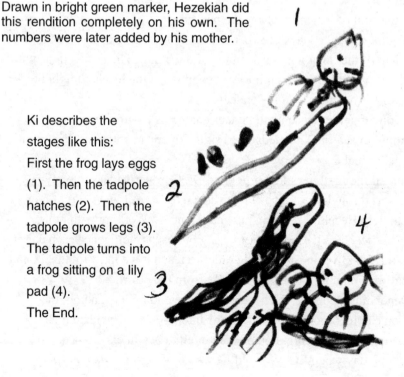

Ki describes the stages like this: First the frog lays eggs (1). Then the tadpole hatches (2). Then the tadpole grows legs (3). The tadpole turns into a frog sitting on a lily pad (4). The End.

intelligence areas. A complete learning involving all intelligences and all senses was experienced. This is one of the reasons Ki remembers the *"Metamorphosis"* song.

Being familiar with the structure and function of the mind is a great asset in interpreting Gardner's eighth point, the intrapersonal. The entire course in self mastery taught at the School of Metaphysics is devoted to developing this internal spark of intelligence that fuels all the others. Gardner's work is one of the inspirations for me in developing an educational model I call the Learning Bagua that I hope to write about next year.

The third objective for multiple intelligence – *celebrating* – affirms the completeness of respect. As we respect ourselves, we have the skill to respect all of life. When we are validated, our experiences and viewpoints respectfully considered, we learn how to give this to others. We can learn to see from another's point of view, and day after day our world expands.

I am learning so much from interacting with the students and teachers at the College of Metaphysics in educating our youngsters. To experience the freedom of learning from what life brings us, is refreshing and challenging. Cooking meals becomes an adventure in math and chemistry and nature. Frog eggs gleaned from the nearby pond become natural scientific laboratories here on 1500 acres of God's country. Stories become paintings and songs and improvisations. Gatherings bring people of all backgrounds, ages, and ideas to play, sing, act, live, love, and laugh together for a few hours or for a lifetime. The whole, functioning Self uses all of mind, these eight intelligences expressed on seven inner planes of existence.

As Multiple Intelligences becomes a part of the training and experience of more teachers, we will find ways to appreciate our mystic children and give them what they need. Multiple Intelligences is a way to open our minds to the potential of human beings, while serving the needs of souls who want to evolve. By honoring intelligence in Self and others, humanity evolves.

At about the same time people in the Midwest were exploring the frontiers of mind and consciousness, so were others around the world. One of them is Tony Buzan author of fourteen books, including *Use Both Sides of Your Brain, Use Your Perfect Memory,* and *Speed Reading.*

Since the '70's Tony has explored and developed how we see and use our brain power. Mind mapping is his brainchild. He has refined it over the past decade, teaching it to people from all walks of life from corporate executives at IBM and Hewlett-Packard to Olympic coaches and athletes to government officials. "Only during the last few centuries have we begun gathering information about the structure and workings of our brains," Buzan writes.

Mind mapping is a dynamic mental tool for using your brain's full potential. His **Mind Map Book** is highly recommended. It includes dozens of mind maps, one done by a homeschooler concerning her child's studies and several about academic subjects. The facing page is a mind map of the biography Ki and I read about Albert Einstein's young life. On the following two pages is a mind map illustrating the enlightenment of the mystic child in eight areas of Multiple Intelligence.

Mind maps can be made on any subject and for any purpose. Using this mental tool calls upon more of your mind thus lighting up your whole brain!

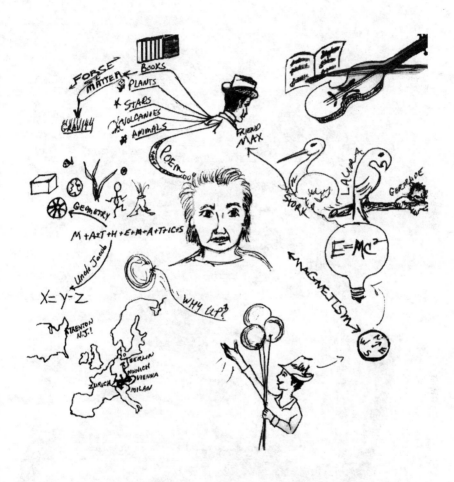

*Mind map of Albert Einstein's foundation years
fashioned in place of traditional word outline*

*Mind Map of Multiple Intelligence
expressing through four, then eight,*

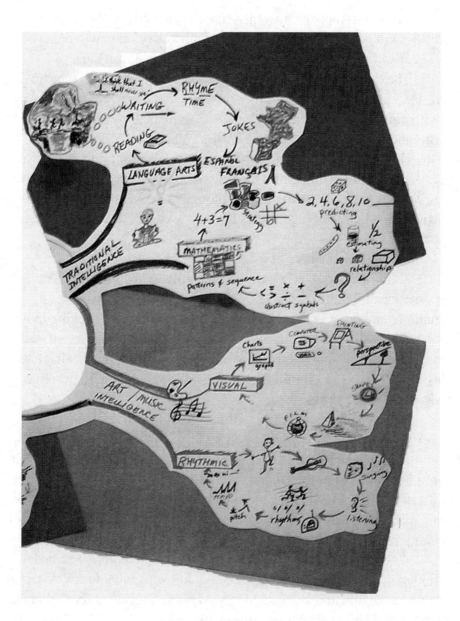

*with core image of the enlightened child
arenas of intelligence.*

A Different Kind of Memory

I was preparing supper for twenty-five people in the College of Meta-physics kitchen. Ki had been playing with "Gary", a newly-engaged 30-year-old who planned to half-jokingly have a dozen kids.

The time to serve the dishes had come. I turned from the stove to see Hezekiah coming toward me surrounded in a black cloud, eyes swimming in tears, a scowl on his face. Immediately, I held out my arms and lifting him in my arms I said, "What's happened?"

He buried his head on my shoulder, as I rocked him. My eyes scanned the room behind him looking for Gary or another adult who might shed light on this trauma. Although there were people there, none seemed directly involved in Ki's distress and, therefore, were as puzzled as I.

"What's the matter?" I asked.

"I don't want to tell you," was his reply. This was not a new response and, because I had learned the relationship between heart, emotion, and brain in me, I had discovered what was happening in my son's mind when he would say this. Saying "I don't want to tell you" meant he needed and wanted time to experience, to absorb, what had just occurred. This assimilation process would help him to describe it, talk about it. Later.

We stayed a few moments until I felt him relax a bit, then I said, "Let Mommy get the food ready then I'll hold you more."

He waited. This was the first time he was willing to stand nearby until I could finish what I had started. As I reached for serving dishes, I looked through the window into the Great Room for evidence of what might have happened at the play site. Briana, an older friend, was calmly picking up blocks. Gary was nowhere to be seen.

As dishes were handed to those who wanted to help, I turned to Ki who was ready to be held again. Not knowing what to say, I started humming to him and we walked around a bit. I signaled for the others to go ahead and begin eating without us.

Eventually Ki and I settled on the couch where we could see the tables where people had gathered to eat. Four of them, stretching 30 feet down the room. Half way sat Gary. I could catch snatches of the conversation he was having with the other adults near him. "He's going to have to learn it sometime," I heard him say. "Gary!" one of the women smilingly reproached him.

At one point Gary turned around smiling sheepishly at Ki who did not look in his direction.

I didn't know what had happened and Ki wasn't telling but I had heard the "so-and-so-will-have-to-learn-it-sooner-or-later" many times through my life. By different peoples, in as many different places. Each time the sentiment masked hurtful intentions their owners wanted to disavow by projecting them onto the innocent.

After 15 minutes, I could engage Ki in a *Click Magazine* story about octopuses. In time he relaxed climbing out of my arms to sit next to me, and eventually getting off the couch to begin marching back and forth as he made up his own story. The initial reaction time had passed.

Once dinner was finished and Ki was playing with a friend, I sat down at the table to grab a bite myself. Gary came up, I thought to tell me what had happened, but it was for another reason, which I found odd. Many of his actions this day were an education for me just by contrast to what my own had been in similar situations. A child in my care who was upset, I would comfort. If they left me because I was what they were upset with, I would follow them when they sought their parents, making sure they were safe and cared for. I would have let the parents know at the first available opportunity what had occurred so they would know. So they would be able to respond with knowledge.

When Gary's reason for coming to me had nothing to do with what had happened less than two hours before between him and my son, I asked what had occurred. "We were wrestling and I kinda pinned him, holding his arms back, while Ann and Pat (two 20-year-old girls) tickled him. He said, 'Stop!' and this strange look came over his face. That's when I let him go and he left."

Having described what happened, Gary now looked a bit more concerned than he had while talking at the table. My first urge was to ease his mind, for I could tell he was now wondering if he had done the right thing. We both knew it was questionable at best. "It's happened a couple times before, where Ki will feel trapped. It possibly relates to a past memory," I said, offering Gary more information for reasoning.

At that Dr. Sheila Benjamin, a School of Metaphysics field director who makes frequent visits to our College and Ki's adopted aunt, told about a time her husband was playfully holding her down and she panicked. She said it was the first time she had felt such fear and it was overwhelming. While my attention was directed to Dr. Sheila, Gary seized the opportunity to make an exit, and it would be some time before the opportunity arose to pursue it with him.

My learning with this sequence of events continued. It stuck with me and I knew there was something to come to terms with, something I wanted to understand. I thought about what had happened off and on through the next couple of days. I knew sometimes Ki would experience something and not talk about it until a day later, so I decided to be patient and not bring it up again for a while. He didn't awake with nightmares that night, as he sometimes did after a real or virtual experience scared him shortly before going to sleep. I received that as a good sign.

The next morning I taught the second session in multidimensional mentoring, a year-long training in ministerial counseling arising from seven schools of yoga. This session developed one of the hatha yogas—bhakti yoga, the yoga of devotion. Here, within the context of this session, I would gain another perspective deepening my understanding of Hezekiah's experience with Gary.

The previous month students had written papers concerning a polarizing report in *USA Today*, a national newspaper, on the upcoming execution of Tim McVeigh, an American who had set off a bomb in downtown Oklahoma City in 1995 killing several dozen adults and children. The assignment was for my students to read the article employing self counseling and other counseling concerning the thoughts and feelings that might arise or that were expressed in the article. Then they were to find the lines of relativity to this and *Walking Between the Worlds*, an excellent book on transcending polarity by Gregg Braden.

It had been a month since they had seen their papers and reading them aloud proved revelatory for each of them. So did the counseling which followed. This was the subject beginning today's session. Sharka Glet (one of the students) talking about her realizations brought

Hezekiah back to my mind. Sharka had written a brief report. One page. Much shorter than her usual reports and the shortest in the class. What she brought out in the paper, however, would be life changing.

She began by saying as she was reading her paper in class, she did not remember writing any of the words at all. It was as if it was the first time she had seen the page. She was also struck by how, halfway through the page, she wrote sentences that didn't make sense. This shocked her. Living the first 25 years of her life in Czech Republic, English was a language she adopted much later in life and one that still required her attention to use. Doing so was a point of pride for her, so her seeming illiteracy puzzled her.

In yogic fashion she explored these elements of consciousness. Thinking about McVeigh's execution had caused childhood thoughts about death to surface. This was where she had learned to deny suffering, Sharka said. From that point of cause she described several different threads that had stretched through everything important to her for 50 years. She was awestruck by what she saw, and freed by her willingness to stay with it. She was no longer willing to turn away.

Within seconds of sharing her experience, the events of the day before came back to me and the pieces came together. I decided to describe Hezekiah's experience to these students feeling certain they would find it useful in ministering to others in the future. The reality of youthful experiences that continue to live far beyond their expected lifespan is at the root of many karmic patterns.

As I told the part of the Gary and Ki's story I knew, I saw it from another perspective. Only through relating it to a group of teachers did I fully cognize that had I been in Gary's place, and seen the look on Ki's face that Gary described, I would have done more than let him go. My heart would have told me to do so. I would have stayed with him. My head would have told me to do that. I would have been with him to help him understand the experience he had just had; the experience I had brought to him.

Later that evening, I brought the memory back once again. This time remembering JW. JW was some relative on my dad's mom's side. I don't know who he was to me in terms of relation but I know he signified losing freedom to me for years. I was around three and my mother, dad and I were visiting grandma's. Many relatives had come, one of them JW. The time came for him to leave and I was being encouraged to hug him. I didn't want to. I remember he was a big man, but that could have been because I was so small. I remember he had red hair which I had not seen before. They kept encouraging me to hug him and I shrunk behind my mother's skirts away from him. I wanted to run into the house but for some reason I stayed. He could have got into his car and left but for some reason he didn't. He came over to me and I ran into my dad's arms, thinking I'd be safe. My dad gave me to JW. I was terrified. I screamed, and when he let me down I did run into the house, disappearing into the back of a closet refusing to come out for over an hour.

I still don't remember why I didn't like JW, maybe it's still buried, maybe it's tied to a past life. I don't know and I'm certain when it matters I will know.

What I do know is from that time forward I never again wanted to see the man. When the grownups would talk about him I would leave the room or think of something else so I didn't have to hear. If he would show up where we were I would purposefully hide until he was gone. I consciously avoided him throughout my childhood years. I have no idea if he even noticed.

I do know this was where the seeds of betrayal were laid that would build an unconscious wall of hurt between me and dad and provide anger as a fuel for rebellion in the years to come. My dad never knew. There was no reason for him to have known, unless he had followed me into the house that day. I have learned with people of any age that when we need to learn something, it will be presented to us, and all we can do is give our best, in every moment to every one.

My situation with Dad handing me to JW was my learning of forgiveness. Dad intended no harm in it. It would take me years to realize this. It was the inner voice, that heart connection, that encouraged me to keep trusting Dad all the while my head tried to deal with the protective edge of cynicism I grew. The resolving of this through my early adult years freed my head and heart to work as one, but it took having a child in a similar situation with hopefully different results to become more conscious of where I had come from. This is the level of self awareness study at the School of Metaphysics can afford. I know I am a much better parent, teacher, and counselor for it.

This is the consciousness every psi counselor nurtures in Taraka yoga. It is the consciousness of the archetypal hero, who doesn't stop to think about whether what s/he is doing is right, will work, will jeopardize self or others. A hero responds without condition, in the moment, because the whole Self is functioning as one. The head feeds information as required. The heart provides the motivating surge of energy bringing unparalled compassion or monumental endurance. This is the consciousness we are becoming, and children will benefit from it.

Whether remembering our own childhood experiences or helping someone to respond to their own, teaching others to be present-minded when with a child was a lesson each of us took deeper to heart that day through the experiences of a fifty-year-old woman and a six-year-old boy.

As for Ki and Gary, as far as I know they have yet to meet since the great wrestling match. I do know Hezekiah avoided Gary that night at dinner. Of this much I am certain, whether Ki will continue to avoid Gary, like I avoided JW, will have much more to do with Gary's attitude than with Hezekiah's. And fortunately, I will be there to help them both.

L
I
S
T
E
N
I
N
G

Briana at the keyboard in the College of Metaphysics studio

Turning Your Life Upside Down

We were visiting Granddad's and some of the many relatives were over visiting on a Sunday afternoon. I had been outside with Ki and two of his cousins, a nine-year-old boy and a 10 year-old-girl, watching them teach five-year-old Hezekiah how to play T-ball. As I came in, I heard Daniel's dad saying to his sister, "Dan likes someone to be with him all the time."

It was an accurate evaluation. Daniel seemed to want it more than I, for sometimes I would encourage alone time for Ki – not the faddish "time out" alone time, but real alone time: Self reflective, Self discovering, Self developing, Self liking time. I have found in teaching Self awareness to adults of all ages and backgrounds that alone time is the greatest challenge for most. "How can I embrace alone time?", "Am I worth the time?" and "I don't have the time," are major hurdles for busy-ness people and parents.

Underlying it all is the question: "How can I face myself?"

This is in large part a product of public schooling. John Taylor Gatto named it "the lesson of the bells" meaning when the class period is over, it is over. Drop whatever you are doing and move on quickly to the next class. No matter how interesting what you are learning is, no matter how much you want to stay and complete what you have started. Ringggg! You're done for now, move on! This and other programmed responses are learned day after day, hour after hour for 12+ years. The programming (ie. nothing is worth finishing, don't get too excited because it will be over soon, if I can just last a bit longer it will soon be over) becomes unconscious then the setting where we learned it is no longer needed for the mental/emotional conditioning to dominate our thinking.

Public schooling does not teach or even foster alone time. Everything is group, even showers. We learn to be alienated in school, from ourselves and of course this will transfer to our view of others – think cliques, razings, and shootings.

This brings us back to Granddad's comment. It stuck with me for weeks. I don't mean I dwelled upon it, but it came back to me for perusal and each time the illumination was greater.

It came together for me during our next visit some weeks later. The occasion was a niece's wedding. This would be the first wedding Ki would remember. He had attended one when he was two but recalled it as candles and lots of people and an angel rather than a complete event human man calls a wedding. Now six, Kiah's brain had significantly grown to be able to accept the elements present and come up with a whole. I smiled as I realized it's basic math: one angel + one Hans Solo/Luke Skywalker + lots of relatives + candles + music + vows = a wedding!

After the ceremony, I stood outside watching Ki and several cousins around his age. They ran up and down the hill, exploring the ant home in the hole of a tree and throwing the tiny bells they had received at the wedding into the air.

Later, when the music was turned up for dancing and the bass became too loud, we would go outside and explore. "Dan likes someone to always be with him," echoed in my memory.

In this moment I realized this simple statement is a common desire of all parents. That's why there is day care and schools. We want someone to be with our children and we want them to be learning something valuable. These institutions are attempts to fulfill the children's need and our desire.

Life has taught me there is a difference between kids running into a house tears streaming down their faces, angry with one another and with two conflicting stories, and eyewitness mediating "elders" responding in the moment. When you are absent and the stories come tumbling out of two or more children, who do you believe? Sides are formed. Judgements based on previous experience may be far from the truth of today. When the children are different sexes, such prejudices are often to the boy's detriment. The boy should have protected the girl, should be nice to the girl, etc.

Being present with any child gives you awareness. We all need time alone and time away from one another. It is part of our learning in life. This is why Daniel and I want someone with Hezekiah. It is more than someone. We want people who have something to give, to teach, people we have a growing relationship with. This is how raising children becomes part of the consciousness of the community. It is what is missing when you feel the need to lock your doors at night. When we know each other, when we are invested in each other, we treat each other differently.

Many times I have asked Ki, "Where did you learn that?" Being conscious, I am aware of what I say and do in his presence, and I am sufficiently aware of Daniel's thoughts and actions. I can easily tell when Ki comes up with something that didn't originate with us. When the source is identified, I can understand the context – which is often missing in Ki's interpretation or use – by asking because I live with the people who are influencing Hezekiah daily. With hours of television and more hours of school, I can understand how parents often get to the point where they feel like their children are strangers.

Sooner or later, we have to ask ourselves, "What is most important?" Being around your spouse and kids and neighbors or two (or more) phones, two televisions, two cars, two houses, etc.? Sometimes the answer may mean turning your life upside down, often that's what you and the people in your life needed all along.

I have a mug on my desk that says, "One hundred years from now it will not matter what my bank account was, the sort of house I lived in, or the kind of car I drove, but the world may be different because I was important in the life of a child." When Ki was born my world was turned upside down, and I moved my consciousness to welcome the learning. It is rich.

I am finding the more simply we live, the easier it is to raise an Indigo child. It is also much easier to be present, and when you are present you know your Self and your child knows you.

Listening is science, the benefit of uniting the first four essential life skills. Respect is what directs the attention toward the one communicating. What keeps the attention there is a desire to receive from the other. Our concentrative powers are in direct proportion to that desire. When we can sufficiently hold that attention steady for the duration of the discourse we can remember what the other person said.

Remembering what *we* said in reply is another act of respect. Now the art of listening becomes clear. Listening to Self we become our own teacher, giving constant feedback to determine how and when our words and pictures match. Have you ever received directions from someone who had never been where you need to go? The chances of you reaching your destination increase with someone who can give you the brain info (street names, numbers) *and* the mind experience (landmarks, experiential details).

Listening occurs in the mind; hearing happens between the ears.

Indigos know the difference. They know when you are listening and when you are not. They can follow lines of attention, and they need your attention.

Becoming Collectively Conscious

*Will Glennon is a wonderful man to know.
You'd expect that from the mind who brought
Random Acts of Kindness to our hi-tech
world. Will is also an attorney, an author, a
publisher, and a father of two. When I asked
Will which books he had read that influenced
him greatly, that he would recommend to
other people, an entire discussion began that
will illuminate the way you see yourself and
how you understand where you came from. It
may help you to view and accept your
upbringing in a new light, thus bring healing
to you and your family.*

Will: I think that the single most powerful thing I've done in my life and the
thing in which I feel most truly myself is in being a father. No question about
it. I love it. I've loved every minute of it. Every horrifying minute of it.
Every painful minute of it, every exhausted minute of it. I've loved the times
when my kids are fighting with me. I've loved them as teenagers. I loved
the whole process. I can't imagine a better role, and in another time, all I
would do, was have kids. I would just live on a farm somewhere and be a
dad.

That's a part of my life that I feel like I was given this gift, and this is sort
of a weird thing to say but partly in compensation for the fact that I was
gonna have to work my butt off for the rest of my life for other people, so I
was given this one part where I got to really, really just relish the process of
it. And I do, I absolutely love it. I have learned more from my kids than I've
learned anywhere else. Sometimes I think that they were put into my life
precisely to teach me. It's like, "You are too dumb the way you are. You
really need help, so we're going to give you some kids because we need some
work out of you!"

This is also gonna sound weird but that if the answer to what book would
you want someone to read, if that someone is a man and is about to become a '

father, that book would be my book, called *Fathering* which is about the experience of being a father and how to do it right. To me the greatest tragedy in this country is that we have essentially severed fathers from the process of raising children...It's such a massive, massive history of heartache on the part of all the kids who didn't have their fathers. They have to look at them as these far away people. Like the struggles that build in real relationships (reaching out) was really hard to do for most people and on the other side the dads were dying (for contact).

For that book I interviewed about 150 fathers. It was a fascinating experience because these guys - the youngest was 15, God forbid, and the oldest was about 88 - they are American guys and they cross the spectrum. They are truck drivers, university professors, grocery stores cashier guys. They were from different places in the country, different races. When I originally started setting up the interviews I thought well this will be real interesting to correlate all this information and figure out what the differences are and why some people could do this better....

There weren't any differences. The experiences were so frighteningly identical, it was stunning. And the experiences were almost all tragic. Men who love their kids more than anything. I mean adored their children and did not know how to deal with it. Didn't know how to reach them. Didn't know how to talk to them. Didn't know how to love them, didn't know how to make them feel loved...

That is the tragedy. They don't realize until their hearts are broken, until it's all gone, it's all passed. Their kids are grown up but their hearts are broken. They blew it, the very thing they really wanted more than anything else, to love and be loved by their kids, to just be in their lives. They didn't know how to do it and they didn't do it. Interview after interview after interview... men don't cry right?...one hundred and fifty interviews I did, every single man with the exception of three was in tears before the interview ended. And embarrassed by it, you know, because they don't cry and they are going "I never do this." I go, "Hey, this is about your kids" and they go, "Oh yeah," and they're just bawling. One guy - the interview went for four hours because he couldn't stop crying, and I'm just trying to calm him down. Unbelievable.

Barbara: Don't you think that's kind of the male story, particularly the last century. You could probably do the same kind of interviews with their wives and the same revelations would appear. Men were learning their lessons, women were learning their lessons. What I see so much is an evolution to it...

Will: right...

Barbara: ..where men are willing to cry a bit more, activate that heart. And women are willing to take charge a bit more, using that head.

Will: That's where the next two books come from. The next two books are about raising girls and raising boys and their different issues. They're really different issues because what we (as humans) have done, and there is a reason for it.

If we go back in history and look at how this all developed, there is a reason why we raised our girls the way we raised them. We raised them because we were concerned about the survival of the species. We were concerned about the survival of our family. We needed nurturing people. We needed people who were going to be emotionally attuned to all these things. We needed people who were going to stay with the kids, take care of them, make sure that they were okay because if these kids weren't okay, we were history! So you needed full time nurturing, loving women who were going to really focus on childrearing and keeping the home safe. You precisely did not want them strong and tough and nervy because if they were strong and tough and nervy they may stand up and try and fight the bad guy when he comes in and get killed, and then the family is history. On the other hand we had to train our boys to be warriors. They had to be tough enough that they could go and fight the tribe next door because they were going to come in and take our women.

These patterns built into an age-old cultural tradition on how to raise boys and girls. Your girls are supposed to be sweet and docile and nurturing and emotionally attuned to what's going on but they are not supposed to be strong. They are not supposed to be confident. That then sort of evolved, and by the way they're supposed to be beautiful so that they attract you know a man so that they can procreate and have kids. So this whole cult of beauty started and every aspect of our culture is now geared towards doing that, towards producing women that do that, from ads, motion pictures, television I mean everything...

Barbara: in spite of the whole women's liberation movement...

Will: In spite of everything it still goes on.

On the other side of the picture, we sever our boys from the entire world of emotions before they are seven years old. I mean cut them off. You cannot have access to your emotions. It used to be direct. You had to be tough. You do not cry, it was a very overt kind of thing. Now it's not so overt but it's still there. People today don't think they are doing that. You know they think, "No, I want my daughter to be strong and to be able to grow into her self, who she really is, and I want my son to be able to know who he is and access the emotional information he has."

Here's what happens: take a four-year-old girl, four-year-old boy. They're in a tree, they're climbing and they fall out. They hit the ground. They are scared to death. They jump. They come running through the back door. "Ahhhhh, fell off the tree!" If it's your daughter you enfold her in your arms, "Oh, you poor thing!" and you comfort her, stroke her and let her cry. If it's your son, first thing you do is a quick scan, make sure his pieces are there right - he's not dead, he's not bleeding, he hasn't broken an arm - then you give him a hug and say, "You're okay." The message is "You don't get the comfort. You are okay, now stop crying because boys gotta be tough. Boys gotta be able to fall out of trees, jump up and say I'm fine!" Girls, it's "Oh you poor thing, I bet you are really scared, and why were you in that tree anyway? Don't do that again!" That's how we are. We are still doing that today in this country and you know every time I use that example people are going like....yeah this is what I do and I mean, that's how deeply engrained that kind of thing is.

Barbara: It's all unconscious, collectively unconscious.

Will: In the process we give our daughters all of the emotional information they need, all the access to the deeper parts of themselves so that they in fact could figure out who they are and how they can blossom. But we don't give them the strength or courage to actually use it. In fact, you know, we imprison them in this sort of myth of beauty, that you have to be this thing. We diminish them so much that they get sort of removed, they lose the ability to ever become who they are supposed to be, to ever have the strength, the courage to say this is who I am and I'm going to follow it.

With our boys, they have all the strength and courage in the world to do this but they have absolutely no access to it, none! It's like "What do you want to be? What excites you?" "Well, I want to be a lawyer." "Well, why?" "Because it makes a lot of money." "No, no, no! What excites you, where is your passion?" "What do you mean passion?"

You talk to most men and you say, how do you feel? They look at you like, "What are you talking about? I'm fine!"

Barbara: "My body is okay."

Will: Yeah. Give me some texture to what's going on here. And they don't know. So, those books were written specifically with that in mind. Techniques to try, it is all common sense stuff really.

Barbara: Unfortunately it's not all that common though.

Will: Exactly. The idea with the books was to put it again in a way that would ring true with them, "Yeah, I want my daughter to have good self esteem. Yeah, I want my son to be emotionally intelligent, that's a good thing, I really want that." Then they start to read it and nothing is scary and intimidating. It's not telling them they're bad parents. It's saying, here's how you can do these things, this is really exciting.

Underlying both of the books is if you really want to do your job right as a parent here's what you do:

• Love your child.

• Show your child that you love them.

• Show them that you love them in a way that *they get it*, because they're different. You can show your love, but if they don't get it then you haven't done your job right. You know, it doesn't matter how much you love them or how much you think you're showing them, if they haven't gotten the point you have failed as a parent on that score.

• Be fascinated with them. Be totally, totally fascinated with who they are and what they're going to become and what are the things that interest them.

• Then live that way together, and if you do that everything's going to be fine! It's not so hard!

As a culture we have this, this pattern of parenthood that really is about control. You know it's do this, don't do that. I'm your teacher. I'm your instructor and I'm also, you know, your maid and your cook and I have all this work to do and I'm so busy doing all these things that I don't have time to actually be your parent. But that's what we see on television, so people do that. In the process of doing that they forget to do the only thing that's important which is to get down on the floor with them and be just absolutely fascinated with who they are. So fascinated you can't wait to get up to see what they're going to do the next day.

I did an interview today about how to parent the "different" child. And it's like, they're all different, that's the point! They're all extraordinarily unique! It's your job to find that uniqueness. Support it, nurture it, love it, be fascinated by it and let them teach you with it. Give them that experience of teaching you that kind of stuff.

I'll tell you a quick story. This is from my daughter. My daughter has done a better job at teaching me than anybody, because she and I are as much alike as oil and water. We live in different universes, completely. So everything she ever says to me and anything we ever do together is this massive learning curve. She was a huge athlete, volleyball player, and she was really good. And I used to go to all of her games which was on one hand an enormous undertaking, because she's loved this damn sport from the time she was twelve. She got a scholarship to Georgetown with it but never ended up playing in college because she had knee surgery from playing it too much. It was her freshman year in high school. Whether her team won or not, which it almost always did, largely depended on how she played. She was their star defensive player. So, they play this game and they lost, and she sucked. It was like one of the worst games she'd ever played. And I'm dying, watching this thing. After the game, they finish their meeting and she's coming over and she's in such a scowl. I was like, oh man, oh man I don't want to talk to her. And I'm trying to be nice and supportive, all that. I said, "Shawn it's okay, you played alright."

Barbara: And she knew she hadn't. How dare you say that to her!

Will: She looked at me and she said, "Dad, that's bullshit!" She said, "I sucked and you know it! Don't you ever tell me that again!" And I said, "I'm sorry. You sucked, you really sucked." She said, "I know, I can't believe it." She was like that her whole life. Everything, anything, she was so good at teaching me stuff, so good. Children are a gift if you let them be, but you have to be engaged in their lives.

So many people today, they think they want to raise their children well, they think they're raising them well. They're giving them all the things. You know, buying stuff. Buying stuff and giving them soccer lessons and they are taking care of them, cleaning and nice clothes. They do some organized activities with them, spending quality time. In the whole gamut of things that people do with their kids, almost the only genuine really good time they have with them is when they read them books, because that's one of the quality time things that actually works. Everything else that they do is just junk, it's worthless. The problem is even while reading books is a great thing, it doesn't allow you to find out about them. It doesn't allow you to do the most important part, which is to find out who they are and then dive into what they are and support who they are. Nurture that part of them and get excited about it so that they get excited. So they think, "Oh, I'm cool, I must be cool. My mom and dad think I'm pretty cool."

It is how things outta be, but you know what I have learned is, the better you get at really hearing very clearly all the messages you are getting and paying attention to them, the better you get at that, the more all of this is just natural. That's the way in which my kids really completely changed my life. Because I knew who I was, I knew what I was supposed to be doing before they came along. But I didn't realize that I was getting messages on a regular basis until they started reporting to me stuff that was going on. It was like "Whoa! Ok, I'm not listening very carefully." Just by engaging them, just by going into their world, it brought me back to the place. It became such a natural honed skill that it's the same as hearing with your ears, you know?

It's extraordinary, really extraordinary because the universe is always trying to work that way. It's constantly trying to bring people into the right place, at the right time, to do the right thing.•

Studies say children with involved fathers are:

• *more confident and less anxious in unfamiliar settings*

• *better able to deal with frustration*

• *better able to gain a sense of independence*

• *more likely to become compassionate adults*

• *more likely to have higher self-esteem*

• *more likely to have higher grade-point averages*

• *more sociable*

source: National Center for Fathering as reported in USA Today 6/2002

The Magic House

The Magic House in St. Louis, Missouri, is an Indigo paradise filled with grown-up places like the supermarket, mind teasers, and electricity coils, and kid places like the huge bubble making machine, the firehouse, and the waterworks room. It had been almost two years since we had visited, and Ki's memory was keen.

His favorite spot was the fishing pond. A wonderfully creative design, the rockbed pond is stocked with four inch fish that are magnetically drawn to fishing poles. Children catch the fish then take their catch some ten yards away to the spring's source. They drop their fish in and trace their journey back to the pond via an inch-thick glass covering the "stream." It is a wonderful cause and effect experience, like Pooh sticks. Every boy and girl enjoys the discovery.

Ki had already caught six fish and recycled them. He was learning to return the pole so others could experience the same enjoyment he did. After one trip, we returned to the pond to find all poles busy. Not liking to wait, Ki complained a bit about this. While presenting alternative ways of seeing the situation – watching others, learning from them, getting excited with and for them – a pole became available. Ki was so busy lamenting his desire for something he didn't have, he missed his chance to claim it. So envy is a seven-year-old phenomenon I noted, cataloguing the new info for future use.

When I encouraged him to claim the free pole, it took him a few seconds to change tracks. By the time he reached the pole, another younger boy also claimed it. They both stood their ground. Ki looked at me and I indicated to give the pole to the younger boy. He looked away, still holding onto the pole. Then I saw it cross his face, he had decided to bear down entering the stubborn zone.

I never told Ki about the stubborn zone. I gave it a name for my benefit not his. He had visited this attitude many times. Becoming quite attached to something seemingly innocent and fairly irrelevant, but to him it was as if his life depended upon him having that particular thing. It could be a toy in a store, a frog from the pond, or spaghetti at a restaurant. Today it was that pole at the Magic House. I saw it. Daniel saw it. He moved to help Ki give up the pole.

Ki let go of the pole physically, but emotionally he was entrapped. His eyes welled with tears, and no reasoning with him was going to change his mind. He was in the grips of losing something he had had. Intermittently, Daniel tried to reach him. Then we'd give him space, then I would try. We walked to another part of the Magic House, away from the scene of the offense. Seeing the market, I rushed to it hopefully. Hezekiah had taken a shine to fake fruits and vegetables ever since finding an assortment in a mall during the Christmas holidays. I thought, perhaps this will help. When he saw the apples and pineapple and ice cream and videos he was tempted to come out of it – but no.

It was as if the movement away from that emotional hurt caused him to lose something and he became more stubborn in his refusal. This time it came with words: "I want to leave this place."

I was heartbroken. I knew how much Ki had looked forward to this trip and how much he wanted to play here. To leave just a half hour into it was to sacrifice that desire, like a punishment for something that never happened. I felt so helpless during these times, wanting to reach Hezekiah, to help him. I'd learned when to stop teaching the alternatives, but I had yet to learn what to do in place of that. I had learned that giving him space helped, but you give too much space at the Magic House and you will lose your child. It's a big, busy place that is full of children.

Daniel and I worked as a team. I went ahead and he stayed behind so we could keep Hezekiah between us. I entered into the water room. If anything would break this spell, it would be water. At first he wasn't fazed by it. I started playing, and in time he began walking around the tables where water flowed past dikes, dams, and banks you create with shunts. Then Hezekiah did something I will always remember. He walked over to the corner and crouched there hugging himself. It was such a noteworthy move – never had anyone told Ki to sit in a corner but here he was doing it to himself.

I walked over and sat beside him. I told him a story about what his Grandpa Bill did one time when I was so adamant about leaving a place. The story didn't matter – Ki still wanted to leave. I stopped talking and just sat there a while with him. He wasn't going to change easily on this one.

"Oh, Ki. I'm disappointed because you were looking forward to being here and I just wanted you to have a good time." I surrendered in that moment, letting him know my complete thought.

We started making our way out of the house. In the next room was the ceiling to floor ball pit, also a favorite, but not today. He watched the children laughing and having fun and I just followed his lead. We entered the sand room and I crossed over to a child-size wooden truck. He came over and leaned against me, watching another child play with the sand. I started pushing buttons on the truck, and soon he sat inside it and began exploring. He was still slow to move.

I went over to the sand table and began pouring sand through a wheel that whirred with the weight. Slowly he began to play too. We stayed there about ten minutes, then he came up to me and said, "Let's go to the ball pit."

"Okay," I replied and he spent the next half hour with children of all sizes, shapes, and colors having a great time. When he was sufficiently happy, I ventured, "I'm glad you decided to play." Then it was the waterworld, followed by the market. We were retracing our steps back to the scene of the hurt.

Once back at the pond, he grabbed a pole declaring to anyone in listening range, "I learned two rules here: 1) no more than two fish at a time, and 2) put your pole back so others can use it."

It was an amazing movement in his consciousness. Ki had never run into rules before. He didn't understand a no-thinking response. That's what "that's the rule" translates to in many people's minds. Now he could see there was a purpose for the rule: so everyone gets a turn. Even him.

More important to me by far than the rule lesson was the shift Ki made in his consciousness that day. By retracing his steps, going back to where the hurt had started, he was finding cause. He was updating what had happened and his emotional reaction to it. On his return to the pond, he even gave his pole to another child. The Self initiative was the act of a mature thinker far beyond his physical years. These were the actions of a wise soul.

It is important for Indigos to be in control of their giving – part of their learning is unconditional love, and Ki being such a willful presence with a strong mind certainly has many conditions on his love even at seven. Loving him means being willing to give him the space he needs to work it out. For, given that, he does. Ki went on to play another three hours, until Dad and I were famished and tired.

I am not certain of all he put himself through in that half hour or so, but I do know his father and I stayed with him. Listening. Just being there until he was able to move himself into the Light. So much of parenting is the patience borne from a love that accepts completely. A love that has learned how to give respect.

Brain Food: Listening to Your Body

I became aware of my ability to listen to my body after I graduated from college. My studies at the School of Metaphysics taught me how to hone this awareness in several ways. One is the discipline of fruit day, a weekly exercise of eating a true vegetarian fare, fresh fruits and vegetables, only. The concept of fasting was not new to me, eating only plants was. It taught me about my desires, my limitations, my fears, my will power. And it gave me back a sense of listening to my body that I had lost sometime around puberty.

I know the value of this intuitive art and I wanted to cultivate it in our son. From his birth, I was keenly aware that I was teaching him about food each time he would be exposed to anything edible. His first edible food was applesauce, and apples remain a food he often grabs for a snack. His body has always responded well to the pH balancing effect of apples, which I learned a couple years after Ki was born. I am often grateful he learned this early.

When I became pregnant, I became more conscious of food, its place and importance in our lives. Starting a soul out can remind you that whatever this child learns to like or love or repel or resist is in large part owing to his environment. Ki isn't hooked on soda pop, candy, and chips because we rarely make them available. He knows what they are but for the most part isn't interested. He likes chocolate chip cookies, if we make them, and ice cream of all kinds. Here it's a matter of choosing healthy ingredients. Fresh cream and butter from the College dairy, organic meat, stevia in place of white sugar, and whole wheat give the body natural vitamins and minerals that are easily digested.

By the time he was four, Ki had favorite foods. I happened upon a list of *"10 Foods for Longevity"* that was published that summer in USA Weekend. I was pleasantly surprised to find many of Ki's foods on that list. In order they are:

1. **Tomatoes**. Like a lot of kids, Ki's favorite way to eat tomatoes is in sauce for spaghetti or pizza.

2. **Olive oil.** Most of our cooking is with olive oil or peanut oil.

3. **Red grapes**. Ki loves them. They have to be ripe, and preferably seedless. This began when Daniel fed Ki from the grape vines growing in the College orchard. Father and son often "graze" in the garden during the summer, giving both the best possible source of life force and nutrition available.

4. **Nuts.** Dad started Ki on nuts. His first favorite were cashews, then pistachios for a while, and now peanuts. He'll often eat them with an apple in the evening before settling down to sleep.

5. **Whole grains.** Although Ki had outgrown his daily bowl of oatmeal, he had replaced it with corn grits or brown rice.

6. **Salmon and other fatty fish.** The omega-3 fat oils are essential for mystic children. Ki loves salmon cakes. We make them with celery, parsley, onion, eggs and crackers which gives him some additional healthy nutrition. We're still working on tuna.

7. **Blueberries.** Every June we pick blueberries at a local farm. Fresh, they taste like candy, they are so sweet! We freeze them in quart ziploc bags and Ki eats them ice cold, year-round. They are a powerful antioxidant with high degrees of chromium, essential for pancreas function.

8. **Garlic.** Ki doesn't know it but he eats it in just about all his foods. Garlic is a natural antibiotic.

9. **Spinach.** He loved it when he was 2-4 but shuns most greens at the age of 7 unless they're garden fresh.

10. **Tea.** Only for medicinal purposes right now.

Shortly after I read this article, a science editor on a network show had his own list of helpful foods for children. These included some of the same foods and some new ones. Pineapple and blueberries headed the list for their enzyme properties. Buckwheat pancakes and corn chips were also noted. A list of brain foods included the following:

1. Omega 3 fatty acids found in sardines, tuna oil

2. Tyrosine essential in the chemistry of the brain for reassembling molecules. Source: spaghetti

3. B vitamins, the brain's telegraph operator. Found in raisins, bran, molasses, romaine lettuce

4. Magnesium, the telephone repairman balancing the negative-positive charges in the brain and body. Found in raisins, bran, molasses, romaine lettuce

5. Acetyl-l-carnatine which converts food to energy. Source: meatballs

When Ki started eating whole foods we watched his choices, what he would gravitate toward or ask for repeatedly. In most cases we allow him whatever he wants filling in any gaps that may arise throughout the day. If we're short on dairy, we may snack on cheese or have a homemade shake. If we need vegetables, we'll eat ripe olives or hominy. In the summer, Hezekiah and dad often graze in the chlorophyll richness of the College garden. If he needs B vitamins, we'll have organic meat. We focus on what he likes, its nutritional value, and a balance of foods throughout the day.

It seems to work well as evidenced by his growth and the fact that, unlike his father and me, he has never carried a storage of fat anywhere on his body.

We also make food available when he is hungry. This has contributed to his use of food rather than attachment to it. Kiah's response is typical of mystic children. Given a thoughtful environment for choosing healthy food and allowed to do what comes naturally, these children use energy completely, wherever it comes from and in whatever form it is provided. They have an innate sense of energy that is beyond ours which requires more patience, understanding, investigation, and conscious thinking on our part. Otherwise we end up chemically altering the bodies of souls who as a result are no longer able to fulfill their purpose. Listening to the body is a much preferred alternative and leads to another essential life skill: breath.

Some people are beginning to realize that biofeedback is an effective tool for the energetic soul. When we learn how to listen to the body, we have direct experience with the connection between thought and substance. In turn, that connecting link - energy - is directed, and Self-direction is preferable to self-medication every day.

*Tommy as Boy and Briana as Babaji
in the 2001 outdoor presentation of "Radiance"*

The Apple
by Dr. Laurel Clark

I was sitting in the computer room, typing, when one-and-a-half-year-old
Hezekiah toddled in. Since he was an infant, Hezekiah's father had carried
him in his arms, talking to him, telling him the names of everything. Dr. Dan
would pick up a can of corn and say, "corn." He'd point to the refrigerator
and say, "refrigerator." He would touch a chair and say, "chair." Hezekiah
made sounds but did not yet speak.

The computer I was working on is an Apple. Hezekiah walked over
next to me and pointed to the logo on the printer. Apple computers, monitors
and printers have a bright-colored logo that looks like an apple with a bite
taken out of it. It is rainbow-striped, green at the top, then yellow, orange,
red, purple, and blue stripes beneath. I thought at first that Hezekiah was
pointing to the logo because it was so brightly colored. I said something like,
"It's pretty, isn't it? Look at the colors." Then I named the colors.

Hezekiah made a sound to get my attention, pointing more insistently,
obviously not interested in my comments about the colors. He loudly indicated that I pay attention to him!

I wanted to know what he wanted and felt frustrated because I wasn't
getting it. I calmed my mind, gave Hezekiah my full attention, and suddenly
it struck me that the logo was in the shape of an apple. Although I had
worked on these computers for years, and knew that they were called
"Macs", I had never really noticed that the logo was an apple!

In the same moment I "got the picture." Hezekiah wanted an apple and
did not yet have the capacity to say the word "apple." So he pointed to the
logo to show me that he was hungry and wanted to eat an apple! I went to
the refrigerator, got him an apple which I cut and peeled, and sure enough,
that's what he wanted.

I was amazed. How advanced that seemed to me, that he could first of
all see that the logo was an apple (I hadn't even noticed it!), and then to
understand that the two-dimensional rainbow-colored image represented the
same thing as the actual apple he wanted to eat! I still marvel at his advanced

capacity to communicate. He could understand the picture language, he could see that a two-dimensional symbol represents something else, and he was able to use the symbol to let me know what he wanted before he had developed the skill to say words.•

An author, teacher, minister, and outstanding speaker, Dr. Laurel Clark dedicates her life to teaching adults how to develop and use their whole mind. Having known Hezekiah since he was hours old, Dr. Laurel is one of the influential teachers in Ki's experiences.

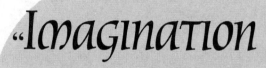

"Imagination
is more important than
knowledge."
–Albert Einstein

Imagination is the creative faculty in man. To be able to imagine something different from what we already have experienced is the great impetus for invention, evolution, growth. Imagination opens us to the possibilities of what could be. It brings awareness of the future, and cultivates desire.

The image-making faculty in humanity separates us from all other animals. We have enough intelligence to be self aware. We have enough memory to know what happened yesterday. We have enough will to draw on that memory today. We have enough desire to image something different for tomorrow. This we call progress.

The faculty of asking "what if...." is the impetus for every imaginative endeavor. With imagination, we are free to respond to our world openly, differently. Imagination allows us to know ourselves as mental creators.

W. Somerset Maugham said, "Imagination grows by exercise and contrary to common belief is more powerful in the mature than in the young." Wise counsel for teachers, parents, and all of us, for we live in a world of children who look to us for guidance and wisdom. How important it becomes for us to still our minds so we may imagine with forethought and with purpose.

Boys and Girls
by Laurel Clark

I grew up with two sisters and no brothers. My parents were pacifists at heart, and we were not allowed to play with guns of any kind. My mother would not let us watch *The Three Stooges* because she thought it was too violent. She did not think it was funny to have people hitting each other. I respected what I was taught and grew to appreciate the reasoning that motivated my parents' choices.

At first I was taken aback by Hezekiah's playing that his "guys" were shooting each other, or fighting each other, or battling each other. I observed that the male college students who played with him also enjoyed the combat kind of play, whether with light sabers or swords.

I wanted to find some way to direct energy in a different way when I was with Hezekiah. Although I recognized that he didn't want to hurt anyone with his play, there were times that people did get hurt, being struck hard by a play sword or being kicked in a mock battle. My biggest concern was that playing war could lead to future imaginings of war, battle, and conflict. I had heard of kids who played violent video games and then imagined themselves shooting classmates and did it. I knew that Hezekiah was not violent, just energetic. I also know that thoughts are things.

One day, when playing with his "guys," (I learned that's what boys call what girls call "dolls,") Hezekiah was making his "zhzhzhoo! Kshh!" sounds while the "guys" were engaged in some battle. I said, "Let's have them become friends." Hezekiah paused the play, turned to me, and said, "No, I like action and when there's fighting there's action."

This shed a whole new light on what I was looking at as "violence." In Hezekiah's mind it was just action, energy, motion! It was my own judgement that interpreted it as negative or destructive. It helped me to identify what Hezekiah was learning and stimulated some ideas about how I could engage him. I began to look for ways to be energetic with him: playing a game where one person walks or hops or moves in a certain way across the floor and the other people follow suit with similar motions; racing to the cedar tree and back; walking to "the little valley" behind the main building which involves going up and down a steep hill; flying a kite.•

The Tool for Change

I was engaged in animated conversation with members of the Missouri Writer's Guild. I had finished an address on "Dreaming as a Creative Writing Tool" where I gave five points for more fully using dreamstates for inspiration, insight, and entrainment of soul.

I saw my husband in the corner of my eye and then "ZING..BING....KURKURKUR" I heard, then saw, my six-year-old pointing a transparent toy gun at a lady. In the moment, my thoughts were stolen from the gentleman I was talking to - the floor could have opened up and swallowed me in that moment of embarrassment.

I know this was a success-failure polarity in me. Ki and I had visited the gun lesson before. He knew what I thought about guns (they cause harm and death) and felt about guns (needed in rare cases, not something to play with).

I kept talking and Daniel directed Kiah elsewhere until mom was done.

When I came out on the college grounds, I saw Dan and Ki under a tree, then heard this loud beeping, zinging noise like the sirens on police cars or those annoying backing-up tones commonly used these days. I said, "Ki, cut it out. That's too loud, someone will think you need help."

Once in the car, I looked at Kiah, and he knew. The small smile creeping across his face revealed his thoughts quite clearly. "What?!" he exclaimed in that imitated voice of incredulity.

"Hezekiah, you misused your daddy," I said.

"What do you mean misuse?" This was a new word and concept to him.

"You know if Mommy had been with you, you would not have bought that gun. And since you were with Daddy and he wants you to be happy, you misused that."

Ki paused only a few seconds and laughed saying, "I tricked Daddy." Emotionally I was shocked to see his glee, but I also knew my lesson was to keep things in perspective.

"It's not funny, Ki. You misused Daddy. He deserves more respect than you gave."

This episode started a series of lessons over the next few days. He would revisit the misuse question four or more times in the next twenty-four hours. He was ready to learn something about thoughts being real, thoughts meaning something, and intentions being important.

These were lessons on how to treat others. "Just play" can be easily misinterpreted by others who feel threatened by aggressive energy not intended to help them or energies that don't even respect their space.

The next day, we didn't talk about the gun. It was still in the back seat of the car in his bag with a few other toys procured on the trip.

When we got home, Ki wanted to visit everyone and everything to make sure they were still here. He went to see the tadpoles and frogs in the ponds, he helped water the vegetable garden and played with his friends. Then he wanted to go to the barnyard with Dr. Laurel. She told me he wanted to get his gun to fire at the chickens. She said, "No, Hezekiah, that will scare them." He was learning. It is from the adults in his life that he collects the information that will form his opinions and ideas.

The next morning, we were reading *Missouri Conservationalist* and he asked about his gun. "Where is it?" he asked.

"In your bag in your room," I said. Then I thought a moment. "Hezekiah we don't have guns at the College of Metaphysics."

"I know that."

"So, if someone comes with a gun, they check it in with the chancellor." He looked at me. "Do you know who the chancellor is?"

He knew. "Daddy."

"Yes. So when you see Daddy later, I want you to give him your gun."

For a little while Kiah didn't say anything. Silence meant he was assimilating, thinking about what had been said or what had happened.

Then, "I got it because I want to use it for special effects in movies." I had heard the sounds and they would make good effects. Kiah had demonstrated all the makings of a budding film director since age two. He was being serious when he said this.

"You can check it out from the chancellor whenever you get ready to make your movie."

"I might want to use it in plays too."

"No. Guns are not to play with."

"I'll leave it in the car." His reasoning skills are improving.

I knew it wasn't a good idea, but I had to think it through. Kiah was thinking now and he deserved more than an outright, close-the-door no. "Kiah, if Tad (a College grad-student) had a gun and wanted to leave it in his car, what would you say?"

"Give it to the chancellor." He knew the answer and he was quiet, because he also knew what it meant. We left the subject behind.

An hour later we were drawing in his room and he said, "I want to make a gun, a laser."

"Good," I said, somewhat uncharacteristically. "That's a creative endeavor!" I explained. "You can build something productive."

"I'll need a light bulb, wire, and explosives."

It was fine until the explosives part, but I also know he's seen the *Star Wars* movie and read the special effects book and has a 30-something science genius as a friend, so he's aware. So I have to be too. That's part of raising an Indigo, too. You won't know everything your child has absorbed, but the more you are with him or her, with full attention, the more you will be aware of, and that counts. What you are aware of, you can respond to.

We've not heard the end of the gun ideas I'm sure. Continued instruction is the essence of teaching. You cannot overdo it.

As self aware people we must come up out of the "over and done with it" training. This is one legacy of lessons learned in a given grade. It is also the emotional approval in dumbing us down.

We need to make a big deal when they make a big deal. This will lead to the head and heart being entrained. Mystic children of all ages need both.

Coming out of pretend into real stuff. Pretend is finger or stick or sunflowers as laser guns. A manmade gun moves out of the world of pretend and into the world of imagination which causes physical manifestation. The truth is when you are old enough to want to play with such things, you are old enough to be taught and to learn the lessons.

Knowing the men, ranging age 20 to early 30's, in Ki's life who encouraged these games is helpful. I know their conscious intentions are productive. They are the major influence in the sword fights, Jedi quarrels, and blaster stuff. On one level it is the updated version of cowboys and

Indians and combat armies, no longer politically correct. It is all still war whether on the Earth or in the stars. There are sides and they are still fighting. Still killing.

I have learned that what begins as liking big fire scenes can become something else. It can evolve and it can be used. Like the times Ki and I spent making up a new story to the *Star Wars* death of Darth Vader. It took Ki a while to reconcile that Anakin became Darth and that Darth is Luke and Leia's dad. To this day he will not watch when Luke takes the helmet off Vader in *Return of the Jedi*. We went through stages with it. Why would Luke's dad turn to the dark side? Why would Luke's dad hurt him? Why did his dad die? How Vader went into spirit, helped when it counted, and took a place alongside Yoda. The eternal redemption theme for age five.

By six we were ready to write a new ending. In our story Darth doesn't die. He's whisked away by Luke to meet Leia. Together the children nurture Anakin, healing him with their love. Anakin in return teaches his children what he has learned, thus improving their command of the force. Through such interaction the head and heart are united and all prosper. It's a good story, well illustrated, too.

The eternal conflict of good and bad is so ingrained in humanity that the genetic spark of Indigos presents quite a challenge. We must strengthen our own capacity to move beyond the entrapment of polarity.

Sports and competition fuel this win-lose, human man exhilaration and pain which leads to greater engrossment. The thrill of victory and the agony of defeat has been lauded by Olympic promoters for a century. It is a living illustration of the pairs of opposites, the polarity of physical consciousness. Sports feed it, rather than curing it. We must learn to forgive, to allow, to love unconditionally. To care for another as we care for ourselves. To unite our souls so we may know the multidimensions of our own consciousness. Mystic children insist human man mature.

Ki and I made real progress today on this same vein.

We were watching a *StarGate* television show taped over the weekend. It was an interesting plot about a planet polarized by two groups. One group, the rulers, were like Earth-Darwinists/Creationists saying all life was indigenous and had evolved under a deity. The other group believed intelligences from another planet had come from the stars to seed the planet. When the

Earth probe comes through the newly unearthed Stargate, the conflict begins.

As we get into the story the Earthlings come and are caged by members of Group 1. Earthlings explain, sharing what they've learned, saying they are peaceful explorers. The Group 1 people use electricity to zap one of the Earthlings, hurting him. Kiah said he didn't like this and to fast forward, meaning to get to the grand finale of the episode which he calls fighting.

I tried to explain this dialogue was action also, and what would lead up to the end. We'd covered this before so I knew he'd heard it and done whatever he was capable of doing with it at this point.

We went to the end where the Earthlings manage to escape with the help of one native midst much stun-gun electric shooting. Suddenly I could see what I'd missed before. Here was the tool to teach Ki the meaning of his words. The part he didn't want to see, the hurting, was the reward of fighting. The final part with all the sparks and fireworks was exciting to him. It was adventure, not fighting. To teach Hezekiah I would first need to change my ideas. The way to do this was by seeing from his perspective. His viewpoint is very simple, very open and honest, real. His brain is uncluttered. He has yet to learn about world wars or people breaking their promises. The TV guns produce bright lights and cause people to fall down. They don't leave children fatherless or maimed in Hezekiah's reality. I had a better way to interpret the energy of his experiences and I could pass that on.

He listened but he still wanted to call it fighting. I let it drop, thus giving him time to think about it. As for me, I knew I'd opened a significant door that would lead him and me into deeper senses of purpose, and greater understanding.

Make Believe

Fantasy is a part of most people's lives. We practice it early. We make believe that we are a character in a book or movie. What we make believe has everything to do with what we are exposed to as a child. We make believe we are like an older sibling or family member. We image scenarios from what they say and do in our presence. We want to be a fireman like Uncle Joe or a veterinarian like Dr. Chris. In time, dreams of Cinderella and her prince, Dorothy and Harry, Joe and Chris, give way to being a rock star, an astronaut, or a world leader.

The significance of what we pretend when alone is the window into our soul it provides. Through years of researching the mind and consciousness, we have found that what we imagine ourselves being and doing before the age of seven captures the inner, subconscious urge for the lifetime.

Mine was creative interactions. Conversations and all sorts of plays with "imaginary" friends was intermingled with schooling my stuffed animals. Hezekiah's is creative communication. It expressed in his artwork at two, his photography at four, his directing, filming and editing video at six. My soul was telling me and anyone else who knew how to listen that my life would be about connecting people with the inner worlds. In every phase of my life my greatest fulfillment has been found in those endeavors – teaching, counseling, ministering, giving intuitive reports, writing, composing, directing, and so forth. I respect what Ki's soul has revealed to us and I expectantly watch his unfolding.

The power of imagination is part of what makes us human. Our ability to think "what-if", to see alternatives and possibilities, is the essence of creative urge. Imagination gives variety to our reasoning. That's why ten people can be given the same problem and solve it in ten entirely different ways!

One of the greatest killers of imagination is peer pressure. Peer pressure ruled much of our thinking before the year 2000. Indigos are so connected they do not relate to peer pressure in the ways you and I have. They do not need the stimulus of "What do others want? How can I fit in? What do I need to do to belong?" Mystic children already belong. We must recapture our power for imaging. Visualization can replace daydreaming; honesty: pretending. When it does, the guidance we can offer our children will better meet their needs.

Erin

A friend's niece visited us when Hezekiah was just eight months old. Erin, a sharp four-year-old Indigo, had heard Aunt Laurel talk about Hezekiah and was eager to meet him.

Finally, after a get-acquainted day, the two sat together on the floor of Ki's room. They were surrounded by stuffed animals, paper and markers, and wooden toys. Erin immediately began teaching Ki about alphabet blocks. Passing on what is learned, teaching, is one of the earliest ways mystic children share. They are attuned to group thought, connected. When viewed in this light, what is sometimes interpreted as the know-it-all-tendency is one of the purest expressions of love.

Erin showed Hezekiah how to spell her name. First she chose an E. Then Ki, imitating her physical actions, offered her another letter. She would take the letter and put it back down. Ki then tried picking up the letter she had already showed him. I could see him thinking, "She did it! This must be fun." Erin made it clear she wanted the E to remain where she had put it.

Ki backed off, not playing with any of the blocks. Erin did something unexpected. She kept telling Ki to leave the E alone. She would rummage through the letters, not paying attention to him, then look back at him and say, "Don't touch that." She even moved his hand away. At first Ki looked at her, the next time he just ignored her.

After several times of this, I realized Erin was using this "don't touch" as a distraction. She did not know the next letter in her name. There were several R's available but she would miss them. Diverting the attention to Ki was a way to pretend she knew something she didn't.

I asked her if she knew what "R" looked like and she said, "No."

"I might be able to help," I replied, picking up several blocks. Finding an R, I excitedly presented it to her. Her broad smile told me how pleased she was and she moved a bit closer to me.

Once I understood what was happening, I could help her add to what she knew. Since she was not able to tell me what was going on, the only way I could find out was using the Essential Life Skills with my own mind. As I watched the interaction with a still mind, I could let my own distractions go, and open my attention to Erin's thoughts. This is how I knew she was searching. She thought she should know and because of that, it either didn't occur to her to ask or she didn't want to because then we would know she didn't know.

Knowing this enabled me to respond without threatening her already shaky security. We could become partners in this endeavor.

Iris

One day Hezekiah complained, "Iris pretends all the time!" He was right. At three, Iris had become a very strong pretender, living in endless fantasies of queens and shops and dress up. This was more than the difference between girls and boys, this was a difference in stimulation.

"Hezekiah," I replied, "Iris is doing what you do. You call it play, or doing a play. She calls it pretending."

"I want to do other things," he said. I knew what he meant. Ki was as prone to catching frogs or watching a video or drawing or listening to a story as he was to doing a play. His life was filled with variety which matched and fed his quick-minded aptitude. His disappointment in not feeling like Iris would do other things with him prompted an exploration of imagination.

"There are many ways to use imagination," I told him, giving him several examples – making up songs, drawing, figuring out a way to catch minnows.

Ki quickly chimed in, "Yeah, or making spaghetti dance (a recent kitchen experiment) or solving a case (solving a mystery)." Imagination was not a new topic for him to consider.

"There are an infinite number of ways to picture people and things in your mind." We had a great talk. Iris was within listening distance. When Dr. Pam came to be with the children, I left to answer email questions to dreamschool.

When I came to the kitchen before dinner I saw a half dozen old mustard and salad dressing bottles on the table. They were filled with oil and colored water mixed with glitter. Ki came running up. "Do you like what Iris and I made, Mommy? They're lava lamps!"

"I never made a lava lamp!" Iris exclaimed.

"These are great!" I said hugging both of them. "Good job," I told Ki. Then turning to Iris, I remarked, duly impressed, "I didn't know you were interested in science, Iris!"

She smiled, "I didn't either, but this was really fun!"

So clean, and honest. It was a beautiful moment for them both.

The next time Ki and Iris were together, it was Iris who was per-turbed at Ki. She wanted to play house and Ki wasn't interested. Ki had let her know that all she wanted to do was pretend and this time she was listen-ing.

"Oh, I know you know how to do many more things than just pretend,"

I said reassuringly. "I've seen you sing, quite beautifully I might add, and dance! Yes, you definitely do more than just pretend. Have you done some of that today?"

"Well, not really," she said. "Dr. Barbara, what's wrong with pretending?"

I saw a door open to give encouragement and to teach something new. "Iris, it's not that there is something wrong. Did you know there's a difference between using your imagination and pretending?"

She shook her head no.

"There is. And that's what Hezekiah is learning. He doesn't really understand why you use the word pretend. You do say pretend a lot, did you know that?"

She nodded.

"There's a lot more to life than pretending," I was aware that I was talking to a four-year-old Leo. I had learned quite a bit about using astrological information for learning, and my life had been well-populated with Leos, so I understand that creative urge. I want to help Iris understand it too. "Did you know some people pretend again and again until it becomes the same old thing they do or talk about. And you know what that's called?"

Her eyes were wide, "No, what?"

"Memory!" I said with a laugh. "What began as pretending becomes memory. Not imagination."

"So what's imagination then?" she climbed on my lap, sincerely wanting to know.

"When you do something different each day, that's imagination. Like wearing different shoes or reading a new book or eating different foods. Some people get up and they don't like going to work because it's the same old thing. They don't like it because there's no imagination there."

"I know," Iris volunteered. "My dad doesn't like getting up to go to work."

I hadn't expected the confession so I was taken by surprise. I chuckled. Iris went on, "He's grumpy in the morning."

"He probably wants to be more imaginative, more creative."

"I think so too," she agreed. She gazed over at Ki across the room. He was playing with his Star Wars characters, making them talk and interact. Iris looked up at me with her big brown eyes and said, "Dr. Barbara, I have free will. And so does Hezekiah. So how do I get him to play house?"

She was so serious. This was the moment when she could learn something about the difference between pretending, which often excludes others, and imagination, which is always open to others. I thought for a moment then said, "You will have to be attractive, Iris."

"What does that mean?" she asked.

"You'll need to make playing house look so good that he'll want to do it."

Undaunted, Iris immediately replied, "I can do that!" and she went off to join him.

I enjoy having these grown-up talks with children. I stoop down or sit beside them and we talk. Such conversations are quite natural for mystic kids. Sometimes they ask the questions and I listen. Sometimes it's the other way around. It is a most enjoyable way to pay them respect while planting and watering those seeds of the skills they will use every day of their lives.

Briana

When Briana was eleven, an Intuitive Health Analysis offered incredible insight into how to prepare her consciousness for puberty. Physically, puberty is the initiation of physical procreation, the ability to father and mother offspring. This is a wonderful metaphysical area in and of itself. What causes puberty is a blend of genetics and mind control. Whether puberty occurs at ten or at fifteen depends upon the mental attitudes of the individual.

Briana's health report described her mental and emotional attitudes which are discussed in the Intuition section of this book. The report cited a "deadening of the imagination." It went on to describe in detail the attitudinal cause and how this was occurring:

This is because this one is not releasing the dependency of infancy to embrace the change of growth, but this one is trading the dependency upon external factors for a dependency upon habits. This retards this one's reasoning for this one does not use imagination when this one is stubborn, this one is only using memory and will. Would suggest therefore that this one's imagination would need stimulating. We see that this one can be highly creative, this one has a great potential in that regard, but we see that it is not part of this one's nature to stimulate the Self in that regard, therefore this one is dependent upon the environment to provide it. (510971bgc)

One avenue those around Briana could help came in the suggestion for ballet. The recommendation came during the analysis of her physical body and as a remedy for the needs present there.

We see that the direction of the thinking, being able to concentrate the thought energy would aid greatly. The stimulation of the use of imagination and this one's ability to create would be very helpful in causing there to be a greater balance in the utilization of the endocrine system growth. We see that physical movement is very important to this body. This one needs to learn how to wield the body gracefully. Would suggest therefore that ballet would be very helpful to this one.

It would be two more years before dance would enter Briana's life. While living on the campus of the College of Metaphysics, Briana began dance lessons at a performing arts school in nearby Lebanon. She learned tap, jazz, and ballet. Her natural talent was obvious both in her dedication to practice and in how her energies multiplied when on stage. Usually outwardly quiet and nonassuming, Briana was a powerhouse waiting for an avenue of expression. Dance offered her this. It became the core of her life. She even entered a beauty pageant just so she could dance.

I was teaching Briana classical poetry and practical mathematics, and we were exploring Nobel Prize winning female scientists during this time. On several occasions I was able to take her to dance class and I witnessed her development, and potential. I made it a practice to read books with her in the evenings. From Shakespeare to Dia Calhoun, we covered a broad area.

I came across an intriguing book in Chinaberry's catalogue, called *Shiva's Fire.* The description sounded perfect, a young girl named Parvati born during the worst monsoon in decades who has an inner urge to dance that will not be denied. I ordered the book thinking it would expand Briana's knowledge of India as well as feed her imagination. What we read ignited both of us.

Shiva's Fire is a wonderful story of love, trust, dedication, integrity, desire, and commitment. It teaches the best of humanity while opening the imagination to the power of reason. It fed my imagination as much as it did Bri's. Its description of yoga and gurukulams (schools for yogic movement), planted a seed of interest in Hinduism in Briana and fueled a desire in my mind for integrating mental and physical form and posture.

I had been focusing on the seven major yogas for two years which had led to the creation of Taraka Yoga. During this time I had drawn upon ancient mudras, postures for the hands and body, for the development of multidimensional consciousness. I began exploring these with the intention of integrating them into a dance that I could teach Briana.

I knew at fourteen she was becoming tempted by what she saw and read. She was already fantasizing going to New York or London and being in a national ballet company.

I also knew the parents she chose were high-minded and spiritually committed. She, the soul she is, had chosen them for these ideals and her schooling at the College was part of this whole Self training. Through Bri, my vision of the schooling of young souls expanded greatly. I knew we could teach dance – sacred dance – in a way that would express the whole, divine self, and touch the soul of all those present.

The first manifestation of this came a few weeks later when Bri decided she wanted to be a counselor at the 2002 Camp Niangua, a summer camp on campus for youngsters 10-15. Briana had attended five camps, and being willing to take on this new responsibility was a signal that she was ready to think more, be more, do more.

She was leaving for a week-long trip with her mother to Dallas. Before she left I talked with her about creating a dance. She had the basics of movement, plus several mudras we had practiced. We had talked about sacred dance and she had already told me she wanted to learn. I gave her a copy of Deva Premal's song *"Om Shree Sache"* with the translation of the meaning of the words and told her to explore, move, have fun. When she returned we would go over what she had come up with.

While she was gone I worked on transcriptions from interviews I had done with her mom and dad several years before. This led me to this Intuitive Report. There it was! The ballet, the need for movement like yoga and mudras, the benefit for her of sacred dance.

We see that there could be some benefit derived after this one gains a degree of control of the balance of the body in the pursuit of martial arts, particularly that referred to as aikido. In as much as when this one develops some development of the mind and the body, both, then this one would be prepared for that kind of integration of energies and it could be quite progressive for this one in terms of her own development.

When Briana returned we were excited to share what she had done. What she showed me brought my heart into my throat and tears to my eyes. The music repeated the core chant seven or eight times. What Bri had envisioned was herself and Elizabeth, a good friend who would be at camp, dancing to the music. The first movement was filled with classic Indian yogic poses, like those you see in Hindu statues and paintings, performed singularly. The second movement included a veil dance for two which was repeated in additional forms later. It was breathtaking!

The theme of camp in 2002 was Peace. Here was the finale for our ensemble of peace stories, prayers, songs, and dance from around the world. Once the campers arrived and we began practicing and developing all the parts, an intriguing spiritual experience was created. We experienced it in the giving, and those in attendance experienced it in the receiving. It was

centering, balancing, transforming, revelatory.

Briana experienced creation from the beginning as a thought to its manifestation as an offering of love, particularly to her parents who were present when the dance was performed publicly for the first time. As I read her report once again while writing this, I see the wisdom it offers coming to life through our experiences.

We see that at the present time period, however, there needs to be a sense of being able to work with the body as it changes, as it changes its center of gravity, as it changes in form, as it develops and builds. We see that there needs to be a cultivation of this not only in terms of the physical action but also in terms of the mental and emotional attitudes as well, looking forward to development and the physical demonstrations that (indicate) change is occurring in the mind. Those around this one particularly the females closest to this one could have a profound effect upon this one's attitude in that regard. (510971bgc)

It was a moment of self respect and thankfulness to know that I am one of those females who in some way has fed the inner flame of her soul's desire.

The Tortoise Shell

The sun was relentless on the August afternoon when several families gathered at our Dream Valley House. The House had just completed its most recent incarnation under the careful hands of loving souls who had transformed it into a fairy tale come true.

Two blue-roofed turrets reached for the sky as the house spread her wraparound porch skirt into the grassy lawn. It is the kind of porch boys like to test their aerodynamic skills upon while girls swing around the columns or sit daintily with legs dangling from the side. On this day the shade it provided was the greatest drawing power.

We'd come from every direction, for "PeaceMakers" a day of worship, fellowship, and fun. Some had come from the city, in large part to spend an afternoon in what I love to call God's Creation. The name serves as a reminder of the evidence of things unseen. It fills my heart with appreciation for every living being and a gratefulness for That which runs through. Prosperity was a theme of the day, expressed through songs and games and the story of one of the richest men our country has ever known...John Chapman.

Born in Massachusetts in 1774, John Chapman was a good man. It is in large part due to his efforts that many early settlers had the seeds that produced the trees that provided food for their families. A devout Christian missionary, Chapman was a follower of Emanuel Swedenborg, a Swedish philosopher who believed that we must live simply and in harmony with the natural world. John Chapman was said to have shown little interest in his personal appearance or in his possessions, but he had a great love for all humanity and all living things.

By the age of 23, his love for all - the native Indians, pioneering American settlers and wild creatures of the forests - led him across Pennsylvania, Ohio, and northern Indiana. John was especially fond of children, sharing his adventures with the younger members of the households he visited. The settlers gave him the name most people remember: *Johnny Appleseed.*

On this day, in a beautiful Missouri valley, Johnny came alive. Students and teachers of the College of Metaphysics had spent several weeks planning for the afternoon. Songs, stories, costumes, and foods were lovingly prepared. But by far, it was the arrival of Johnny Appleseed that made the biggest impression in all our minds. From three-year-old Iris to fifty-something Pam, it was Jonathan Duerbeck's rendition of Johnny Appleseed that lingers in our minds.

Our Jon came to us across the field, a figure out of the past in his check-ered shirt, blue jeans, and straw hat. "Did someone say they were hungry?" he asked with a smile, gently lobbing an apple Dr. Dan's way.

The youngest children squealed with joy as "Johnny" passed out his apples, while the older ones admired Jon's incarnation as the famous horticul-turist. It was in fact Jonathan's extensive knowledge of nature, plants and trees that made him perfect for the part, for in so many ways Jonathan wasn't imitating Johnny Appleseed, he was realizing a spiritual bond with a kindred spirit from our shared history.

Today he was going to share the spirit, that love of humanity and all living things, with us. Gathering us with his tales of oak trees, raccoons, and herbs, we found ourselves moving with him, to better see where he was pointing or to be able to hear when his head turned away. He looked like the Pied Piper of Hamlin leading the children and adults across the lane and toward the grove of trees several hundred feet away from the house.

It was sometime later when "Johnny" and the youngsters returned, their arms filled with nature's bounty. On the porch they found posters and matboards of every hue, scissors and glue of every size with which to fashion their newly gained treasures into nature collages. Briana, Roxie, Dalton, and Maggie went straight to work while Gabriel and Desiree found it more fun to eat the elderberries they'd collected than to make a picture from them.

It was Nathan's treasure that captured everyone's fancy. While traveling the dry riverbed, he had discovered one of the country's greatest finds, an abandoned tortoise shell. The shell, a recently vacated home, had been untouched by weather or other animals. The outer "skin" was a dark green tinged with cocoa brown, and a gentle shaking turned the prize into a percus-sion instrument! The children were fascinated.

"Want to see the shell I found?" Nathan called to four-year-old Hezekiah who was having the greatest time running arcs on the lawn surrounding the porch.

In a perpetually curious state of mind, Hezekiah raced up to Nathan. His eyes grew wide as awe filled his mind. This was the first time he'd seen a green shell with nobody home! "Can I touch it?" he said tentatively.

"Sure," Nathan said. Hezekiah held it gingerly at first, and then as four-year-old boys do he became more vigorous. When he heard the clicking sounds he became investigative. Cautioning him to care for someone else's treasure, I lowered his hands so he could return it to Nathan.

Not too interested in artistic endeavors, Nathan, a city dweller, knew opportunity when he saw it. Here, in this beautiful, unspoiled place, were living creatures. To his way of thinking the reality of an empty tortoise shell paled in comparison to the possibility of a real, live lizard!

"You can have my tortoise shell," he said, placing it in Hezekiah's surprised hands.

All Kiah could do was smile and look up at his new seven-year-old friend and with his mom's urging softly say, "Thank you!" It was a touching moment for all who witnessed it, yet it was only a new beginning.

None of us yet knew just how far this one act of kindness was going to go.

As Nathan dashed off toward the creekbed with Matthew, Hezekiah suddenly became very popular. The girls raced over and it didn't take long until the tortoise's greenish-brown overcoat began separating from the hard grayish shell. It didn't tear in strips nor did it come off in large pieces, rather they came off in the geometric shapes characteristic of a tortoise back; the rectangles and triangles. They gleamed like translucent gems!

With a little more activity, the front part of the underside came unhinged allowing the mystery of the click to be revealed. Out spilled tiny pieces of skeleton about the size of navy beans, over a couple dozen! Soon thereafter the other two thirds of the underside came free from the domed top as well, and now the perfect tortoise shell was no more.

The magic was just about to begin.

The children scooped up the pieces immediately envisioning them as appropriate additions to their collages. One of the underside pieces became a perfect flower vase in Briana's picture. Maggie quickly followed suit with the companion piece to hold her wheat and milkweed and elm leaves.

Segments of the spine appeared as stars or even flowers in Gabe's and Grace's artwork. One larger piece resembling a pelvic bone in minature ended up floating in the air of Kiah's creation. The gemlike "skin" was in every picture made that day. A beautiful reminder of the gifts of God and a young boy named Nathan.

I don't know what happened to all the collages made by the "Peace-makers" that afternoon. I do know one hangs in the dining room at the College of Metaphysics and one is found in Kiah's room. I also know I will forever be grateful for Nathan's kindness to my son for that kindness continued far beyond the two of them, in ways we never imagined but in ways we will always remember.

We, all of us, do indeed live in a perfect universe, where the generosity of a single child can touch the lives of so many, transforming us with the Truths of creation.

Sunflower
a painting in the style of Georgia O'Keefe
by Miranda Mobley, age 14

The Secret of Life
sung to the tune of "Bicycle Built for Two"

Ideal is the image we have in mind
of a brave world noble, peaceful, and kind.
We image a world of sharing
a place of love and caring.
Please join us now,
we'll show you how
to envision the world we see!

Purpose is the power to change your mind
Inner knowing, eternal Self divine.
The secret's in why we change things,
embracing lessons life brings.
To know I can
be who I am
is a wonder for all to see!

Action is the duty within our mind.
Sacred yearning throughout all humankind.
Imagine a dance together,
united in endeavor.
Come sing your song,
and you'll belong
to the Fam'ly of Man we see!

Ideal, purpose, and activity,
elemental lifetime philosophy.
The keys to successful living,
soul growth is in the giving.
Ideal, purpose,
activity
is the secret of life, you see!

–from *PeaceMaker's Songbook Vol. II*

B
R
E
A
T
H

Peace Pole planting ceremony
with Chancellor Dr. Daniel Condron
at the College of Metaphysics

Self Acceptance
by Dr. Laurel Clark

Hezekiah and I were walking through the woods, talking about the upcoming Family Weekend when students and their families were invited to come together for learning and fellowship. We would pitch tents on the College of Metaphysics campus land and cook meals over an open fire. Hezekiah remarked that he had never stayed in a tent and would like to. I told him about the first time I had stayed in a tent when I was about Briana's age. We spoke of other things, the woods, the lizards, poison ivy, and trees.

I was relishing the camaraderie and conversation, feeling the great love pouring between us as we walked hand-in-hand. I turned to Hezekiah and said, "Hezekiah, I really like you." He looked up at me with his wide blue eyes and said, "I like me, too."

It was so beautiful and refreshing! He was so innocent, so accepting, so genuine. He exemplifies what it means to "be yourself." How different he is from how I was at that age. I can remember going to kindergarten and making a conscious choice to shut down my natural urge to be myself so that I could get along with the other kids. I misinterpreted the desire to cooperate by "checking out" what I thought I had to do for approval. I behaved outwardly as I was expected to do and turned away from cooperating with my own inner urge. It has taken me many years as an adult, practicing metaphysics and learning to still my mind, to re-discover who I truly am!

Every time I am with Hezekiah I realize how fortunate he is to have chosen parents who have taught metaphysics for 25 years, who know what it means to "love you just because you are" and who allow his spirit to soar.

We all know things get better when we pay attention to breath. We're more in the moment, more present. Breath is what gives us life. Breath is what ties the soul to the body. Breath is our connection with our Creator.

When the mind is restless, the breath is disturbed. When we are frightened, hurt, lonely, shy, it is reflected in the way we breathe whether we are two, twenty, or one hundred twenty. The way you breathe determines how you speak, walk, work, use money, make love, and even how you die.

To be centered in Self, to be at peace with our connectedness with others, is to breathe rhythmically, gently, intuitively.

Indigos are naturally connected. It has been called a hive mentally. I teasingly call it Borg consciousness (from the *Star Trek* shows), and as with the Borg, resistance is futile. Surrender is the lesson of the breath.

Emotions

Our own emotional state is vital. It can mean the difference between success and failure, health and illness. In our interactions with others emotional equilibrium is the spark for cooperation or rebellion, peace or war. Yet most of us receive our beliefs about emotions unconsciously. We absorb emotional attitudes from the environment without even knowing it. This is why you can be having a great day then go into a restaurant or office and suddenly develop a headache or feel depressed. If this can happen to you, imagine or, better yet, remember what it does to a five year old with limited powers of reasoning.

Emotional energy is present in everyone. Emotions are what bind the outer conscious mind to the inner subconscious mind. They enable your thoughts to become a physical reality in your life. That's what the process known as visualization is all about, learning how thought is created and manifested.

How we learn to express emotion as a child has a great deal to do with how our lives turn out fifty years later. It also influences how we interact with others. The beliefs we hold about the emotions influence our well-being for they determine in large part how we understand the polarities of our world – good/bad, happy, sad, fearful/courageous, introverted/extroverted, warm/cold, and so forth. How we understand the emotional level of mind determines in large measure whether we experience success or failure in life.

Emotional energy will be expressed. When the conscious mind is still, the energy flows easily. We give and receive. Good things happen to us and when the not-so-good comes, we receive it for our learning rather than deny, rebel, reject, and otherwise try to push it away. Stuff your emotions long enough and you'll explode, saying and doing things that with a clearer mind you would think twice about. Or the explosion can happen in your physical body in the form of disease. The energy is generated *by* you, it is *in* you, and it will be expressed *through* you someway.

Conscious choice is always the best way to express emotions. This is how 26-year-old Adam Campbell, one of Ki's favorite teachers thus far, learned about this.

The Inner Teacher Awakens:
Hezekiah Condron and the Vinegar Volcano Mess

by Adam Campbell

Hezekiah and I spend time together every day. He is a brilliant, sweet, dynamic child of seven years. Recently, Hezekiah, fourteen-year-old Briana, and I were creating a play with his dinosaur figures and a baking soda / vinegar volcano. We made quite a little mess on the floor. He wanted to leave the room with Briana and continue the play while expecting me to stay behind and clean up the mess. I told him that we should all help clean up the vinegar. He reacted and ran off.

I followed after him and asked him if he would at least come in and be with us while we cleaned. Briana suggested we just go clean it up and then follow him upstairs. We did and when I approached him asking him if he wanted to be with me, he ran upstairs, yelling "I don't want to be with Adam!"

I was shutting down emotionally when I walked away and out into the dining room. His mother and father were there and I told them what happened. From what Dr. Barbara pointed out, I realized I had forfeited my authority when I asked him *if* he wanted to be with me. Dr. Dan reminded me that I am to teach him, not to just play with him.

So, I went upstairs to where his room is and waited in the hall. The door was closed but I could tell he was in his bed and did not want to see me. I stayed there projecting love and light to him. He opened the door once then slammed it. He opened the door again and peered out long enough for me to tell him I loved him. Then he darted past me, down the hall and downstairs.

I followed him into the great room. We passed Dr. Barbara, who seeing my distress, told me to be direct and honest; to keep Ki's best interest in mind. So I sat.

My head was swimming. I've learned to shut down and close myself off from others so I expected him to do the same. I knew I needed to get my attention off myself and on him. He was sitting next to his dad pressing buttons on a calculator.

I came over to him saying, "Hezekiah, I need to talk to you."

He looked up and said, "Okay." His voice was so sweet. I was surprised by his openness.

I pulled up a seat next to him and shared my thoughts. I told him that I didn't mean to make him mad. I didn't realize cleaning was such a big deal to him. I thought we would clean up really quick and continue with the play. Cleaning up is part of play I told him. Then I mentioned that I was there to teach him drawing and art.

He made some unpleasant grunting noises that seemed to indicate displeasure. I had no idea what would become of the situation. Would it be okay or not okay? I just didn't know.

So after I had said these things to him I sat there quietly, wondering what to do next. I didn't know what to do, so I just sat there.

A few moments later, Hezekiah got up and told Briana that he wanted her to draw with him. He seemed happy and centered. I could tell he had released the past so I approached him and sat down nearby on the floor. I'd just begun to draw some pictures when he asked me how I spell my name. I showed him and noticed that he was writing something on a little piece of paper. There is a collective effort in our community to teach Hezekiah how to write and spell. This is a lesson he has been stubbornly resisting, so the fact that he initiated learning and writing my name showed a willingness to be in harmony.

When I realized what he was doing I felt the tears build up in my eyes. I was so happy. He made a little envelope for me with a little letter inside that read; "Hezekiah Yes Adam." This was his way of letting me know that he was ready to be with me again.

I'm going to keep it as a reminder for me as a teacher that it's okay when the student reacts emotionally. I just need to keep their best interests in mind and be honest.•

Holding Your Breath

What do you do when an Indigo digs their heels in about something? Certainly stubbornness is not new for any child or parent at any time, any place. It is present whenever will is present without benefit of intelligence. The battle of wills that can ensue with these children is astounding. I learned about this early on, some of it from Ki's resistance to reading and writing that Adam mentioned.

My lessons in this have revolved around patience and acceptance and self-discipline.

I learned the patience lesson because we purchased the *Hooked on Phonics* learning kit when Ki was about a year old. We listened to the first few tapes often, then my dedication waned. Other things became more important.

At two he picked up the *Big Red Barn* book and turning the pages read the entire book. At first I thought he was reading the words, then I quickly realized he was reciting the entire text, page appropriate, from memory! The teacher in me stepped forward. Since memory is one of the essential life skills I was more impressed about this than if he had been able to read physical language.

I believed this meant he would probably read on his own in the months to come. Week after week passed. Ki had hundreds of stories and books read to him in the next few years. He was far more interested in drawing pictures than stick marks with occasional circles attached which represented words. This is where I learned acceptance. I love and respect Ki. I know his mind aptitude and I was certain he would learn. Dr. Pam said, "One of these days he'll pick up a book and start reading and we won't be able to get him to do anything else! He'll fall in love with reading."

I trusted her experience with children, and this helped me let go. Letting go of my emotional attachment to my child reading early, and then on par with other children, gave me a clarity about myself. These were the lingering effects of intellectual and emotional approval that had led me to be an "A" student but left me with all kinds of emotional scars. Although I'd become conscious of many of them, I was finding out what work I yet needed to do through my attitudes with Ki.

I started asking the right questions, "Why is it important to read before the age of 5? What does it mean? What is Ki doing that is more important to him? Is it feeding his character, his soul? Is he building the skills he will need to be able to read when he is ready?" Answering these questions gave me resolve, which in turn led to emotional calm, even when tested by well-meaning relatives. No longer perturbed, afraid, or otherwise imbalanced, I could breathe again.

I learned self-discipline through acknowledging and answers the questions in my mind, and I learned it by watching what Daniel did with Ki. For over a year when he was five to six years old just about every morning Dan would sit down with Ki and write one word. He would then help Ki copy it. Just one word. Every day.

The beauty of this discipline, combined with what everyone else was doing, is laying Ki's foundation for mental as well as physical language. The summer of his sixth year, he proved he could write any letter when he wanted to. This came in the making of lemonade signs to raise money for the bearded dragon he wanted and then for the building of the Peace Dome on the College of Metaphysics' campus. He would ask how to spell "Lemonade for sale! A quarter a glass" and made sign after sign.

Sometimes he would write Happy Birthday on a card and sign it or write a note like "please do not move this box." He was learning the purpose of communication, which was more gratifying to me than knowing ten languages.

When Ki turned seven his dad made *Hezekiah's Happy Book, Part II* complete with pictures and words that Ki knew. Hezekiah read it for all of us at supper and boy, was he surprised at everyone's emotional response! He could see he had made us happy, and at seven that was starting to make a difference in his consciousness.

After that I imitated what I learned from Daniel. Ki and I began reading together each night. Sometimes it would be a story. Ki would choose one word to read. Sometimes he would recognize another word and gleefully shout it out. Sometimes he would want to say a word he already knew rather than add a new one to his reading vocabulary. One night something happened that turned on a light inside me.

From birth Hezekiah was a night owl. He could stay up until past midnight and be up a few hours later. His daily naps stopped before he turned two. By five he would get up around 8 and go to bed around 10. I learned how to adjust to this, cooperating rather than laying down the law that he would never understand or respect. Now I was going to learn how to use it.

We settled in at 10 and he wanted to read a story. I said okay and got the phonics book out. When he balked, I said, "Okay lights out!"

"No, no, no," he said.

"Okay, the sound of *a* in apple, and the sound of *t* in tent," we sounded out the letters together then he added the beginning sounds that make the words b-*at*, c-*at*, h-*at*, m-*at*, s-*at*, etc. by adding the sound of the first written letter. He had done this orally since the age of two. Here we added the element of seeing it represented on a piece of paper, through typed words.

We covered several different combinations including words ending in -*ag*, -*an*, and -*ar*. After several words he began to be lazy with his attention, starting to sing or saying, "You do it."

I would just reach for the light saying, "Okay, lights out!"

"No, no, no!"

"Okay, then what's this word?"

He would focus and begin again. It became a kind of game and we laughed about it. What amazed me was the pure unadulterated action of the mind at work. Ki is so bright, as are all children, and quick. He can multiply four times three in his head and tell you the life cycle of mammals, birds, and amphibians. When his full attention is directed he can accomplish anything within his power. His full attention is directed by the same element that controls anyone's attention: desire. When the desire is present, the will is engaged.

I learned a great deal about motivating people as a teacher of adults. People enjoy learning what they want to know, and given the opportunity they enjoy learning. Absorbing something new puts us in infancy, a wonderful mental state of love, expectation, and accelerated learning.

By feeding Hezekiah's mind with the basics he needs, then waiting until he desires something, I found ways to make learning fun for us instead of frustrating. Self-discipline, acceptance, and patience. They fit together very well, giving me the mental clarity I need to separate my thoughts and feelings from Ki's, and the emotional equilibrium to love us through it. Growing pains have evolved into growing gains and we can both breathe!

9-11-01
A Child's Perspective

I turned on the television in the bedroom a couple minutes before eight in the morning. I had made this a practice, my time to check in with the world for a few moments before rousing Ki for the start of our day.

Live footage of a smoking World Trade Center Building in Manhattan, New York filled the screen. As the story progressed it captured my attention. I watched as the second plane circled the second building exploding into it. The commentators were unaware until the flames burst forth. Another man-created disaster was unfolding.

After a while Ki stirred and began listening. Then he wanted to see. He came over to the bed. "Wow!" he said, impressed by the fire display.

"It's really happening Ki," I said gently. "It's not a video. The building is really on fire."

"What happened?" his big eyes held the question more than his words.

I explained how one plane had flown into one building, then a second plane into the second building. I paused, and his silence told me that was as far as he could go with it for now.

We continued to watch for a few more minutes. Ki grew restless and moved to play. My attention moved to what was happening. All we didn't know yet. Memories of 1993 bombing of this same building. Oklahoma City's Murrah Building bombing. Waco. Columbine. All the acts of violence and harm that had left their imprints on American consciousness in the last decade.

My thoughts moved to the increasing energy levels in our universe, the shift of the ages, occurring in our world. I thought of forgiveness and allowing, and knew this to be another test of the collective consciousness of Americans and of the world. Teaching my child, leading our community, required an alignment of consciousness.

News of another plane crashing into the U.S. Pentagon shook me and I recognized the testing of my reasoning skills. It was the uncertainty of where this might lead, how long it might continue that entered into my mind

Hezekiah drew several pictures of his experience of the events in New York City on September 11, 2001. This stark black marker drawing has a bright yellow background with orange flames coming from the word he printed at the bottom of the building, "HELP!"

for a moment. Hezekiah responded to this shift in energy with "Come on, let's go! I want to go downstairs."

We proceeded in the morning ritual and Dad came inviting Ki to go out to the orchard to take part in the cider making. He happily went off with his dad.

Christine would later tell me, when she was at the sandbox with Ki that afternoon, he had wanted to build dams to keep the Pakistans out. No one here had talked about Pakistan. Even the television coverage we had watched had yet to bring up the country. Ki knew his continents and some countries where we have friends, but as far as I knew he didn't even know where Pakistan was. It was a direct reception of thought foreshadowing what would occur several hours later.

At dinner Ki announced, like some of the people interviewed on TV, that he wanted to get whoever did this. I understood his pain, his instinct to lash out when hurt, to protect in human fashion. I also knew what I had learned about forgiveness and repentance and grace, and I want to teach this to my son.

I told him we would find out who did this. I asked him what he wanted to do with the people when he got them. "Stop them. Kill them so they can't do it again," his reply seared my heart. I understood his words were a reflection more of our frustration, collectively, than his own personal opinion. I was becoming more and more aware of how to describe what I know.

"That won't stop it, Ki," I replied.

"What will?" he asked.

"Love." It was an answer I would have thought terribly sappy and idealistic ten years before, but I knew love's power increasingly every day. It has been demonstrated over and over, through Gandhi and the British soldiers, through Jesus and the Jews, through every mother and father and their newborns.

The destruction of the World Trade Center was an opportunity for us to be who we imagine ourselves to be at our best. A collective learning experience. And the focus of the media was fear. The real lesson of all of these recent tragedies played out on satellite TV around the world was not fear, nor was it the shattering of pride or the evil of humanity. The lesson I can see is about who we are. This lesson is a test of what we believe individually and collectively. And more importantly what we want to know. Every "disaster" has shaken beliefs, all for the purpose of separating beliefs from what is known through experience. By knowing the truth of our experience we can love one another. We can allow the physical world to be what it is without reaction that leads to our own darkness. We can learn to be in the world but not of it.

Certainly our individual mastery of self affects, directly and by example, the pattern we give to all children.

Ki finally settled into bed shortly after 10 p.m. I was transcribing an intuitive report across the hall and Dad was putting him to bed. It didn't take long for him to fall asleep.

About an hour later I came in and quietly turned on the television. I had wanted to watch President Bush's remarks I had taped earlier that evening. Ki began to stir. Then cried out, "No!" I knelt by his bedside comforting him with soothing words and a carress. He moved around under the covers, at first quieter then agitated again.

He sat up, then turned around, eyes wide open. "Ki, it's okay, Mommy and Daddy arc here," I said with directed thought. I had seen him do this several times before. The pop term for it is night terrors. Having researched the mind for years, including dream phenomena, I understood what he was experiencing.

He alternately calmed and reared. I gave him water. He relaxed for a few minutes then cried out again.

Dan came in offering his comfort and a drink of water which Ki again accepted. He knew we were both there and laid back down. In a few moments he was back up and I offered to hold him. He came into my arms and I endeavored to lift him. Being dead weight I sat in a nearby chair and he stood up, still not conscious with eyes wide with expression, trapped in the emotional level. I expanded my mind to be where he was, a familiar presence for him. It was the way I had learned to lull him to sleep in the first few months of his life.

Dan picked him up and carried him up and down the hall. He laid Ki on our bed and we both soothed him. He settled in under the covers. It was like swimming underwater. He would fade and begin to drift, then cry either aloud or in muffled whimpers. I knew I was hearing the sounds of those who had died so quickly in the past twenty four hours as well as those who were still alive. Emotions, raw, confused, distorted.

At one point Ki sat up, looked toward the door of the bedroom and yelled, "Stop!" He was obviously afraid.

"What do you see Ki?" I asked. He looked at me, then back to the door. "What do you see, tell Mommy and Daddy, we can help you understand." He relaxed, laying back down, saying "I don't want to tell you." I had learned this meant he didn't know how to talk about it. I did not ask again, and for the most part he was calmer and able in minutes to move into a deeper level of sleep.

He slept through the night between his father and me.

The next morning when he awoke the television was again filled with information. Ki came over so he could see it and said, "Again. They're still talking about that?" I explained there were still many questions everyone wanted to know the answers to and so they would continue talking about it for a while.

Later some of the teachers at the College and I would talk about the difference in the energy as experience moved forward. Yesterday was shock for just about everyone. Collectively that instinctual pulse that aligns the mind to do what it must because of crisis was felt. It seems ironic when you realize that same alignment is what we inwardly crave, and can attain at will, at any time, through meditation. Because most remain in human consciousness, they are buffeted by their experiences, sometimes rudely forced to experience repercussions of what their thoughts cause. The way they experience is emotionally. This second day was a day the emotions became pronounced.

One of the teachers had awakened and cried for an hour. Some were feeling out of sorts, upset stomachs, turned solar plexuses. Others were channeling the energy into their work, cleansing and aligning their minds through concentration, prayer, and meditation. For them, this was a day for living meditatively.

Throughout this aftermath day, Ki stayed close. Even before getting dressed for the day he took off downstairs to find daddy. He wanted to know where we both were. After lunch, I passed his room heading downstairs and he came running out to tell me to "Stay up here, Mommy. Don't go." I reassured him I would stay. He just wanted us near.

For a young child, being present is everything. It makes me realize anew just how close we are as children to the Truth.

When I shared this writing with the college students,
Laurie asked, "Why did you put this in the section about breath?" I figured if she asked, you might, too, so I'll explain.

Breath is energy. Energy moves in, around, and through every living form. Even when we are unaware of the energy we are using, that our very life depends upon, it is still available for us to use.

Shared experiences produce large amounts of energy. When directed – as in prayer, an orchestra or choir, or even a sports team – the energy is palpable and its power is made manifest. When unexpected, as with the events of 9-11-01, the energy can be scattered. Much of the good that came from 9-11 was because people began looking for it. From a crisis, came learning and growth for those who wanted to wake up. Some people have stayed awake.

I know there are many people who love their kids who did not understand 9-11 in their own minds. This makes it very difficult to be centered and still to receive your child's needs. I remember watching some news feeds of a Manhattan mother and child who were unable to communicate for several hours after the buildings came down. After coming together again, the young girl said, "I feel like the mother. She (her mother) doesn't want me to leave her sight."

So it is with Indigos. They often function as parent. I understand that part of Indigo from my own upbringing. It is the inner wisdom coming forth to comfort, heal, help, lead. Those who care for Indigos need to know about this so they can understand its manifestations in their own lives.

What good is it to teach our children about peace and love and compassion and respect and reason if we fail to practice these principles in our lives?

We are all connected. Indigos experience this because they live it. Every day. Experience gives them an elevated sense of what we do to each other, we do to ourselves. Experience however does not automatically bring understanding. The sooner we understand it, the better off we will all be.

"I didn't even breathe!"

by Dr. Laurel Clark

Hezekiah had just turned seven. It was the weekend of a Spiritual Focus Session and his parents were both doing intuitive reports in the chapel of the main building on campus. Hezekiah, active, energetic, and vocal, was running around playing and wanted to go upstairs to see what was going on.

Since Hezekiah lives on campus, he is used to being up in that room as a playroom where he runs around, sings, shouts, and paces back and forth telling stories. The intuitive reports are a sacred experience. The room needs to be quiet for the participants to concentrate and listen.

I wanted to encourage Hezekiah's curiosity and desire to learn. I also know the importance of having a parent and teacher as a model "to be like." It is probable that one day Hezekiah will himself conduct intuitive reports. I know that my first stimulus for being an intuitive reporter was seeing them being done. Very firmly, with a clear, directed thought I said to Hezekiah that he could go upstairs and watch if he was completely quiet. No talking, no whispering. And he would need to stay near the side of the room. He said okay and we went upstairs.

When Hezekiah walked up the chapel stairs he was very quiet. He stood at the top of the stairs, looked around, smiled, waved at his Daddy, and then came down the stairs. He ran down the hall and out the front door. When he was outside he shouted triumphantly, "I didn't even breathe! I knew I needed to be really quiet so I held my breath."

I was proud of him for his desire and willingness to do whatever he could imagine to cooperate. I have noticed that parents oftentimes becoming embarrassed by their children and in public places they tell them to be quiet or say "Shhh!" or worse, "Shut up." The other day I was in a bathroom at Wal-Mart and a young girl was with her mother in a stall. She was talking loudly. I couldn't understand the words she was saying. She sounded as if she was about two, just learning language. Her mother, somewhat harshly, said, "Shhh! Be quiet!" I thought, "It's no wonder adults have such problems with communication! They learn that it's wrong to talk." When they emerged, I smiled at the little girl and said to her mother, "It's great that your daughter is so verbal. She must be fun to talk to."

There are times, like when intuitive reports are being done, when it is important to be quiet. There are other times when the sound of a 3-year-old's singing or a 7-year-old's rambunctious shouts of joy are stimulating and delightful. It is a matter of respect, for the child and the adults, to determine what is needed when and where.•

Breathing is so natural to the human body we don't think about it until we don't have it. Having the wind knocked out of you, or gulping too much water when you're learning to swim, or laughing until your stomach hurts tells us about the power of physical breath.

There is a mental breath, too. Mental breath is reflected in the way we use money and space, in the way we talk and move, in the way we interact with others and ourselves.

Naturally, babies breathe connectedly. The inbreath and outbreath create a constant cycle like a mechanical respirator that moves in and out, only this respirator is an inner spark of life from the Source. When this inner spark is dimmed, thwarted in some way, the breath becomes restless or hampered or trapped. It is estimated that a fourth of our kids are asthmatic. They have difficulty breathing without help. Maybe the help they need is wise teachers who teach how to wield the power of breath.

When Hezekiah was four, the infamous "O'Guinn temper" began to make itself known. When thwarted he would become angry, sometimes hitting or throwing something. Our first talk was about behavior: you never hit or throw out of anger. You can hurt someone or something. The anger can cause you to do something you'll regret later. For a while it subsided. Then it returned.

The lesson was repeated. Now Ki had experience of what being hit with something, albeit accidentally, is like. His capacity to understand had increased, but his anger still rose when he feared he would lose something. We had been reading about the lives of American presidents and I asked him if he knew what Thomas Jefferson did when he was angry.

Ki said, "No."

"Jefferson once said that one of the standards he lived by was when he was angry he would count to 10 before saying or doing anything." I knew he could count to ten, so I asked, "Do you think you can do that?"

He wasn't sure.

"Well, you know how to count to ten. I believe you can," I replied.

Ki thought about this for several days.

Weeks passed and again he did something thoughtless in anger. When I asked him what happened he said, "I forgot."

"Why?" I asked, truly curious as to what he thought and felt.

"I was still angry after 10."

I smiled. "You know what else Jefferson said about anger?"

"What?"

"That when he was really angry he would count to 100!"

"I don't know how to do that!" Ki cried.

"I will teach you, Ki. In the meantime I know something else you can do."

Always willing to learn, he was interested. "What?"

I taught Ki a mudra, a posture for his physical body, designed to calm the mind and a breathing pattern that would help him regain his center and focus.

Some days later he was raising his voice about something and I said Kiah, "Remember your mudra." Ki knew this was new to those with him. They didn't know what this was and they were curious. He went over to his favorite chair and sitting in lotus position with arms crossed in front of his heart, he closed his eyes and breathed.

When he was done he went back to playing as if nothing had ever happened.

A Collective Sigh
Meeting the Educational Needs of the Indigo

Indigos need guidance. The old educational structures are not going to work.

Their incredible energy is present from birth. It expresses in their willfulness. We can dumb them down and dope them up, altering the connection with this innate energy or we can be the change. We can learn so we can love and teach and help guide these souls into their own brilliance.

Staying the same will not enable us to do this. We must love enough to change ourselves so our children can receive the benefit.

Change does not happen as a matter of time. This is why societies and nations can repeat the sins of their forefathers, again and again and again, seemingly never learning.

Change is thought revolution. The 1960's were filled with thought revolution. From "make love not war" to equal rights for all to exploring altered states of consciousness, glimpses of what could happen were everywhere. Seeking alternatives to materialism opened the mind to possibilities – the food for thought revolution, the fuel for change.

In 1999, we started looking for the revolutionaries for the new millennium. We wanted to aid the talented and gifted among us, this time in the form of a nationwide search for a worthy recipient of $50,000 in seed money we desired to give away. As before, our search for those who teach the gifted among us, the potential inventors, scientists, artists, statesmen and yes, even mystics, enriched us all.

We learned of a growing number of purposely small schools, from coast to coast, who are seeking to reach the soul by teaching the whole person. We were inspired by the people we met and the work they are doing. There are good people doing outstanding work in meeting the needs of the future leaders of our planet. They need to be recognized for their work is innovative and inspiring.

We created what we called The Maker's Dozen, twelve of the top schools we discovered in our travels. Each has a unique approach to learning and teaching. Each works for the teachers, parents, and students because they form a community and community is essential to learning. Community is where our experience is rooted.

These schools work because people give their energies - be they time, participation, or money. They literally breathe life into their relationships with the children. By being willing to give in your own community you will find the educational gem in your own backyard or create one! That's how each one of these schools began: *someone is dreaming a dream they are willing to make come true.* Hopefully hearing about one of them will inspire you.

1

Oak Grove School in Ojai, California
Unique quality: International Students
The only school in the U.S. founded by spiritual teacher and author J. Krishnamurti draws upon all ideas that work to give the best education for the whole person. Preschool to high school, Oak Grove welcomes students from all over the world. Nonprofit, self-supporting students raise money each year for scholarships. 160 students.

2

Providence-St. Mel, Chicago
Unique quality: Work/study program
Teaches children how to use initiative, to be responsible, to understand cause and effect, to believe in themselves and to work for their dreams through a unique work-study program for 1-12 grade. A wonderful example for this day and age, showing that self esteem comes from creating and putting forth effort, not welfare or pity. 97% of Providence-St. Mel's students go to college. Since 1972, nonprofit.

3

Sycamore School, Indianapolis, Indiana
Unique quality: Parent-founded school
Only complete talented and gifted school in the state of Indiana. Started in 1984 by parents to meet the needs of their children. Within a year, 50 parents were interested in beginning a school with 110 students. Now 400 students, preschool to eighth grade, learn leadership by teaching others. Students paint ceilings as Michelangelo did while parents devote time to teaching in their areas of expertise. Nonprofit.

4
Post Oak, Houston, Texas
Unique quality: Teaching whole person
A 35-year-old Montessori school for 14 month olds to 14
year olds. Well-established school that illustrates what these
teachings offer. As with many of these schools there is a
maximum number of students (350) enabling the student-
teacher association, essential to learning, to flourish and
grow.

5
Waldorf Teacher Education
Unique quality: Teaching teachers
Waldorf education, based on Rudolf Steiner's teachings,
educates the whole person in 120 schools worldwide. As
well as arts and sciences, Waldorf philosophy teaches
children goodness, beauty, and truth through an ascending
spiral of learning that includes experience, application, and
service. Many idealistic conventionally tooled teachers
discover the Waldorf philosophy is compatible with their
own and liberating for they have the freedom to be the best
teacher they can be. Training teachers will enable this
education to become more widespread and flourish. Six
teacher institutes in the United States and in Canada

6
Upland Hills, Oxford, Michigan
Unique quality: Community interaction/involvement
Outstanding quality is their desire to be a model for other
schools based on love, community, and drawing out the
genius of every child. Toward this end, Director Phil Moore
is writing a book chronicling his 30 years with Upland Hills.
This school provides hands-on experience, teaching concepts through practical application. This kind of education
aids children to live better lives. Founded in 1971.

7

Community School #1, Kansas City
Unique quality: Community School of Future
Based on the philosophy that a child learns best when he or
she is able to teach others. One room school for wide interaction of students is not going back but moving forward as it
reflects the society we live in. This school teaches the importance of community by giving the students the chance to live
it, essential for spiritual man to flourish. 1982. K-6th grade.

8

ABC-123, Republic, Missouri
Unique quality: Early learning
The only school on our list that serves pre-school ages 3-5.
The dedicated teacher who does her own building mainte-
nance, says she has been waiting all her life to do this! "This"
is teaching 65 children in buildings owned by a Methodist
church in this rural Missouri town. Her efforts are both a
testament and a response to the reality that learning begins at
birth.

9

St. Louis Children's Aquarium, St. Louis, Missouri
Unique quality: Learning is Life-long
With its on-site aquarium and Internet access it may seem a
strange nominee, but its ideal of teaching teachers while
educating people of all ages makes it outstanding. When
Jacques Yves Cousteau looked for a place to donate his library,
St. Louis Children's Aquarium was his choice.

10

Belin-Blank Center, Iowa City, Iowa
Unique quality: International and comprehensive
International in scope offering individual classes,
summer programs, Saturday programs, live-in programs. Teaches teachers and parents along with children. Includes public, private and homeschooling.
Started 1980. Nonprofit housed at University of Iowa.
3-11 grades.

11

University of Human Goodness, Winston-Salem, North
Carolina
Unique quality: Service Education
This program, although not specifically for talented and
gifted children, educates the soul and teaches the
importance of contributing to the lives of others. This
all volunteer, 501(c)(3) educational organization, is
dedicated to teaching children how to be of service to
others. Personal responsibility is taught through its
hospice program and the respite programs. Noteworthy
for its humanity in an age of technology. 14 years old.

12

Brisbane Academy, Charlotte, North Carolina
Unique quality: College Preparation
Incorporating regular school hours, this college prep
school espouses academic guidance, social and emotional mentoring, and unconditional love for each
individual as a being of light. Founded by tutors who
wanted to continue to foster brilliance in their students,
Brisbane began in 1995 with 11 students. Currently 90
students who average three grade levels higher than
public standards.

Each school on our list inspires each of us toward loving more, teaching more, giving more. In every instance they are living testimonials to the power of the individual to make a difference. Those who teach are examples of what is being accomplished, right here, right now.

Awareness of rapid growth from one generation to the next arises because that growth is caused intentionally. Intentional growth is what it means to raise an Indigo child, a mystical child. Since the children are intentional, we, their teachers and examples, must also be intentional. Our own minds are the ones to discipline. Our minds are the ones to still. Indigos need to be heard and understood. They need guidance from talent and genius that understands itself.

We are preparing ourselves for the task, whether that child comes from your own genes or someone else's. All of us influence these mystical children. Very soon, we will live in a world of them, and they will be the ones making the choices that affect all our lives. How they understand and use energy – personal and interpersonal – then will be the result of the example we are giving right now. This depth of thinking places labels like "hyperactive", "bi-polar", and "schizophrenic" in a different light.

By being open to being a bridge, you understand all people. You strip away the colors that others have painted you and allow the Real You to shine. This is the honesty Indigos expect and demand. Indigo is not a limiting label, it is the expression of a way of thinking, an inner strength of the soul, a consciousness being brought into the world, to cause change.

Those who are already a part of the change understand this and are ready.

R E A S O N I N G

One of Hezekiah's first attempts at wielding computer technology. Today there are many exceptional programs available to supplement learning.

Gratitude
Prerequisite for Reasoning

I was looking forward to working in the studio with Paul Madar. We planned to lay the foundation for a CD of Atlantean music. Produced by dulcimer strings, the vibrations would align consciousness, opening the listener's mind to ancient healing methods.

We were ready to go and I was preparing Paul's frame of mind. I thought of the metaform, a revolving geometric form, that might facilitate focusing Paul's attention. I quickly went to the upper room to retrieve it.

While coming down the narrow wooden spiral staircase, I realized I'd be better served to move the metaform from my right hand to my left. This would free me to use the right hand to steady my descent. I was thinking this as I was already a quarter of the way down the stairs. As I reached with my left hand, the shift of weight was just enough to allow my left leg to skim the step. The nylon of my stockinged foot easily slid off the polyurethaned step and into the air. My right hand wasn't yet free so there was nothing to grab onto for support or even steadiness. In a second, I knew I was going to fall and everything started moving in slow motion.

I knew I'd gone into the sixth level of consciousness.

"You have to come out and deal with this," I reprimanded myself immediately, but not soon enough to reason to let go of the metaform in my hand. The compulsion was to save what I was holding – childhood echoes of "Don't break it!" took over and rather than let go of that model I held onto it as I tumbled toward the wicker chest on the floor about four feet below.

My next thought revolved around the experience I was having. I felt pressure and heard something pressing into the left side of my face. "My eye!" The anxiety rushed forward. It felt like whatever I'd hit was going through my face. Knowing the power of thought, I quickly banished that one with "you're okay" and action. My hand came up over the eye and I began directing energy – prana, chi, ki, life force – through my palm into the injured area.

"Breathe!" I thought and breathe I did. I know the power of breath from pranayama experiences and rebirthing. In assisting people in learning how to connectedly breathe, I had witnessed changes in asthmatic conditions, headaches, and even blindness. I knew thought control and breathing were the best mental actions to bring mind and body back to balance.

I got up off my knees, steadied myself, and moved toward the bathroom. I was doing fine until I saw the blood in the sink. The panic thought came back, "My eye!" It is not in my nature to live in fear. I want to know, so I immediately looked up in the mirror. Lowering my left hand, I could see the eye itself was fine and I could see through it. The blood was coming from an inch gash across the cheekbone and a smaller cut on the eyelid.

I knew the best thing I could do was keep breathing connectedly. I did for half an hour, as I gently rinsed the area with cool water. The only time there was pain was about five hours later when I made the mistake of eating. I wasn't really hungry, but I ate anyway, moving muscles that didn't need the stress. As a result, I experienced a dull ache for about three hours that was more annoying than distracting or devastating.

There were many times in this experience that I experienced gratitude with my head and my heart. Breath had gotten me through the experience, giving me a healing focus. Now it was time to understand why this had happened, beyond the outer clumsiness. I knew it could have been worse, and I knew it was in my life for a reason. One of those reasons came to light during a session with a health practitioner over a week later.

I knew jarring my skull the way I had meant I was in need of energetic and matter rebalancing, just to get the bones back in place. To evenly redistribute these energies, my mind focused on the fall, what I thought about it and how I felt about it.

The attitude the practitioner fed back to me was "gratitude." He said, "Be grateful for the things in your life! Be thankful for what is in your life."

My first thought on hearing this was an exasperated, "I've already been doing that!" as if there is an end to gratitude, a point where you don't need to do that anymore.

As he kept muscle testing and reestablishing polarities, my mind drifted to my upbringing. I saw a mass of thoughts best described as others telling me to be grateful when I already was. Whether it was being grateful for food on my plate where children half a world away had none or being grateful that someone else loved me even when I was less than perfect or being grateful to live in the United States, my elders always sent me a message that I should be more grateful. I received this as not being grateful enough and I rebelled against that thought.

As a youngster I was not quite strong enough to hold my own in a household of four adults telling me I wasn't something I knew I was! This memory began to unlock a chain of Self reflective thoughts.

From that beginning I had built a resistance to people telling me how I think or what I think. Anytime anyone – family member, instructor, boss, advertising executive, "experts" – tried this I saw it as an invasion of something very precious to me: my right to think. I had no resistance to learning or receiving instructions. I did resist others trying to control my mind by pressing their desires and will onto me. As I got older, I began to understand that the mind to control is your own, and that when you control your mind, you no longer fear others controlling you. Nor do you feel the need to try to control others' minds. In recent years, I have learned this is a lesson shared by every talented and gifted Indigo soul.

In this moment I was separating my *feelings* of being controlled, which were exemplified in the health practitioner telling me something I already knew, from my *thoughts* about gratitude that I knew were true. Reading, studying, and counseling hundreds of people through Intuitive Health Analyses taught me the difference between and the connection of the mental system and the emotional system in human beings. Today, I was drawing upon what I had learned to make a significant change in my life.

I could mentally see that gratitude is timeless, endless, fulfilling. I knew in that moment that my impulse ("feeling") to emotionally reject someone else telling me what I already knew was the barrier between partial knowledge and complete understanding. I let go of my resistance. The truth of the moment washed over me as a healing wave.

My mind expanded and I could see how my interpretation of this experience was tied to my experience of raising Hezekiah. I want to teach him how to be whole, connected, appreciative. This barrier limited me, making me far less effective as an example and as a teacher. Just the day before, Daniel had brought Hezekiah his usual breakfast of grits, sausage, and blueberries. Ki was so enthralled with the *Eyewitness* video we were watching, he gave no attention to dad. This was not the first time. Even with encouragement, he kept his attention and eyes on the television set. Good humor evolved into frustration that Hezekiah would refuse to acknowledge someone else's presence. In an effort to get his attention, I did something I hadn't done before. I turned off the television.

Ki erupted!

I gave him my full attention and looking him straight in the eyes, I said, "Kiah, people are more important than things." Then I turned the television back on.

Since he and his father are both males, both Aquarians, I often rely upon my husband to enlighten me about our son's thoughts, moods, and learning. One thing Daniel has taught me is the source of Kiah's eruptions. Dan says they happen when Ki thinks he has lost control. How familiar that sounds! My scientific research of self and others has proven the truth in this sequence of thought events. Certainly, when I terminated his TV show, Ki knew he had lost control. This action was something I had never done before. Punishment is not an acceptable motive in my mind. I turned the tv off so Ki would break his attention which would free it to be placed elsewhere, in this case on learning something new. It was momentarily unpleasant, and I didn't know until the next day how Hezekiah had received the whole experience.

The next morning when dad brought breakfast, Ki said, "Thank you, Daddy" and I knew he was on his way to understanding the message.

Gratitude is a cornerstone of humanity because it is intrinsically linked to experiencing and expressing love. It has been a life long lesson for me, rich and spiritually textured. It is the power that enables me to surrender completely. I know its importance in reasoning and opening the mind to intuition.

Through children, particularly those I live with, I have learned gratitude is essential in their development. They are so very bright and quick that the need for all facets of love is keen. Love is what connects them with Self and each other. It softens the explosive energies of the talented and gifted which might otherwise prove harmful to themselves and others. "Please", "I'm sorry", and "thank you" are more than social amenities and good manners. They are the seeds that enable us to become whole.

Since Ki was born I have been increasingly grateful – for him and for my husband, for very good friends and students and teachers. Everyone in my life is generous and helpful in many ways. I have made it a point to say "thank you" often. This day I realized what more I could do to help my son open to gratitude. I realized, if I want Hezekiah to be grateful, I need to show it, to be it, as well as talk it. How was I acting when dad came into the room with breakfast? Was I immediately opening my mind and heart to include him or had I inadvertently failed to do so because my attention was on our son? Did I show him how to express love with others by being the first to hug others? I knew I hugged Ki often, and this was good. How good was I with others? Years ago I hugged often, and I knew I hugged much less these days. How could I be better? Did I just leave Ki with a brief "Mommy and Daddy are helping people" when we would go to teach class or give intuitive counseling? I knew from teaching adults that more words describing my experience would lead him to understand his own. I could do better at helping Ki to develop and integrate his perceptions of experiences.

I affirmed in that moment, lying there in the health practitioner's office, to let go of the barrier I had created that kept me from experiencing ever-increasing levels of gratitude. I would be a living example of what I had realized today. And in time, Ki and others might emulate that example.

The old saying is, "The apple doesn't fall far from the tree." I am committed to being the best tree I can be.

*"What the good man ought to do he
does; for reason in each of its pos-
sessors chooses what is best for itself,
and the good man obeys his reason."*
–Aristotle 384-322 B.C.

Reasoning is the power in the waking, conscious mind. The science of reasoning is found in its
universal principles – memory, attention, and imagination. When combined, these three mental skills bring
freedom of thought and action. Reason is what
enables us to learn from our experiences. Reason is
what chooses experiences from which optimal learning can be gained.

Reason is how man knows himself as a
creator. The art of reason brings hope that man can
do more, be more. "What a piece of work is man!"
declared Shakespeare. "How noble in reason...in
apprehension how like a god."

Reasoning, well employed, begets the direct
grasp of truth known as intuition. It opens our eyes to
discern the workings of the universe, and we come to
know our place in the grand scheme of things.

The ability to bring the past and future into the
present moment to uplift the spirit in a new understanding is the epitome of man's reason. Dante said
it well, "We should rather marvel greatly if at any time
the process by which the eternal counsels are fulfilled
is so manifest as to be discerned by our reason."

Beyond Your Own Limits
Getting out of the Child's Way

by Dr. Pam Blosser

When Hezekiah was three and four years old he liked the stories about a blue bird and a chipmunk in a magazine we read together. These stories were the kind that had little pictures among the words. I would read the words and point to the pictures for him to read. The bluebird's name was Bonnie, and the chipmunk's name was Chester.

The first time we read the stories together, I told him that every time I pointed to the bluebird he could help me read the story by saying Bonnie, and every time I pointed to the little chipmunk it was Chester. We began to read and Hezekiah obediently said Bonnie every time I pointed to the bluebird and Chester every time I pointed to the chipmunk.

The story was going along smoothly when suddenly Hezekiah changed. When I pointed to the little bluebird Hezekiah said Chester and when I pointed to the chipmunk he said Bonnie. My first thought was, "Hezekiah is giving me the wrong answers," and instructed, "No. No. That's not right. This is Bonnie and this is Chester" and pointed more adamantly at the pictures.

I was somewhat perplexed because he had been identifying Bonnie and Chester correctly, and now he had reversed them. Why did he continue to give the "wrong" answer? Why had he changed his answer? Why would he even want to? He was doing it very purposefully neither as a joke nor as a refusal to obey. How curious this experience was for me and I wanted to understand.

This was amazing to observe because it set off memories of what I had been taught when I was going to school. Giving and getting the right answer was how you succeeded in life. I had learned giving the right answer was how you played the game. Right answers brought rewards. Those rewards were praise and acceptance from the teacher, good grades and good marks on your report card, and special privileges. Right answers meant you were smart, good and a host of other admirable qualities. The more right answers you gave the smarter you were and the higher up the pecking order of good and successful. Giving the wrong answer brought chastisement and the stigma of being stupid. Wrong answers and something being wrong with you had become equated in my mind.   When I was going to elementary school I wouldn't have even thought of giving the wrong answer. In fact, we would shoot our hands up in the air with the right answer hoping the teacher would call on us first so we would be the one to give the right answer first and be rewarded with a smile, nod or that's good from our teacher.   Even today if Hezekiah were in school and gave the answers he had just given, he would have been labelled. But the labels today are more insidious than in the fifties because any behavior different from what is accepted as the norm is a psychological problem and needs to be treated with drugs.

Hezekiah is an extremely bright child, asking a million questions and always eager to learn about anything and everything. This was the key. Focusing on him with my full attention and the intention of discovering what was going on in his head, I sensed no defiance, no battle of wills, dullness, or practical jokes. What I did notice was an exploration of events for the purpose of learning, like a scientist setting up the conditions of his experiment and observing them with keen interest and curiosity as to what would happen next.   He had learned the "right" answer and he had learned what happens when you give the "right" answer. Now he was learning what happens when you give an answer other than what you've been taught is the right answer. Once he knew which one was Bonnie and which one was Chester he reversed them to see what would happen if he gave a different answer. Hezekiah was not entrenched in right and wrong. He was entrenched in learning.

This was such a different concept for me. How freeing to be focused on learning rather than entrenched in right and wrong. What an adventure to deliberately give what I would call the "wrong" answer for the sake of learning. A door in my mind that had been slammed shut began to open and light streamed through the tiny crack.

Another experience that opened my mind was also when Hezekiah was three years old. This time it was about doing the "right" thing. The two of us were drawing with Briana, ten years old at the time. He wanted Briana to stop drawing because he wanted her to do something else. In order to do this he took the paper she was drawing on and tore it up. I knew this had upset Briana because she had been concentrating on and giving her energy and attention to her creation for quite a while.

I said to Hezekiah, "When you tore up Briana's picture, you hurt her feelings."

He answered in his usual curious way. "How come I hurt Briana's feelings when I tore up her picture?" Hezekiah had neither remorse, nor regret. What he did have was an extreme curiosity and a desire to understand why tearing up Briana's picture would hurt her. What I observed was Hezekiah's keen desire to understand and know why this would hurt somebody else.

Again I felt my mind opening up as I observed Hezekiah. I had just gotten out of my box. I had been stimulated to think in a totally different manner. Hezekiah had pushed my "wrong" buttons, leading to being a bad girl, in trouble, fearful, and punished. As I had grown into adulthood I had continued the punishment. Now it was not an authority punishing me but myself inflicting punishment on myself. When I did something "wrong", the way I punished myself was making myself feel ashamed, sorry, guilty, or regretful to the degree of the wrong I thought I had committed. When I had finished emotionally executing myself, my penance was complete. I was relieved of my guilt, and I could let the wrong action go. What was totally left out of this masochistic process was the learning.

Hezekiah's ego was constructed in such a way that he wasn't ashamed of what he had done. What he was doing was seeking to understand. What would have stimulated in me a shame or a guilt did not stimulate that in him. It opened my mind to how I had been trained in limited ways with playing the right and wrong game. If I did the right thing, I expected to be rewarded with kindness, promotion, acceptance, esteem, and so on. If I did the wrong thing I was bad and deserved to feel bad. Hezekiah was not thinking this way at all. He wanted to learn and understand the cause and effect of how his actions influenced another.•

The Little Red Schoolhouse Turns Indigo

One of the most brilliant people I've come across thus far is John Taylor
Gatto. He's the New York Teacher of the Year whose in-the-know insights
set the establishment on its ear every time they are presented.

For example, when Daniel and I gave his sisters, who are public educators, copies of Gatto's book *Dumbing Us Down* the only comment one of
them would offer was "sounds like a burned out teacher." Appropriate
feedback in this age of cynicism.

I am a teacher of adults. I understand the call to teach and what happens
when you respond. I have met many teachers, and I hear loud and clear that
it's a battle trying to teach anything in the public school system. I also hear
how one man did something to help his kids, often defying the system to do
it. When you are fulfilling your purpose, for Gatto it is to teach, you don't
get burned out. You learn.

Gatto's learning is tantamount to coming out of Plato's cave.

When I read *Dumbing Us Down*, I shared it with everyone – my dad,
friends, School of Metaphysics teachers and students. I knew for Dad it
would help explain why we are not sending Ki to public school. For friends
it might inspire them to break free from the well-oiled system and think for
themselves. For potential School of Metaphysics students it might inspire the
urge to know thyself that living metaphysics requires.

When I first read the chapter entitled *"The Seven Lesson Schoolteacher"*
I was filled with admiration for someone who could so clearly elucidate the
experience of millions. These common experiences learned 40+ hours a
week for most of the year for 12+ years laid the groundwork for the majority
of adult Americans living today. I often tell my classes, "Whatever twenty-
five years of teaching metaphysics and self counseling hadn't illuminated for
me, *'The Seven Lesson Schoolteacher'* did."

"The Seven Lesson Schoolteacher" describes exactly what it says – the
seven key lessons Gatto, as a public school teacher, was expected to teach his
kids. Beyond reading, 'riting, and 'rithmetic, these are ways of thinking
ranging from class position (be happy and grateful for where you are) to
intellectual dependence (always seek an expert). These are socialization
skills intended to make it easier for society to function.

A favorite for metaphysics students is the lesson of the bells. This lesson defies the intrinsic laws of the universe by teaching disconnection and chaos. Its message that you need to follow the rules may intend to instill discipline and cooperation but to the intelligently engaged, the bells signal a disruption of self discipline, with a completely opposite effect. The bell says, "This class is over, now move on." The student who wants to stay is in an immediate emotional quandary, even an ethical dilemma. How can such a youngster grow into a vital, creative, Self disciplined and Self aware adult when what they have practiced for years is something less?

For most, over time, the bells teach that nothing really matters. Why even risk being invested in something that is going to be pulled away from you? Gatto writes that more than one high school drop-out has told him they could never master the lie of pretending to be interested when they knew it would be over before they could finish or, in some cases, even start.

When you realize what 12+ years of this has done to *your* thinking, it is easier to understand why some people cannot sustain a commitment like marriage or how a student/employee can walk into a school/business and shoot his fellow students and teachers/workers.

Indifference disconnects humanity. Humanity is necessary for a reasoner to evolve. Humanity provides the basis for heart-centered connectedness where respect, love, concern, forgiveness, allowing, generosity, prosperity can be born.

The lesson of the bells is finality. It is all things must end, and they end without your input. It is too physically rigid to teach the individual. For individual creativity to mingle with discipline, for the student to find his passion and live it as long as it will carry him, he or she needs freedom. Reasoning requires concentration, sustained attention at will. Experiencing the freedom to complete what you begin encourages individual responsibility.

The problem is not what is taught in schools, nor is it the teachers who almost unanimously want to aid the kids. The problem, and even the teachers tell you this, is the bureaucracies. Those who have little if any contact with the schools they create: government representatives, administrators, labor union execs. The problem is schools are so big the individual gets lost. Children are taught to externalize their sense of self worth, well-being, health, prosperity, creativity, intelligence, humanity. They learn to look outside where these valuables will never be found.

For anyone to learn to know themselves they need time to be with themselves and with others. When children learn intimacy early, it becomes a talent, a part of them they carry throughout their entire life.

Grouping children by age is unnatural. It cuts them off from parents, family, friends, the very people they live with. Their community becomes a very limited one. When children are given opportunity to engage younger kids, they help, they teach. When given a chance to pair with elders they learn from the purest founts of wisdom life provides, the experience of others. Here they learn respect, how to view self and the world through many eyes, many points of view.

Gatto talks at length about the artificial environment of public schooling. Even likening it to a prison. This hit home in several ways for me. One was remembering images of the Columbine School in Colorado, the footage shot from a helicopter showed a complex of brick buildings, square, and with police combing the area. The scene looked like a prison! I was amazed I had never seen it before. The musty chemical cleaner smell of my 16 years in public (elementary through college) school comes back to me even as I write this. The hallways had a particular smell, the lockers, the gym. Yes, mass schooling affords us common experience, but at what price? And was it a price I was willing for my child to pay?

When I first read Gatto's words another "prison" memory came forward in my thinking. This was my first day of first grade. My parents managed a motel where we lived. In the 1960's the big chain hotels were just getting started so, like many things in our history, there were lots of mom and pop businesses, from corner soda fountains to cleaners to motels like ours.

Living in this environment was an adventure, always meeting new people, getting to do grown-up things like answer the business phone or register people in a room long before I was an adult. It also meant my neighbors were not families with kids close to my age but Sally, the waitress at the restaurant next door, and Jeri, one of the maids.

When mother drove me to school the first day, it was a long, long way from home. It seemed we were in the car for hours. House after house passed by us as we twisted and turned on the hilly streets. I had no idea where I was.

Then as we crested another hill I saw it; a long grayish building, bigger than any building around it and stretching forever. Being a new school, the grass hadn't taken root yet so it was on an island of dirt separated from everything around it.

Hundreds of kids – most older than me – swarmed in and out of this hive. Even at six, I knew something was wrong and it wasn't because I didn't know who these kids were. It was *because* I did not know them. I'd never seen any of them before, anywhere. We hadn't grown up together. I didn't see them at church or the grocery store.

I knew how to make friends. Church gave me an opportunity to learn that, as did meeting relatives who lived far away. Half-day kindergarten closer to home the year before had strengthened these social skills. Making friends wasn't a problem, being a stranger was. Here I was overwhelmed. Here the seeds were planted for things I would be seeking to understand all the way through college.

My mother was the next to the last mother to leave. I did not want her to go, to leave me with these people I had not learned to trust, surrounded by kids I didn't know. I was petrified, but I tried to be brave. I wanted to be a "big girl" as mother kept encouraging. Looking back she must have been torn, since she would not have anticipated my strong emotions. After all, kindergarten hadn't been like this, and she was doing what she had been told was best for me.

When mother walked out the door, I wanted with all my heart to run after her, but I didn't. I swallowed my fear and began my long school career of courting the favor of teachers. Yes, I excelled at learning because of this well placed desire. After all, I could have decided to court the favor of the kids – at probably a high cost.

I didn't know about prisons at age six, but when the door closed behind mom I experienced it. I was trapped with no way out. I didn't know where I was or anyone here, but I did know when I was supposed to get out. 3:30. Little did I realize it was a twelve year sentence.

I had very benevolent teachers – some mentors like J. T. Gatto. But what I would not recover until I found the School of Metaphysics was my sense of community. Young and old, rich and poor, all inclusive. Much later I would realize that the great failing of mass public schooling is the segregation by age. All the children of a particular age are forced to be together. It is not natural.

So Daniel and I asked ourselves, how can we best educate Hezekiah?

Even some of the students who have lived here at the College of Metaphysics were shocked to hear me say, "I would never homeschool Hezekiah." They look at the way we live and come to the conclusion that Ki is being homeschooled. For people making such judgements it is a lesson in how appearances can be deceiving.

I have a great respect for those who homeschool, but I want Hezekiah to be exposed to as much wisdom as possible. Every day his father and I imagine what will enable this to occur. Here at the College of Metaphysics, Hezekiah lives with different people every six months while always having the security of mom and dad and his extended aunts, uncles, godparents in Pam, Paul, Laurel, Sheila, Teresa, Christine, and young friends ranging from seven-year-older Briana to year-and -a-half younger Iris.

He has lived with people of different races, from several countries, bringing experiences I would have loved growing up. Ki became familiar with Spanish by hearing Paulina, a student from Chile, speaking her native language on the phone every day. The surrounding countryside is his science lab where the entire life cycle of a frog is eight feet from the backdoor and the natural stone driveway can become the Amazon under the direction of Dr. Pam or Paul Madar. The clear night sky becomes a planetarium revealing every planet and star in the heavens for a budding astronomer enthralled with all things *Star...Gate, Wars, Trek.* He learns writing every day with Dad and practices it when he wants to make a sign for his lemonade stand or a birthday card for his four-year-old friend Iris.

Here Ki is surrounded by ages four to seventy-four. His teachers include youngsters and teens in public school and homeschooled. Some hold degrees – in geology, agricultural economics, women's studies, journalism, recreational therapy, science, business, psychology. As new college students arrive, the worldly experience of his community grows. What a great environment to raise an enlightened soul! Everyday I am so grateful for this opportunity for it is surely a treasure trove for any Indigo.

One evening students and faculty were gathered to share dinner. At six, Ki would eat a couple bites then pace, creating one of his plays, like a screenwriter in a creative frenzy. Daniel gave everyone present some food for thought when he asked, "If Hezekiah was in school, would he be allowed to walk around, singing and talking, like he does?"

We talked about our own upbringing and how unnatural it is to expect children, particularly boys, to sit still for long periods of time. It used to be accomplished, and any old timer will tell you this, by reward/punishment, promises of teacher's smiles and good grades to take home or threats of harm and physical reprimand. It now reminds me of how we train animals. The sad truth is corporal punishment has been traded for a much more malicious and insidious form of external control: drugs.

The dinner conversation was rich that evening and everyone seemed to see the difference for a child that environment can make. The biggest difference I saw was the ratio of teachers to students. This means that at the College of Metaphysics everyone is a teacher, even Hezekiah! At most public and private schools, the age discrimination eliminates this experience of giving and receiving of knowledge and wisdom. Every day we pay for this as a society.

The next day, Daniel and I were talking and he said, "That's why the Little Red Schoolhouse worked. Everyone was a teacher except the youngest. The teachers taught everyone, the kids taught other kids the basics of life and learning. The community was formed because people learned to live together."

This is the high price of schooling as we've accepted it, Gatto says. We have lost community. Community is what I had lost when I was abandoned to first grade. My community had changed from people of all ages – grandparents, friends, and strangers who became friends by staying at our motel, to a handful of middle-aged adults and lots of kids my age. No grandparents. No babies. Not even any teenagers until I became one myself. I couldn't describe what I'd lost, but I felt it for years.

I've slowly realized the depth of what we are forging with the College of Metaphysics. Yes, it is a university for spiritual, intuitive man that serves this world. More and more I see it as serving those from the inner worlds as well. We, people who are applying metaphysical principles, are building a community based upon spiritual enlightenment. This place encourages multidimensional living. It invites the soul who wants to accelerate spiritual growth.

Such a community is a daring concept to some. For me, for Daniel, for Hezekiah, and for the people we share a great deal of our life with, it is what we are on the planet to do.

Ki, the paleontologist, on a dig at the Kansas City Science Center.

Lessons I Learned from a Six Year Old
by Shawn Stoner

Hezekiah. Where do I start with Hezekiah? There was so much that I learned from and continue to learn from him. I first met him when I went to the College of Metaphysics in 1998. I remember very distinctly him wailing during a talk during the 25th anniversary celebration for the SOM and seeing Dr. Barbara walk around holding him as he cried.

I have always loved children and have pretty easily connected with them. I have had very strong opinions about how a child should be treated, and have been known to walk up to people in stores who are ignoring their crying baby or dragging around their three-year-old by the arm and ask them if they would like it if someone twice as big as them did that to them.

I knew that Hezekiah was special from the beginning. I mean, my Lord, how could he not be? He chose to incarn into a family made up of some of the wisest spiritually enlightened people that I know and to live in an environment in which all of the people surrounding him are actively trying to elevate their own and others' consciousness. Just given those conditions, you have to figure that he is a strong soul, with many understandings, coming into this lifetime with a definite and strong purpose.

And he is that and more.

He has taught me so many important lessons. Jesus said to come to him like little children and by loving Hezekiah, I have learned more about what that means.

The first thing I noticed about Kiah was how open he was and how different from other six year olds that I had been around. There was a lightness and freshness about him that I hadn't experienced with other children. What this caused me to realize was that I expected children to be a certain way by that age – rather world wise and kind of jaded, already closed off and wary. Kiah was and is still not any of these things. He lives his life with a kind of honesty, an openness of expression that we would all be wise to strive for.

Not so Hidden Agendas

I had an agenda with Kiah – things that I wanted to teach him – how to pick up after himself, how to respect people's "space". I also wanted to share with him my love of science and science fiction. I imagined reading with him Robert Heinlein's *Have Space Suit Will Travel* and Isaac Asimov's *"I, Robot"*. I imagined teaching him of the human body and all its wondrous workings.

What I found is that agendas with this kind of child don't work.

He had his own direction, his own way of doing things and he did not want some other person coming along and upsetting what was already set into motion. You could see this in the way that he would ignore or react angrily at someone who interrupted him when he was in the middle of a story.

Kiah loves to create stories. Sometimes he will pace back and forth by himself, always with a creature in his hand, usually a small plastic dinosaur. At the end of his paces he will sometimes give a little hop and jump and then take off in some other direction. All the while he is talking, creating a story in his own mind. Sometimes he wants you to listen, and believe me, he can tell when you are not paying attention. Sometimes it doesn't seem to matter if anyone else is paying attention. He will continue the story on until it is ended.

He also likes to create stories with others. One way he does this is to draw the illustrations himself and then have you write in the words that he dictates. Creating "plays" as he called them is also a favorite – stories with either people characters, usually himself and as many others as he could gather, or play-toy plays with small plastic characters. Regardless of how he would begin a story, he wanted to complete it and would react when he would be interrupted.

Several times when I was still learning this about him, I would come to be with him. He would be sitting on the floor with Dr. Laurel or another adult, in the middle of creating a story of some kind, and I would ask, "What's the story?" or "Can I be in the story?" something along those lines. Sometimes he would simply tell me, "I don't want to play with you." Sometimes he would get angry and reactive, yelling at me to go away.

I didn't know what to do at first with this kind of reaction in him. It seemed to hit me full force in the stomach, sending my emotions reeling and my thinking in directions that I didn't like....What was wrong with me?......What had I done that was bad?.......What about my identity? Aahh..there was a big one. I had built an identity over the years of being very good with children, very loving and comfortable for them to be with, and Kiah's reactions to me at times was not in alignment with this identity at all.

What I learned was that when he was in the middle of something, to come and sit very quietly on the edge of what he was doing, on the edge of his attention. Just enough for him to know that I was there, but not enough to be intrusive. It was respect that I was learning, respect for where he was and what his experience was and how I could merge into his experience without disrupting it. I learned how to merge in with him – to be with his energy rather than having an "This is what I'm going to teach Hezekiah today" agenda.

The Power of Receptivity

One day I learned about the power of receptivity. Kiah has a stuffed lion and a lion cub that for some reason always seemed to be the victims of a horrible tragedy. When he would play with them the lion was always heartbroken over her cub being taken away and then she would get pounded on. I'm not sure when he started doing this with these toys but I had told him in the past that I didn't like it when he played like that.

This day I tried something different. Instead of trying to convince him to play something else, I grabbed a big stuffed snake, wrapped him around my shoulders, picked up a book and said, "Mr. Snake, you and I are going to read this book. Doesn't it look interesting? I've never read this book before....." Then I started reading.

Kiah was sitting next to me in a matter of seconds, the heartbroken lion laying forgotten on the floor.

Science Fiction

Hezekiah loves *Stargate,* the science fiction series on television. Often times our time together would be us making up our own *Stargate* stories and acting them out either with ourselves as the main characters or with plastic *Star Wars* figures commissioned into action as fill-in *Stargate* characters.

It was a wonderful thing, the fulfillment of my desire to share my love of science fiction with Kiah. We weren't reading Heinlein or Asimov, but we were fighting the system lords and going through the stargate to explore unknown worlds. I learned from this that my desires and what I wanted to teach him was still important, I just needed to adjust to how he learned.

Dr. Dan told me several times that children learn through play, everything is play for them. So I learned to incorporate what I wanted to teach him into our play together. Sometimes I would ask him what he knew about the nervous system, for example, then share with him what I had learned in Healing Class the previous Sunday. For a while he was fascinated with how fetuses developed, so we got a book out of the library that had pictures in it and drew our own pictures of zygotes, blastocytes and fetuses.

Force does not work with a child like Kiah. Giving and receiving openly and honestly does. I learned more about how to make what I wanted to teach attractive and desirable to him, and also how to sometimes let go of what I thought I wanted to teach him and to simply be with him, completely in the moment. I think that's what he taught me the most – how to be in the moment and give my love completely to someone else. When I did this, things always went well for us. When I didn't – when I was focused on myself, what I wanted, what I thought he should do, how I was feeling bad about myself or insecure – it would most often come out in our interactions.

This was very apparent to me one Sunday afternoon. Kiah had gathered several of us together to watch the *Stargate* that had been taped the previous Friday evening. I was feeling kind of off that day, not very sure of myself and rather restrictive. I can't even remember now what the cause of this was, which says a lot in and of itself. Dr. Laurel, Kiah, Briana and I had gathered together and Dr. Laurel was asking questions about *Stargate*, when I made an unfortunate mistake – I answered her question. One of the things that I learned about Kiah is that *Stargate* is his; it is something in his life that he knows the most about and he wants to be the one to share it with people. So whenever someone asks questions about it he wants to answer them.

This is something that I had observed in him before, but in that moment I wasn't thinking and answered Dr. Laurel. Kiah reacted strongly and yelled at her and me, "Don't listen to her! We are not going to watch this today or ever because I'm never going to play with you ever again!" Then he grabbed the tape and ran out of the room. I sat there, rather stunned and realized what I had done. Ordinarily, if I was centered and secure in myself, this situation would have easily been diffused, but I knew that one of the reasons it escalated the way it did was because of where I was.

The next morning Kiah was trying to make a stargate with his dad and I attracted his attention, asking him what he was doing. He said that he was building a stargate so that he could send me a letter back through time (this is accomplished by activating the stargate while there is a solar flare going on; this creates a distortion in the wormhole that sends the traveler back through time) telling me to not answer Dr. Laurel's question.

Then he said that I could do the research to find out when there would be a solar flare. He was doing all of this so that we could be together. Here was forgiveness and respect again.

Eventually he decided that we didn't need to build a stargate. I apologized for answering Dr. Laurel's question and said that I would be more mindful of what I answered in the future.

Shawn Stoner studied at the College of Metaphysics in 2001, the year Hezekiah was 6. With her dharma of serenity, she left an indelible impression on our lives. She now teaches metaphysics in the Chicago suburb of Palatine and plans to return to live on campus in a few years to raise her own Indigos.

The Sapling

It was an open weekend on campus at the College of Metaphysics. People had come from seven states to build friendships with those of like mind, learn from teachers who had been studying for decades, and to help beautify the grounds by planting trees and landscaping.

We met in the early afternoon for an old fashioned weiner roast. A perfect day for late winter, the air was just cool enough to keep you moving and to make the fire inviting. Dan, Hezekiah and I brought the fixin's from the main campus to the backyard of the Dream Valley house where about 30 people eagerly awaited our arrival.

For the next hour Dan and I took turns talking with people and playing with Kiah. At one point I watched them scale the steep hill, Kiah with bag of toys and stuffed critters in hand. Later he circled the seated group, sometimes stopping to say hello or tease someone he knew well.

This particular time of year and setting was coming to be a point of evalution to me. The privilege of seeing our son in the same place, with similar activities, was an excellent way to note the building of skills, particularly mental and emotional ones. Yes there was the greater physical agility of climbing the rocks independently and the ability to use tools as exhibited by using sticks to dig up rocks. These were areas most of the people here were astute in. There were plenty of guys willing to teach Kiah how to play all manner of sports. In fact sports had often been a topic that needed elevating. I knew I had lots of help in the basic physical developmental skill areas.

What I was reaching for was evolved ways of teaching essential life skills, indeed as it is being revealed to me a new system of education that will build the soul, the whole person from birth.

The afternoon was slipping by and it was nearing the time for us to leave. There were three new ladies I wanted to say a personal hello to before we left. After exchanging warm embraces, we talked for a few moments. Kiah had wandered off with another teacher so I knew he was cared for. Being newly six and coming into his own, he felt it necessary to go to one of the three-year-old saplings and gently bend one of its branches to which the teacher immediately began doing what she does best — teaching!

"Kiah!" I said in that knowing tone of parental authority, like God speaking through the clouds.

When I turned back to the women, I felt that odd twinge of needing to apologize. "He knows better." The words were out of my mouth so quickly. I gathered the threads of my attention so my reasoning could function and added what I knew to be the greater truth, "He's just seeing what will happen."

One woman said, "Yes, they all do that."

Another, "Testing the limits."

I found myself being agreeable, and feeling like I was betraying myself in the process. I knew better than I was sharing here. Years of programming of what's good and bad, right and wrong, acceptable/nonacceptable, polite/impolite, supposed to be said/not said, etc. surfaced in these moments. It would be so easy to go unconscious, to ignore it all, to let it pass without comment. My awareness does not allow me the luxury. If I try to remain unconscious, asleep, I will be tortured by the nightmares it brings. If I speak, I risk rejection. This is a polarity experience for me. I know it. I use what I've learned to see the whole picture, to transcend the self imposed limitations.

I know my intentions are loving. I have nothing to prove, no ego payoff is expected. I know the truth I have learned from teaching people of all ages and I surface, realizing what a gift the truth can be for these ladies, and for me. I speak, "Yes, actually what I've found is Ki does such things so he can learn through what the adult does, how they respond or react. It's fascinating how the learning takes place!"

I am breathing again. Relaxed. Still.

We all think about what I've said for a moment. I realize more deeply what I have learned in the past two years about my own reactions. I've never felt like my child was out to see how far he can push something, like I've heard some adults (even so-called experts) declare. I knew some of the people who spend time with Kiah end up dealing with some of that attitude themselves. What has come together for me in the past six months is the awareness that everything this child does is to stimulate learning. What he was learning about by bending the sapling was emotion. It had nothing to do with the tree. He'd already learned what happens to the tree! Today, Ki was learning what emotions are. What they are called. When they happen.

When an Indigo child puts his hand in the aquarium or runs down the hall with dirty boots or bends that sapling branch he knows the action is not desired. He isn't looking for punishment, or attention as some claim, nor to see if he can get away with it, he is looking to see *what the response will be.* Will it be the same in this person as that person? With this tree or that tree? Or will it be different? He is learning, looking for something new that will feed his undying curiosity. He is using his imagination to create experiments from which he will learn. He is maturing as a thinker.

Once I understood this, I was free to move beyond wanting to reprimand, spank, or otherwise bribe Kiah into "better" behavior. I respect how he is stretching his mind, seeking new learning, even creating it! His progress excites me. I began actively teaching him about emotion, feeding that curiosity and asking him for the reasoning behind keeping hands out of the aquarium, taking boots off outside the door, and nurturing the baby tree. It doesn't so much require patience as it requires mental investment on my part.

I've learned when the course I take is right we both learn.

One of the ladies broke our silence, asking if I was home schooling Hezekiah, and I said yes, although I didn't really think of it that way. I teach him and Briana every day, as does his dad, Dr. Pam Blosser, Dr. Laurel Clark, and others living on campus. Someone is always available to teach, and I see teaching young ones as an integral part of the evolvement of the College of Metaphysics as a place where souls of all physical ages can learn.

Shortly after, Kiah came up to let me know it was time to go. I said, "Okay, but first I want you to meet some ladies. This is Joyce, and Grace, and Ann." I repeated the names twice as he looked at each woman. Once back in the truck, I heard him whispering their names and I followed the line of his vision which was directed to the sideview mirror. There were the reflected images of Joyce and Grace and Ann. He was still practicing.

Self Initiated Learning
by Dr. Pam Blosser

Hezekiah is an active four year old who likes to learn because he causes his learning. When he wants to learn something, he will do it over and over, and he will ask to do it over and over until he learns it. One evening we were looking at a calendar in his room. We came across a picture of sea turtles under the sea. At the bottom of the picture was a skeleton of a sea turtle. The caption described a cavern under the ocean where sea turtles venture. Sometimes they are not able to get back out of the cavern so they are trapped inside the cave and die.

Hezekiah was very interested in this picture and what it described. I told him the story over and over again and he kept asking questions about it. "How come the sea turtle gets trapped? What happens when he gets trapped?" He asked to go downstairs and do a play about the turtles. He got flashlights and went into a room downstairs. We turned out the light and pretended to be sea turtles trying to find our way back out of the cave, shining our flashlights to search for the entrance.

He then asked me what happened to the turtle and how the skeleton got there. I told him that the turtle dissolved and the skeleton was all that was left. He remembered an experiment that we had done with baking soda and vinegar, where the baking soda dissolved in the vinegar releasing bubbles of carbon dioxide. He wanted to go do that experiment. We went into the kitchen, got out vinegar and baking soda and proceeded to combine the two chemicals. He used the word "dissolve" several times while we were pouring soda into the vinegar.

One thing I have learned from Hezekiah is that he causes his learning; he wants to do something over and over again, either using the same medium or a variety of media. Waiting until the situation calls you to respond is a slow way to learn.

I used to be intimidated with making pie crusts and I would avoid making pies at all costs. One day Dr. Dan, one of my teachers, showed me how to make a pie crust. When he rolled out the pie dough, preparing it to go into the pie pan, some of the dough began to break. This was the point, when I had made pies by myself, that I had started to panic. I continued to watch him. He calmly unrolled the pie dough into the plate and then took some other dough to patch the breaks. When I saw what he had done my anxiety began to melt.

After that I made lots of pics so I could become confident with making piecrust. I made cream pies and fruit pies. I made round pies and square pies. I was causing my learning. I taught others how to make pies. I taught my niece when I was visiting my sister at Christmas. I taught some of the students here at our college. I taught a teacher at one of the teacher's meetings I attended. I taught them what I had learned: that making pies is easy and fun and it's all in the way you hold your mouth when you're rolling out the pie crust.

You must smile.•

Choices
by Shawn Stoner

One of the biggest lessons came at the end of my time at the College. Dr. Barbara and I had been working on revamping the som.org website and had found a good time astrologically to upload the new site to the internet. The day was Kiah's seventh birthday and the time was when I was usually with him, about 11 in the morning.

This day he came up to me and I could tell that he was excited about what we were going to play together that day. His eyes were shining and he was smiling. When I told him that I needed to go work on the computer for a while, he became very upset. He went and started talking to his mom about it, asking if someone else could do it, or if we could do it tomorrow, or if we could do it later that day.

Fairly soon, I went upstairs to work, and Kiah went to play with someone else. I soon found out that he had said that he was never going to play with me ever again.

For several days he didn't talk to me at all and then one night as he was helping us to serve dessert we started talking about it. He said that I had two choices. One was that I could play with him again and never work on that particular computer while I was a college student. The other choice was that I could work on the computer and he wouldn't play with me.

What was my choice to be? He asked me this several times, "So what do you choose?"

I explained to him that I didn't like either choice and I explained to him what it meant to be between a rock and a hard place.

He still asked, "So what do you choose?"

I told him that I loved him very much and I apologized for not talking with him about what was going to happen on that day sooner. I told him that he was very important to me, much more important than any work that I might have to do. I also explained that I had certain responsibilities with the school's websites, that I was the only one who knew how to do them, and that I wouldn't be able to not work on the computer the rest of the time that I was a college student.

He then said to me, "You know, Shawn, people are more important than things."

I agreed and told him that I wanted both things. Eventually we worked it out. He didn't like that I would be working on that computer while I was there, but we had agreed that I wouldn't work on it during the time that I was supposed to be with him.

Then he said, "How are we going to work it out for us to play together when you move away?" I told him that I would make sure that we had time together. That if I needed to I would either come in early or stay late during the weekends that I was there to make sure that we would have time.

For me this was another lesson in respect   seeing this situation from Kiah's perspective. On his birthday of all days, one of his best friends chose a computer over him! Of course he was upset and didn't want to be with me. But in this case, his desire to be with me helped him to learn an important lesson in forgiveness. And I learned about thinking about my influence and how things would seem from another's perspective. It was good for us both, I think.•

I
N
T
U
I
T
I
O
N

The first PeaceMaker's gathering
in the backyard of the Dream Valley House
on the College of Metaphysics campus.

What is a family?

The English word family comes from the Latin *familia* meaning household. It is akin to the Sanskrit *dhaman* which means dwelling place. So any sense of family is a place to live. A place to dream. A place to share. A place to grow.

Family is our experience of connectedness. A sense of belonging that encourages us to be whole. I am always excited when people request a Past Life Family Profile. These intuitive reports continually astound me in their depth and insight. By drawing upon the dynamics of the family's inner selves, the outer strengths and weaknesses are placed in a new perspective.

Several years ago, a woman from the northeast United States requested a profile which included herself, her husband, and their young children, a boy and a girl. This report impressed me so vividly its universal truth remains with me even now. Here is the purpose of any family.

What would be the significance of that lifetime to the present lifetime for these four entities?

We see once again that there is a great deal of love between these ones. We see that there, at different times, is a great deal of strength they do draw from one another and a way that they rely upon one another that does enable them to find the truth and to have the truth revealed to them. We see the dynamics within the associations are such that there is the capacity for them to overcome limitations, and difficulties, and problems that might arise. We see there is a capacity upon each one's part - that is growing and being revealed - for giving in an uncondi- tional way to one another. There is the capacity to put them- selves aside and to consider what is true, or just, or honest, or what is in the best interest of the other. We see that this is the foundation of what can be built in the present time period for these ones as these ones individually are ready to expand their awarenesses to becoming more attentive and more devoted to the best interest of a group rather than self-serving. We see that this is a kind of developed consciousness that puts these ones upon an equal level. We see that although the dynamics in the present time period are somewhat different inasmuch as the associations are different, and the ages are different, there is nonetheless many of the same dynamics that do come to bear in the associations...

....it is important for the ones of (the mother and father) to respond to what they have created in their lives by bringing children into their life. In some ways the ones of (the parents) would benefit by expanding their vision, realizing that their marriage, their union, has turned into a family, and what that means by openly discussing that between themselves, and then with the ones of (the son) and (the daughter). The ideas that they have of what a family is, and what it does, and what it means are being conveyed to their children in more unconscious ways than in conscious ways, and therefore there is much that is being missed by all concerned because this is not being thought about deeply, or communicated in words and actions. Would suggest this be done so that there can be a much stronger sense of family within all of them - who they are in the family, how they relate to one another in the family, what the family means. [Would suggest to] then transcend this to an even higher degree, as was stated initially in this part of the report concerning the group karma of these ones being to devote themselves and their energies for something greater than themselves. This is how this family will reach its greatest potential.... [21898BGC1]

Intuition is the direct grasp of truth. It is the product of reasoning applied to arrive at a greater Truth in the life of the individual. The rewards of a life well-lived, a virtuous character.

Intuition is the realm of the soul, the understandings that draw us closer to our Maker. Much more than a sixth sense, intuition is the benefit of the soul's comparable senses. People often see visions (the intuitive sense of clairvoyance) or hear voices (clairaudience). Those with a healing touch are drawing on the intuitive sense of psychometry. Then there are those who "sense" something through taste or smell. This is not a physical sensing, but rather intuitive like smelling something fishy or tasting victory.

Intuition is with us every day because the subconscious mind is always present. We need only still the outer conscious mind to hear that inner voice or perceive that greater truth awaiting us.

Several of us at the School of Metaphysics have invested decades into intuitive research, some of which appears throughout this book. By probing the vast volumes of wisdom available in subconscious mind, we have been able to make this knowledge available to anyone through intuitive reports and to teach those who want to learn how to access their own intuitive mind at will.

Intuitive research is the newest science on our planet. One that is destined to accelerate enlightenment for us all.

Creating a Spiritual Focus for Your Family

interviews with the Padillas

Teresa and Ernie Padilla are the parents of a beautiful girl who is now into her teens. In 1997, they attended what is called a Spiritual Focus Weekend on the campus of the College of Metaphysics in the Ozark Mountains of Missouri. Here they gathered with several other parents and a mentor for the express purpose of coming to deeper awarenesses of themselves as parents. The weekend, combining instruction, discussion, practices, and an Intuitive Report on each child, fueled their aspirations and restructured the way they saw themselves as people and their daughter as a soul.

After a few weeks had passed we met to talk about their experiences in the hope their insights might aid others. At the time Briana was nine. The family lived in Webster Groves, Missouri, where Ernie worked full time for a contractor and Teresa worked part time. She was getting close to being financially able to homeschool Briana. Their attendance at the Spiritual Focus Weekend was a loving gift from friends for which they "will be eternally grateful."

In the course of our meeting, Ernie began explaining one of the perspectives that revolutionizes parenting any child. This is the reality of knowing your child as a soul. The timeless idea of the soul is now finding a place where it can best nurture every human being born – in the home.

The Soul You Call Your Child

Ernie Padilla: Part of what helped in the Spiritual Focus Session was the idea of dealing with your child as a soul rather than be attached to it like this is mine.

Barbara: Like a possession?

Ernie: Right. My perspective changed. I have a greater purpose in giving. It's easier to follow through.

Barbara: What's the difference in how you saw Briana, children, before, and now how you're seeing them?

Ernie: I guess I just intellectually knew that kids were souls. It took the weekend of discussion, focus, contemplation for it to sink in. At one point Dr. Pam (Blosser, the session mentor) said, "I want you to take fifteen minutes to hear what your child is saying to you as a soul. What is it they want to learn from you as a soul?" Sitting down and thinking about that for fifteen minutes and then objectively looking at it from that perspective gave me a whole different experience. Instead of her just being a little girl in a body that we're taking care of, it's now more. It's more like I'm entrusted, except it's a different image though. I'm not sure what the word is. It's kind of like an honorable responsibility though.

Barbara: Duty?

Ernie: Duty is closer. Entrusted would be the closest word.

Barbara: You said that you intellectually knew about children being souls, but how did you get that far? Most people, even the most religious, when they look at their children, don't think of the souls in their presence. They think of the little body that is just adorable or is throwing a fit, or the teen who is growing up too fast or running around with the wrong crowd. How did you intellectually form that idea, do you remember?

Ernie: Probably because it gave me a way to be distant and not responsible. Recognizing who I am, and that my example does have an influence.

Barbara: Are you saying it came from you beginning to believe and have knowledge of your Self as a soul? That then you could see that other people, including your own child, as a soul?

Ernie: Yes, I think that would be it. When I heard Briana's analysis say "this one grasps concepts very quickly then she thinks that she knows more than she really does know," I thought, God this sounds just like me!

An Intuitive Health Analysis on Briana's health given during the course of the weekend began in this way:
This one is quite expressive with the thoughts. The mind moves very quickly, and we see this one is able to grasp concepts very quickly. We see that there is some confusion that occurs however because this one does not know the

difference between experience, understanding, and wisdom. We see that this one can grasp concepts and has an intuitive ability to receive images from other people. This one often becomes confused by these ones believing that this one has a greater depth of understanding than she does possess. We see that this does lead this one to false conclusions. It does retard this one's reasoning skill and it does keep this one from causing the kind of learning that is necessary for this one at this point in the development... (510971bgc)

Ernie: Then it talked about the creativity being stifled, and stubbornness.

The report continued.
We see that this one is in the process of attempting to release infancy and the dependency that is inherent in it and begin to embrace a more responsible and freer expression of the Self. We see that this one is having some difficulty in doing so because there is not the guidance or the stimulation to learn how to learn. We see therefore this one's learning is beginning to shut down, and we see that this is exhibiting itself in a variety of ways. It is obvious in a kind of stubbornness this one is beginning to develop through particular habits in the way that this one thinks that are being established and are being well rooted. This is because this one is not releasing the dependency of infancy to embrace the change of growth, but this one is trading the dependency upon external factors for a dependency upon habits. This retards this one's reasoning for this one does not use imagination when this one is stubborn, this one is only using memory and will. Would suggest therefore that this one's imagination would need stimulating. We see that this one can be highly creative, this one has a great potential in that regard, but we see that it is not part of this one's nature to stimulate the Self in that regard, therefore this one is dependent upon the environment to provide it.

Ernie: Immediately I looked at my Self and saw what kind of example I had been setting for the previous nine months. I couldn't deny it, I mean there was the truth right there. I recognized that I wasn't applying the metaphysics that I was learning and teaching. It was just talking a bunch of words, I really wasn't identifying with who I truly am. This realization brought back the memory of something you said to me a while ago: "You have a vision that's very rare, we don't need you at your mediocracy, we need you at your best." That stuck with me because I know times when I am just mediocre, and there are several times when I can be great. To be great all the time is to embrace the greatness as the spiritual being, as the soul. When I heard the stubborn-ness I guess it hurt me. Not only was I letting my Self down, now I was letting down this soul that is in a physical body that's nine years old. That truth hurt me inside, and I wanted to do something about it by using my imagination and will power. I think commitment is the link.

Barbara: Honesty is one of the greatest learnings of physically parenting. You may think you can let your Self down, or your mate, or your boss or your best friend and they'd get over it, it's okay. When you have a child, if you have any kind of Self awareness then you realize that there are certain experiences that they may carry with them for decades. It's one thing to inadvertently be a part of something that a child remembers like that, but its another thing to be aware of a fault in your Self and not do anything about it. It's too easy to use it as a stimulus for you to be the best you can be. Kids remember, and they imitate. A Universal Truth is if you want someone to be something, first be that yourself.

Teresa: It touches me very deeply to see Ernie embracing what it is that we have to offer, and giving that to Briana. That's helped our relationship. It's helped me to trust in something and maybe start trusting as far as both of us because family has always been very important to me and is directly tied up in my relationship with Ernie. The weekend helped us to create together, to have something to create with.

Barbara: Common Goal?

Teresa: Yes.

Ernie: There's definitely greater cooperation, a gentler and kinder responsive-ness with each other and with Briana. Probably the biggest change was recognizing what I do as far as being more trustworthy and using my imagi-nation in communicating with Teresa and Briana. There's more trust in my Self which I think has created a greater sense of peace in my Self so there's a greater love that I'm experiencing or a deeper love.

Briana's Intuitive Health analysis began its report on the emotional system with *We see that emotionally this one would benefit from developing belief and trust.* It was very clear that Briana was absorbing and patterning herself after what her parents were displaying and teaching at that time. For them the report suggested, *that those around this one need to be keenly aware of their own trustworthiness, and their own reliability and to take greater care in how they express their thoughts, for this one is keenly observant and still imitates the environment.* Ernie had taken this suggestion literally to heart.

For Teresa, sharing this experience with her husband, the father of her child, meant the most. Although they saw each other every day, and were leading what would appear to be a normal life filled with work, extracurricular activities, trips and various relationships, a weekend when they could absorb themselves in their love for their daughter and what was in her best interest was very rewarding.

Teresa: Something unique that we experienced in the Spiritual Focus Session that other participants didn't was we were there together. The other participants were either single parents or the spouse was absent. I was greatly appreciative that Ernie and I could share this weekend. We needed this kind of spiritual guidance that only a weekend like this could provide.

Barbara: What aspect did you find particularly meaningful?

Teresa: It was the whole experience. It was the structure that was needed for Briana, Ernie, and I to interact with, our relationships together, also our marriage and us as individuals. This Spiritual Focus Session touched on all of those aspects, and that was what we needed. I felt several times a settling inside of me, "Teresa this is what you've needed for a long time." I'm glad somebody created this.

Ernie: I know how these kinds of spiritual initiations are going to change the consciousness of humanity. We definitely wanted that experience and have had that experience through this weekend and our lives have been changed. We know what it's like to be intuitive man, at least for a weekend.

Another important thing we learned this weekend was creating a place inside ourselves. We had forty-five minutes to write what we thought home is. I was so still and calm and at home mentally that I wrote about it in picture language. It was like writing a song (Ernie is a musician). I remembered what it was like. I almost think of it like writing a Beatles song, it's really great. It's not just mediocre or really good, it's something great and that's what I experienced. We wrote it down so we could read it any time and no matter where we are we can always bring that memory out.

Getting Inside Your Child's Head

At some point every parent thinks, "If I could only know what my child is thinking." Whether in the mind of a new mother whose efforts to soothe her newborn seem to meet with failure or in the mind of the father who watches his daughter leave for her first date, the question is timeless and always the same. The peace of mind of knowing what your child thinks and why has eluded us until now.

What changes this is the availability of intuitive research. Information gained through a controlled use of subconscious mind is bringing into being a new science, a new way to understand ourselves, each other, and our world. This is not mind reading, rather it is a precisely designed means to explore the origin and expression of consciousness. The Intuitive Health Analyses are particularly insightful for they relate the mental, emotional, and physical factors causing imbalance. They also give suggestions for restoring wholeness in all three areas. This information is invaluable for every parent, so much so, that one of these reports is given for each parent's child in attendance at the Spiritual Focus Weekend. This enables the mentor to guide the parents in studying, understanding, and implementing what is given for the greatest possible outcome.

The mentor sets the parent's feet firmly on a growth-filled path so each can carry the new discoveries into their home life. Ernie and Teresa began by letting Briana hear the Intuitive Health Analysis that had been given for her.

Ernie: As soon as we got back after the session we had Briana listen to her reading. Then we talked about it with her. Her stubbornness came out, "Well I know it all already. Well I know." Immediately Teresa and I heard it and we said, "That's what your analysis is talking about," and we talked about it a little bit more and she did it again. We go, "That's what it's talking about!" Then she smiled and looked at us. She knew what was going on. Since then there's been a very dramatic change in her, and she's different. She's learning on her own now. She's initiating a lot more of her learning.

Teresa did one thing where we talked about what infancy was, what adolescence is, what adulthood is, what old age and wisdom is and have her memorize them. So I think she has a different idea now of how to look at those.

Barbara: And maturity. I would think the insight would give her a different idea of what it is to mature because that's going to be important to her. You know, I mean especially when you're dealing with an Aquarian child plus you're dealing with an Aquarian child who has metaphysical parents. She has parents who are continuing to learn all the time. Her choices are different, her soul urge is different, and she is always going to be more mature than people her own age no matter how old she gets. Even now at nine she could probably teach twelve year olds as well as six year olds.

Teresa: I recognized the need for that a while ago. I didn't recognize the need *for her*. When I heard that in the report, I remembered others which said Briana has an understanding of cycles and growth and all different life forms. I guess one of the reasons why she needs to teach people and work with people of all different age groups is that she has some understanding....

   In describing her mental system, Briana's report had described this in a manner Teresa immediately identified and embraced. First what the report said.

...We see that new conditions around the Self are stimulating to this one; they do promote this one's imagination. We see that this one needs to develop skills in regards to working with other people of all ages. This one would benefit greatly by tutoring, by teaching those that do not know what she knows. We see that this would aid this one in many capacities and would in essence begin to teach this one how to learn, which is what this one needs the most at the present time..

Teresa: I've had this growing need to give to (Briana) what we've learned and go beyond that. This was wonderful to hear because it helped me put things together as far as what we're doing that's on track, also what we can do in the future and the expectations that we can have for her. The thought that touches me....I was raised Christian. Before Briana was born I remember very specifically I was thinking about what kind of mother I wanted to be. The thought of Mary (mother of Jesus) came into my mind. I thought well, that would probably be the greatest gift that I could give her if I could be like Mary, and I could teach somebody like Jesus, to contribute something like that to the world. That's what I started cultivating. My grandmother had read me stories about Mary. So I had those thoughts in my mind to turn to.

So when I heard this intuitive report, it started making sense to me about Briana's creativity. The reason why she's very creative and the reason why she chose us as parents this lifetime. How important it is for us to be an example – that was a large part of that weekend was learning how to be the kind of example that you need to be and that kids need to help them fulfill their assignment. This is a line that just keeps on going over and over in my mind, "These ones," referring to the parents, "don't realize the full impact yet of merely being who they are." That just stuck out from the whole reading when I heard that.

Barbara: Ninety percent of parenting is living it, especially at her age, because now she's going to start coming to you with dilemmas, with questions, and you'll have a chance to give her your experience, and teach her how to think, and how to trust her own judgement. The infancy days are over, and now she must use whatever you have taught her up to now. You're there as a sounding board, a counselor, and a teacher every once in a while. The example of the people who you are — how true you are to what you say and how much what you say and what you do are the same, that's going to make all the difference in the world.

Ernie: That also came up in the reading.

We see that emotionally this one would benefit from developing belief and trust. We see that there has been in the past some disruptions of both of these, and we see that this one has developed somewhat of a distance or what could develop into a cynicism because this one has been hurt in the past or betrayed where something was promised to this one and then it was not fulfilled. We see that it is important for this one to be reliable. It is important for this one to know the thoughts and meet the commitments that this one makes. It is part of the strength that this one needs to develop in the Self at the present time period so that this one can develop the trust in herself and her own judgement. We see that this is a process, it needs to be built over time and guidance would be of benefit in this...

Ernie: In the past there was a sense of betrayal in her learning to know trust. I looked back and I recognized some places where I didn't do what I said. Since having the reading, every time I say I'm going to do something, I make sure to follow through on it. It makes a big difference.

Barbara: Like what kind of things?

Ernie: Like, she always wanted to know what time are you going to be home? I had to think about it so that when I tell her I'm going to be home at this time, I'd be home at this time, or if I'm going to be a little bit later, then to at least call and talk to her and let her know what's going on. There are other things like the swing set in the back yard that has been there for a year and has never gotten concrete in it and she asks, "When are we going to do that?" and I told her on Friday. On Friday I made sure I went out and got the cement. We mixed it up together and we put it in the holes, dug the holes out and now she has a workable swingset. It took all of three hours.

Barbara: She'll always remember the day daddy and she put that swingset up.

Conscious Parenting

A teacher of concentration and meditation to adults, Teresa knew Briana needed help directing her mind. This would ease the transition of the soul into the physical world, making that transition more gentle, and easier. What she has to offer about how she worked with her daughter gives all of us a picture of what we can do as parents and stimulates thinking on our parts to become more aware of our influence directly and through example. We call this conscious parenting.

Teresa and Ernie were also aware of the Intuitive Reports offered through the School of Metaphysics and had requested several, two for Briana prior to the report they received as part of the Spiritual Focus Weekend. How they integrated what these reports revealed into their care and direction of Briana is inspiring. Their lives testify to the advantages intuitive knowledge brings, and how an Intuitive Health Analysis can serve as your personal teacher's guide for your child.

Teresa: I helped Briana to bring her attention to what she was doing fully, by using her senses. I would ask her questions, "What does it feel like? What does it sound like?" so she could be fully there and identify that experience. I would show her undivided attention by using it, or (point out to her) when other people were using it. I'd also point out the results when other people weren't using their full attention.

There's an evolvement (in Briana's successive intuitive reports). The first one said that she was malnourished. I remember being shocked about it because we were feeding her just tons of food, and I thought how can she be malnourished? We try to get all these different kinds of food, and have a balance of different kinds of food different textures, more organic, more healthy than we had ever been. What we came to realize was that undivided attention and being together and allowing more time for meals was missing in our lives. We were eating on the go a lot of times. That's what we changed.

The report given during the weekend said nutrition and vitamins are still needed but now there's an evolvement: she needs to learn about the cycle of how energy works.

Teresa is referring to the following excerpt describing the condition of Briana's physical body:

We see that the body needs more nutrition. It would utilize all vitamins and minerals more if there was more given to it, we see that this one needs to learn to appreciate food as a source of energy. We see that purpose is very important to this one at this time, and we see this needs to be reiterated to this one because it has not been given to this one earlier. We see that the repetition of this would be quite beneficial in this one's ability to learn how to learn and in making the transition that has been spoken of. We see that this one needs to understand that there is a relationship between her own body and that of other bodies, root races, in essence that of plants and animals, and that there is a cycle of the expression of energy that occurs through the process of eating.

Initially Teresa describes this in physical terms, but as she continued speaking she reveals a more important lesson that *she* is learning about herself.

Teresa: Briana needed to learn what happens when food goes in the body, even in relation to other life forms; how other life forms use food. Photosynthesis is the first thing that comes to my mind. She needs to learn that it's not only her that this is occurring in. It relates to everyone and everything, more of the purpose behind it. We didn't really teach her purpose in the very beginning because I don't think we understood it. Now we're teaching her purpose. It would have helped to be taught a long time ago.

Barbara: Perhaps, yet we can only teach what we have awareness of and we teach best what we know because knowing comes from personal experience. Also realize by working with Briana about energies now, both you and she will be preparing for what will happen with her in the next three to five years. When her Kundalini begins to become active she's going to be much more prepared to respond to the transitions it stimulates. She will better understand the spontaneous spurts of creativity, having an idea of what's happening, why, and how to channel it. Learning how to learn provides a strong foundation for this. Knowing how to concentrate, how to remember, how to visualize eases the experience of the Kundalini's arousal.

Ernie: The earlier reports talked about the importance of the basics, concentration and so forth. Her second report suggested a reverence for God and building some kind of spiritual foundation. I worked with her a lot. She likes to read books, so I would read her a story at bedtime or do something spiritual. She used to really enjoy reading the sayings of Paramahansa Yogananda which is some really enlightening stuff. I guess one thing I began to realize is the importance of teaching infancy, adolescence, adulthood, old age and wisdom. I knew I'd heard the concepts before and to some degree I had an idea of what they meant and was using all of them. It's really understanding the importance in learning and having that concept of living; it's like breathing. It's something you have to live by.

Barbara: What I hear you describing is the difference between seeing something and perceiving it. The conscious developed intellectual ability is one mental action. It is a skill to observe, to watch, to learn through reading or through someone speaking, and from that to see a concept or an idea. It's a different action to actually know the truth of it, to know the cause of it, to see how it operates in the universe. That's perception.

What you're describing, Ernie, is that you've seen these concepts for a long time, so much so that you took them for granted. Now because of Briana you're beginning to move beyond the point where you're seeing it with your conscious mind to where you're perceiving it with more of your mind, so you actually can observe, participate, experience, directly grasp the truth of the concept. This is how you move from believing something to knowing it.

Where would you say you are headed now?

Teresa: I'll let the visionary go first.

Ernie: I'm really glad that you're asking us to talk about this so we don't take it for granted, for one. We're headed to bringing out the greatness in all of us. Living an example of creating and learning how to learn the most basic or essence. To some degree physically we already live that. Mentally embracing our learning. It's the difference between eating really good food nutrients just go right through your body, and eating really good food and you absorb the nutrients. With our family right now, with Teresa and I, we have a wealth of experiences and sure we have our stubbornness and so forth, but the kind of lifestyle and freedom that we live right now and just using it. Being aware of what we're doing, how we're doing it, why we're doing it, and sharing that with other people.

Barbara: Conscious living.

Ernie: Right

Barbara: Purpose with a very expanded view.

Ernie: It's still just theory now at this time.

Barbara: Most people define knowing as an intellectual endeavor. You know because you had it done to you or you saw your parents do it or all the other parents are doing it or a book says to do it.

Ernie: I was listening to an audio tape of one of your Interfaith lessons where you asked: "Have you ever asked yourself why is it so important to our society, to all of us, that we have relationships. That we have babies. And, if you don't then there's something wrong with us?" It's making more and more sense to me. Why *is* that so important to us? Not necessarily that we're doing it, but *why* are we doing this? I'm going to answer that question.

Ernie was learning one of the essential lessons of conscious parenting. He had moved from ideas of ownership to being rooted in love for his daughter. From this point of view he could open his heart where the answer could be found.

For Briana on Her Eleventh Birthday

When it was time for you to leave Heaven
the angels gathered round,
To learn who would companion you
as you walked on earthly ground.

You would need someone to help you
fulfill your special mission.
Someone you could easily talk with,
one who would always listen.

All the angels were very willing
to go with you that day.
But only one was chosen
to guide you in God's way.

Since that day of your birth
your angel has been near,
Delighting in the light you are
and holding you most dear.

So when you need a special friend
"I am waiting just for you.
Whisper my name in your heart
that's all you need to do.

"I will answer when you call
be it night or be it day
For we are as one, my gentle lass,
connected in every way."

Birds of a Feather

Since he was born I have endeavored to faithfully record significant passages in Hezekiah's life. So far I have filled two notebook size journals with his life experiences and began a separate dream journal when he turned seven. I see this as part of the duty of being a parent. We are witness to the first steps the soul takes on the journey in this world.

Because the first seven years lay the pattern, the foundation, for all that will follow, what occurs in those years is invaluable. I know, from teaching and counseling, that some day Hezekiah will find keys and missing links in these books. They will tell him what he has forgotten, offer him insight into the origin of ideas, thoughts, or emotions. I am a scribe serving a purpose far beyond the present, and in so being I make myself more alert, more attentive, more present in our togetherness.

Living and learning at the College of Metaphysics affords him multi-age relationships, making community the focus of his reality. Daniel and I purposefully choose the situations focused on age grouping. Parks are one of the many places this occurs.

One late winter day shortly after Ki turned seven, he and I went to the park. While he relished the chance to experience others his age, I absorbed the progress I had witnessed over the years. Before leaving the park on this day, I wrote the following.

> *I watched you teach yourself today at the park. We come here about every four months or so when we visit Granddad Jack. Living on a farm, as your Granddad does, doesn't hold the luster for you that it does for all his city grandkids. For you, the cows and pasture, creatures and ponds, are an everyday occurrence. For you, going to Chillicothe to shop, or better yet the city park, is one of the highlights you look forward to.*
>
> *I can see your progression with each visit. It is measured in your willingness to climb all the way up to the top of the two and a half story rocket. It is measured in how you can reach bars more easily, maneuver your body in new ways, and most importantly in how you relate to and interact with the other children present. Sometimes the fascination of the park wears off quickly. Today, you wanted to stay.*

The park was filled with kids ages two to sixteen. You loved the energy. You would move from one area to another just soaking up the vibrations. I decided rather than chase after you, I'd choose a central location from which I could survey the entire play area.

You played on one of those colorful jungle gyms that combine slides with ropes and bridges and tunnels. Close by was a simple "n" shaped set, about six feet tall and eight feet long, that enables the kids to grab onto a ring that slides from one side of the "n" to the other. A quartet, two girls and two younger boys, were playing there. I noted them because you saw them, and my attention followed yours. Then you continued climbing through your tunnels.

Every once in a while I would glance over at the quartet again, observing the dynamics of ages and interactions between them. They didn't appear to be all brothers and sisters although for certain the eldest girl, probably 15, was dominant, the leader. The younger girl clearly idolized her, clinging and imitating, in turn. She was probably around ten. The boys were younger, eight and six, I guessed. They would follow the older girl's direction when she wanted them to do something although most of the time they did what they pleased.

As I watched, the smaller girl lost her grip on the ring and fell into the sand below. I immediately moved toward her. I could tell she was winded and after the shock wore off the tears came. You heard her crying. You stopped, moving closer to her, and stood very still. The natural urge to help was strong in you. Your attention very focused. I had seen this at other times when a child would be hurt - physically or emotionally - and you, and other children present, would draw near, just being there until the pain subsided.

Having participated in the projection of healing energies for years, I understood the need, the response, and the miracle. I also understood that beyond giving your energy, you did not yet know what to do. I knew this was something I could give to you.

I respectfully entered the space between the two of you, touching you briefly then bending down to ask the girl, "Are you all right?" I felt you come closer to me.

The older girl had squatted next to her and they both looked up. It was as if, when a stranger asked she was suddenly okay. She immediately stopped the tears and nodded. She started breathing more evenly and we moved a bit away. The four walked to another part of the playground leaving the offending playset behind.

You wanted to know what happened and if she was going to be okay and why she suddenly stopped crying. We talked about each question and what you might do if something like that ever happened again. Once satisfied, you returned to your play.

About forty five minutes later, the quartet was working together to cover a low, broad slide with sand. The leader was packing the sand as the younger ones would pick up handfuls and drop them onto the slanted surface. Feeling more secure and comfortable from having been around these people a while, you wanted to help. You started imitating what you saw the others doing, picking up sand and putting it on the slide.

After a few trips, the older girl said with a hint of irritation, "Let it drop from the top." You didn't seem to notice her emotion, nor did it seem you listened to her command because you kept putting sand on from the side where you could reach the slide. Instead of showing you what to do, when you came with a handful, she looked you in the eye and said sternly, "Would you stop that!"

You dropped the sand in your hands and moved a couple feet away. You got the full effect of her desire and emotion. You separated yourself and started playing in the sand alone. You were hurt and dejected. My heart strings tugged, and I decided to give you space. I would continue to lovingly watch you and we could talk later.

Very soon after this another boy, a twelve year old new on the scene, arrived. With six other slides available and with no consideration for the quartet's efforts, he ran over and climbed the ladder of their slide. Looking up, the girl was clearly amazed that he was clueless about the work going on. She had the petulant, "can't you see what we're doing here! this is our space!" look on her face. She really believed her glare would deter him.

It didn't.

The boy came down the slide, intentionally wiping down as much of the built-up sand as he could. "Why did you do that?" she yelled. The boy just smiled back at her, infuriating her even more. She stood there, mouth agape, hands on hips, while the boy ran off.

You quietly watched the whole interaction.

Stunned, the girl went back to covering the slide with sand. One of the boys in the quartet threw sand at her, and she asked the same question, "Why did you do that?"

Then another girl who was with the 12-year-old slid down the slide, wiping out the rest of the sand. At that the quartet left, abandoning their efforts. I thought about cause and effect, about karma and intention and how opportunities to learn present themselves as many times as necessary for the learning the soul needs. I thought about how this is the real learning in life, and how the manmade "ologies" we create too often distract us from our purpose in life rather than point us in that direction.

I wondered what you thought about the whole scene, the chain of events that had unfolded before your eyes. I wondered how much you had learned by watching. Soon your actions told me. With the slide free, you felt invited again. You could pick up where the others had left off without fear of being pushed away. You wanted the experience and you had waited until it was available again.

You began picking up the sand, bringing it over to the slide. At first your efforts were solitary. You built alone. Soon a boy about your age joined you. The two of you built together. You or he would slide down, wiping out some of the sand, then you would build again. A little girl joined in, then another. You'd attracted like kind, birds of a feather, a gentle group who worked together carefully, without any prodding, and with few words. It was a mystic kid group, no one person dominant, each one seeing what part they could play, responding to the desires and actions of one another. It was as if everyone else at the park respected the space you created, either contributing or leaving you be.

This was a lesson in observation for you and for me. I could have joined in your park experience at any time – teaching, instructing you or the other children, guiding, influencing the play. Instead, I waited. I'm very glad I did for by waiting I learned more about you than any amount of words can say.

Intuition is the direct grasp of truth. It is learning through observation, from the inner subconscious mind's point of view. When the conscious mind is still, receiving, we see and we know. When we draw upon subconscious understanding we align our minds with a greater truth and we experience ourselves, our children, everyone with the deepest sense of compassion and wisdom.

Some months later Hezekiah, Daniel, and I were driving along the highway. Ki wanted to listen to a tape of Greek myth stories tailored for children. He asked if he could push the tape into the machine. Ki did so gently, but nothing happened. A quizzical look came over his face and turning to me he asked, "Do I push this button?"

Daniel read the words printed on the buttons for him. Hezekiah reached over and pushed the on/off button which does not have letters.

Feeling our surprise he asked, "Do you know how I knew?" He turned to Dan, "I watch you and mommy do it."

The human idea of *"do as I say not as I do"* quickly filtered through my outer consciousness. I was bemused by it. How often do adults cheat themselves and their youth with that thought? The thought holds the distance between thinking ideals and living them. Hypocrisy has no place in the world of someone who is connected to his or her subconscious mind. This is one of the reasons Indigo kids value, and expect, honesty.

Having acknowledged the limiting human thought and I laughed, saying, "You learn through observation very well, Hezekiah." I was proud of myself for directing my attention to a higher thought worthy of a spiritual teacher, and even prouder of Kiah for demonstrating a growing, active, reasoning mind that can learn anywhere, any time, through experience and through observation.

Jade & Andisa cradle the new kittens
during Camp Niangua.

E
N
T
R
A
I
N
M
E
N
T

Iris's Weird Dream

Iris's mom was teaching adults how to understand their dreams in a class in Springfield. Her dad attended his metaphysics class, on the College of Metaphysics campus, on the same night. This gave those of us living on campus the opportunity to embrace another Indigo child one evening a week.

One Wednesday, upon arriving with her dad, Iris proudly announced "I had a weird dream." She was telling Paul Madar, one of her dad's classmates, who was listening with rapt interest written plainly across his face. Brewing tea a few feet away, I could tell Iris's audience was being swept away by her four-year-old charm, completely forgetting their vast knowledge of the subject at hand.

"Why was your dream weird, Iris," I asked.

She lowered her chin, almond black eyes raised under feathery lashes, "It was just weird" she replied.

I knew from previous experience with other Indigos, their amazing capacity of listening and memory far outweighs the maturity level of comprehension, and so words can tumble from their expressive minds generously in flow while empty in meaning. I had learned to still my mind so I could honor whether the image in another's mind matches the words employed or not. I perceived Iris didn't know what weird meant, so I asked her, "What does weird mean?"

She twisted around, as youngsters who have yet to have the joy of learning kindled are wont to do. I stooped so I could be on her level, reached for her hand, and smiled. Iris shrugged her shoulders, which was the way she knew to say "I don't know."

"Weird means something is strange to us. Usually, people think things that they don't understand are weird. Sometimes it's something that's a little scary."

"My dream wasn't scary, Dr. Barbara. It was just...just...weird!"

"Tell me your dream, Iris," I said encouraging her. Iris did tell. She had a dolly that would drink milk if she went poo. Indeed if I didn't know the universal language of mind, the dream language, I would have thought the dream a bit strange too. But I knew it was talking about Iris's need to release old images in order for there to be room to receive new ones. Her resistance was showing even in this short exchange.

Rather than try to tell her what the dream meant, I responded to what the dream told me about Iris' state of mind by saying, "You know what, Iris?"

"What?"

"I've been writing down Hezekiah's dreams ever since he starting telling them to me. When he wakes up, he'll let me know if he's had a dream, and I keep it in a journal."

Her head lifted and those big eyes softened.

Knowing Ben and Dory, Iris's parents, knew how to interpret dreams I felt safe saying, "I'll bet if you'd ask them kindly your mom or dad would begin writing your dreams down, then when you are ten or twenty you'll have a record of all your dreams!" She was twisting again but this time a coquettish attitude had replaced the more defiant one. When I said, "That would be very special" she was sold. She had allowed the new idea to enter into her thinking, and more importantly her dad had been there through it all to hear it. Now it would be up to him to water and nurture the seed that had been planted.

Several months later, Iris ran to me for a hug. I picked her up and as we twirled around she said, "I had a dream!"

"You did!" my voice intentionally reflecting excitement.

"Yes, but it was a bad dream," she replied, head lowered.

"What made it seem bad?" I asked, whisking the hair from her eyes.

"It scared me."

"Ah, I see." Now she had told me the truth behind the judgement. A most important place to ascertain in guiding an Indigo. I had experienced both personally and through observation how easily children are trained to move outward away from the point of cause. And now as an adult teacher I was having the wonderful experience of how honesty made each learning very simple. "So it's bad to be scared?"

Iris nodded. "I don't like to be scared."

I hugged her, reassuring her that we only fear what we do not understand, and I would be happy to help her understand her dream if she would share it.

She smiled, that radiant smile through the eyes that we want to nurture and keep alive. Iris proceeded to tell her dream

We were at Peacemakers (a family interfaith gathering). Mommy and daddy and Jonathan and Adam (family friends) were there. We were in a circle, singing and doing a play, and this man said he was going to kill me. I ran away from him.

"I didn't want him to kill me." Iris said quite adamantly. "He was scary."

"Did you know who he was?" I asked.

She shook her head no.

"Well, Iris, what did your mommy and daddy say about your dream?" As a teacher, the first reference is to learn what the parents are teaching, so you can determine your response and children at age four will tell you to the best of their ability the truth.

"They said it was just a dream and nothing would hurt me."

I nodded, reaffirming the last part of the statement, "That's true, the more we remember our dreams, the more we learn about ourselves."

Iris continued, "And they told me to ask you." By this time Iris' mom had reached us and she affirmed her daughter's statement. Having mom's approval gave me the freedom to teach Iris what I know.

I had grasped the dream's meaning as Iris related the dream, listening to her words and watching the pictures in her mind. Now I needed to determine how to place this in language a very bright four-year-old would understand. Still holding Iris, I looked her eye to eye and said, "That's a great dream, Iris, did you know that?" She looked at me quizzically.

"Yes. It's a good dream because it says you are about to change. You change every day, did you know that?" Iris's eyes were wide with excitement. "Your hair grows. Every day. You're getting smarter and taller. That's what your dream is about."

"But that man was scary."

"He was? That's because you didn't know who he was. That means you don't know yet which change the dream's talking about. But you will soon, and your mommy and daddy will be there to help you." I smiled at Iris's mom and Iris reached over to transfer from my arms to her mother's. She wasn't completely convinced but she wasn't as scared as she had been or would be when another such dream came her way.

Entrainment is a scientific term meaning "to carry along in its flow." An example of entrainment is the phenomenon that when you have a wall full of varying sizes of pendulum clocks, you can start them at different times, and within hours they will become entrained with one another, moving at the same rhythm and tempo.

When used to describe a state of mind, entrainment is the harmonizing of the conscious and subconscious minds, so these parts of mind are synchronized, functioning as a whole unit. Developing the essential like skills brings this entrainment, a reuniting of the soul if you will.

An outstanding way to court entrainment is by remembering your dreams. Dreams are messages from the inner subconscious mind to the waking conscious mind about your state of conscious awareness. Dreams tell you what your subconscious mind thinks about what you are thinking and doing, who you are and where you are going. Your subconscious mind, being the storehouse of your wisdom, acts as your best friend or an internal counselor. This is why dreams can solve problems, tell you of future events, and encourage and entertain.

We dream many things in common, of people, places and things from our waking life in the physical world. When appearing in a dream, your best friend serves as a dream image conveying a specific quality of an aspect of your whole Self. Each dream symbol has a meaning that is both universal and personal. Decipher what the symbol stands for and you understand the language of your dreams.

Interpreting your dreams means you have learned the language of your dreams, the language the inner minds speak. Those who interpret their dreams are more self aware from the practice. They also have a keen insight into others' dream experiences. This is an amazing ability for anyone around children.

Interpreting dreams is a science and an art that can be learned and taught. The School of Metaphysics has been doing so for decades. Since the initiation of www.dreamschool.org, we have corresponded with people worldwide, many of them young people. It gives us a unique window into the consciousness of the Indigo and the people they live with. We share a bit of this with you in the hopes it will inspire you to respond to what your dreams are conveying.

What do Indigos Dream?

I have taught many parents how to interpret their children's dreams. Knowing the language of mind gives you an invaluable window into your child's consciousness. When Briana was eleven I asked her parents, who are both dream interpreters, how often she remembered her dreams. Her mother, Teresa, said she remembered about four every week. Teresa also thought Bri had an idea of what her dreams meant. I encouraged her to listen to Briana's ideas and build upon them. When Teresa said sometimes it was like "pulling teeth to get her to express her thoughts," I suggested she encourage Bri to draw or even act out her dreams.

Description can be expressed in many ways. It doesn't always have to be in words. By being a character in your child's dream, s/he needs to tell you which dream-character you are and what you are doing and even thinking in the dream. This can be great fun for you both, and very enlightening. For the parent or teacher, whatever you have to offer a child about the meaning of dreams will be better remembered when given in this fashion. It teaches the young conscious mind to value the inner subconscious voice. In time, the dream language can be taught and used as an extraordinary means for Self awareness and Self reflection.

The School of Metaphysics has been researching mind for over three decades. In that time we have come upon profound Truths that are both universally and personally applicable. With a worldwide base, the conclusions about the purpose and meaning of dreams is well substantiated. The art and science of dream interpretation is taught in our classes, through correspondence study, lectures and courses at universities, and in books like *Interpreting Dreams for Self Discovery* and *The Dreamer's Dictionary.* We even sponsor an annual National Dream Hotline® the last weekend in April for those who have questions about their dreams.

What we have learned and are learning is described on the internet at two sites: www.som.org and www.dreamschool.org. Here the person who desires to learn will find hundreds of dreams and their interpretations in the language of mind. Articles, book excerpts, and personal accounts of the meaning of dreams in our lives are available at dreamschool.

Five years after talking with Briana's mom and dad, Briana is one of the people who help make dreamschool happen. One of the avenues of her education here at the College of Metaphysics is apprenticing in the receiving and responding to dream questions mailed to us from all over the world.

The internet gives us a means for worldwide communication, it has accelerated our research in all manner of inner level mind experiences, dreaming being by far the most common. Since the site went up in 1998, we have seen an increase in dreams from teenagers. Many of these reflect the evolution of consciousness taking place that is producing the Indigo child. Here is a taste of what you will find when you attend dreamschool. We called this email dream **"Driving Mom's Car."**

hi my name is s*.
i had this weird dream that i was driving my moms car around a track that is around the barn on the farm where she lives. i am 15 and i have driven the car around the track before for practise. anyways i was driving in the dark i had to fumble to put the headlights on ,then i reached one of the horses paddocks and i was scared thinking i would spook them, when i got past them i couldn't see anything and i knew the turn was coming up , i panicked and turned the wheel from left to right over and over again but i could see the trees that were there but everything was dark and i couldn't see where i was going .

Can you help me figure out what's this mean please?
thank you
S Female

Our ***dreamschool response*** is as follows:
It is very helpful that you let us know your age and in a moment you will see why. This dream focuses on your thoughts and feelings about your physical body. There is some sense that you shouldn't have freedoms or opportunities, while at the same time there is an awareness that the control you desire is revealing itself in a natural fashion. There is also the sense that the control is reckless, lacking information and experience perhaps, and there is a recognition that the will needs to be involved in order for you to have the direction of your body that you desire.

During the teenage years, the years of physical adolescence, more is changing than just the physical body. Your dream gives you insight into that more. The thoughts that your dream highlights are all natural and can give you deeper insight into your experience. There are many things that you have yet to experience physically and therefore understand concerning the many chemical and electrical changes causing your body to act and react as it does. Endeavor to be attentive to the changes, even to the point of writing down your observations and experiences. This will help you to link your thoughts to what is happening in your body.

For instance, a day when you feel really good about yourself and what you are doing may result in an enormous amount of energy that makes you giddy and able to exist with very little sleep. A day when you are keenly disappointed by something that happened may put you in a tailspin not only mentally and emotionally but hormonally as well. Fifteen is a great age to begin becoming a master of your own mind and body.

It would probably be helpful and highly instructive for you to pursue yoga, qui gong, or martial arts. These forms of discipline, particularly with a wise teacher, will serve you well in understanding the energy that ties the mind/soul to the body. This is what most teenagers are looking for in sports or dance activities which too often become physical only. You are looking for more, you want more (after all you're driving your mom's car), so make choices that will fulfill your desire.•

Hundreds of dreams are interpreted at dreamschool.org, many from young people who want to know. Their dreams are the experiences of the soul, the thinking being, whose mind expects to be used. These individuals are the mystic children – the Indigos, the psychic kids, those with amazing healing powers. Their abilities reflect in the quality and type of dreams they have.

Some of their dreams like the losing teeth dream, getting married, and dying are among the most common dreams people of any age have. Others, like this next dream, reflect the exceptional abilities these children exhibit, naturally. From lucid dreaming (being aware that you are dreaming as it is happening) to out of body experiences, the capacities of subconscious mind are being discovered and explored during the dreamstate. In increasing numbers we are "awakening" to our inner life, often through our dreamstates.

BEYOND LIFE AS WE LIVE IT

I find your website very interesting and have gained some insight from it. I have recently submitted a dream for interpretation and thank you for your feedback. I'd like to share a strange experience that occurred years back, I have only mentioned it to my parents and no one else because people would probably say its crazy.

I went to bed and felt myself starting to fall asleep, when I suddenly felt "a force entering my body (invisible, I could just feel it and knew it was there and it was strong), I was frightened by this force because I had been taught by my mother (who is somewhat gifted and because of her religious beliefs refuses to develop this gift) that things of this nature are evil. So, as I felt this force entering (through my mouth) I fought it mentally - I recall saying oh my god what is this, no I am not going to let this happen, I kept saying no but the force entered and I found myself in a place (like a dark tunnel) that was the most peaceful and serene "feeling I will ever experience in life as we know" - I do not believe such peace exist. Then I started questioning myself, wondering if I had just died. I thought oh god am I dead? did I just die in my sleep? I kept saying I cant believe I just died in my sleep. I recall thinking if this is death then no one should ever be afraid to die. I felt as if it was like in a tunnel of some sort and felt as if I were floating, I couldnt really see anything but it was all pure feeling, I sort of wanted to stay in that peaceful place, but then just as it entered it left but this time through my chest - I literally felt a force leave through my chest (crazy right?).

This was such a crazy experience I did not understand but the truth is that I was literally aware of everything at that moment. So, I never discussed it with anyone except my parents. I told my mother that such peace does not exist in this life as we know it. I just wondered your thoughts on this "experience" - it was not like a dream but an experience. I was completely aware of everything although I was in a sleep state, a "hyperawareness so to speak". As I write to you I feel that sharing this with you makes me a little uncomfortable but feel that your group probably understands these type of experiences.
Thank you
RD, female

dreamschool response
We are very glad you appreciate the work we are doing and that you wrote us back. Yes, we have a great deal of insight to offer you concerning this dream experience. Here, at the School of Metaphysics we refer to experiences like this as inner level experience. This is based upon a model of consciousness that expresses itself in seven distinct and connected ways. We recognize 7 levels of consciousness, the physical level being the outermost.

The physical level of consciousness is where the waking, conscious mind functions. The next four inner levels comprise the totality of subconscious mind (the remaining two are superconscious mind) where what we call dream experiences occur.

When you sleep your conscious, waking mind is pushed aside. Your subconscious mind is free to do its work of re-energizing mind and body, assimilating the previous day's experiences, and communicating wisdom to the waking consciousness. When the latter occurs, we say we remember a dream. Learning how to understand dreams is part of what we study at SOM.

Our broader study is of the whole Self, the complete mind that determines human consciousness, its past, present, and future. From this perspective we can say that you were experiencing the inner levels of subconscious mind. Others have reported similar experiences here at dreamschool and in thousands of lectures and radio shows throughout the US and worldwide. The movement independent of the physical body and the sensation of floating are characteristic descriptions of out of body experience (OBE) or astral projection. The tunnel is a universal symbol for entering into the inner levels of mind. The feeling of peace and awareness of the separation between this inner world and the outer world is also common for those who have expanded their minds beyond the limits of the physical body and life. The sense of complete oneness with everything is the consciousness of the Enlightened. You experienced it for a moment. It was real and you know it. Now it is time to respond to it.

This is why the School of Metaphysics exists. We teach how the mind works and how to develop skills and abilities in using the whole mind. Most people only use a small portion of their potential. They rely so heavily upon the physical part of self that they often do not even remember their dreams. You are definitely not crazy. You have an attentive mind and a desire to know your Self. You need to harness your curiosity so you can learn to reproduce and further your experiences. This will move you from belief (where fear can often delay, twist, stymie, or color the truth of your experience) to knowing (understanding from personal experience, the height of spiritual knowledge). By harnessing your natural abilities in ten essential living skills, you can open the inner worlds within you where truth, peace, wisdom, and interconnectedness define experience.

Also....in regards to the entering and leaving.....this point of entry highlights your willingness to receive inner guidance and from what happened during your "dream". The force was most probably the energy flows connecting your mind and body. Following the peace and awareness you gained from your experience, the exit was through the heart area, the resonator of understanding, the part of us where we know our connectedness with others.

Keep in mind there is a reason for everything that happens. We just need to develop the perception to grasp it. It always amazes us, even after decades of living meditatively and teaching others, that the predominant beliefs in the world can be that you have to die to experience peace and awareness. It is that kind of thinking that devalues life to the point that it is okay to martyr yourself or someone else.

We think the goal of life is the expanded consciousness that leads to Enlightenment for Self and for us all. Hope to hear from you again soon.•

The entrainment that comes from learning how to interpret the meaning of your dreams, then using your conscious waking mind to fashion an appropriate response to what you have learned, creates a complete cycle of energy in your own consciousness. It produces a centeredness, an inner calm and authority, that cannot be bought, borrowed, or bestowed.

Entrainment is produced by awareness, one thought at a time. It is invaluable for each of us, and is what every child is seeking. Listening and responding to a child's dreams tells you their innermost thoughts, the ones that truly count. They tell you about hopes and fears, desires and concerns. They tell you the level of soul awareness, and whether it is being nurtured or stymied.

Children's dreams can tell us when they are emotionally troubled, and often what about. They can tell us when they are undergoing a major life change, or fighting one. They tell us what the child is learning and how, or if, it is permanent or temporary. Young people's dreams give daily guidance, serving as a compass through the sometimes churning waters of adolescence.

Dreams are one of the most incredible resources available, one we can so easily access. All we need do is respect our dreams. Give them attention so we can concentrate enough to remember the details upon awakening. Then we can hear what that inner voice is saying.

We are Linked by our Dreams

The more we learn from our dreams, the more we can aid others with theirs. It's like learning English or Chinese, proficiency comes with use. Often we dream of children, sometimes when we don't even have children of our own. This is because in the Universal Language of Mind, the language used in our dreams, children represent new ideas or new ways of life.

Sometimes parents dream about their children and depending upon the content of the dream this can be funny, perplexing, or frightening. The following dreams, taken from www.dreamschool.org, give insight into the dreamer as a person while also leaving impressions about their relationships with their children.

When a Parent Dreams about Her Child

The urge to diagnose is strong. Being reasoning beings, we want to separate and identify everything. When this becomes the foundation of Self awareness, we lift our hearts and minds. When separating and identifying are their own end, the labels they produce are heavy and limiting. The following woman was quite open in describing her consciousness. This was valuable to us in giving her insight into the dream she had about her son. We called it....

ANTI-CHRIST AND THE END OF THE WORLD

I have a six yr old son, who for the past 3 yrs has had behavior problems. In the last year and a half we have sought professional help/counseling/meds. He was held back from kindergarten because of his behavior. He has been extremely hard to diagnose, actually so far only possible ADD. My husband and I are strict disciplinarians; between his school, the doctors and everything we've been trying at home I feel we've made little progress. He is a very intelligent and stubborn child, and has taken manipulation to a new level. Consequences seem to mean nothing to him, no matter what they are. Sometimes my husband and I wonder if he's playing us all for fools and has out smarted us all. I had this dream about six months ago.

In this nightmare, I was approached by a man I didn't know. He had shaggy blonde hair and wore geeky black glasses. He told me that my son was the anti-christ, that he must be killed, this had to be done to save the earth. Apparently this man was working on a short time line. This man (I think he was a scientist) told me there were only a few hours left to do this. I was of course horrified at this information and this man and I argued extensively over the matter. I remember being terrified and in disbelief of what he was telling me. He was showing me maps, Biblical scriptures and information that apparently deemed that what he was saying to me was true. I remember watching on a screen "the end of the world" the earth was exploding and I was seeing people dying everywhere. I felt enormous guilt and responsibility, but still in disbelief of what this man was saying to me. He was very panicked and would not let up on pushing me to do this terrible deed; in the same sense was saving mankind.

Then I remember being in a house with this man and I was terrified. I went into a bedroom and my son was there. I still did not want to believe what this man was saying. Then I remember looking into my sons eyes, and they were black and evil. As if I could feel that Satan were inside him and I could see more but I can't remember what. His eyes told me what this man had said was all true. I remember my son looking me in the eyes and he was confused. He was asking me not to hurt him. I remember crying hysterically and slowly putting my hands around his neck and starting to squeeze. My son was looking into my eyes the whole time. I don't ever remember feeling so much emotion in a dream, it was traumatizing.

I woke up and it took me a while to realize that it was just a dream, it felt so real. I felt horrible and wouldn't get out of bed. It was about 5 minutes until it finally hit me, that it was just a dream. I got up and ran to my son's room to see if he were still alive.

I'm hoping this may symbolize something that might give me some insight with helping with my son.

dreamschool response

Your dream is about respect, self respect. Your son represents an idea that you created and have nurtured into a way of life that needs to be changed. Inwardly, subconsciously, you are aware of this for the idea is no longer serving your whole self. Consciously you are fighting making this change until you realize that failing to alter this way of life symbolized by your son in the dream will lead to uncontrolled and unwanted changes in who you are.

You have become aware of the need for change and as you start changing you realize that the cause for the difficulty is your own imagined limitations. What needs to change is your perception and you are using your will to do so. This is why we say that this dream is about respect.

Respect is a mental skill that can be taught and learned. It is the ability to see, to perceive, again. In other words you look at life from a particular set of beliefs and experience. This is your perspective. You may have a twin who has shared many of the same experiences and even the beliefs yet her perspective is her own. Both of you may have a brother who has a third perspective.

The capacity to respect is the capacity to see from other points of view, to be willing to look at a situation, circumstance, memory again and again and from different angles. This ability requires a degree of mastery of attention and will in order to move consciousness from one place to another. This is why respect can be taught and learned. It is so important that it is the first endeavor of each student in the classes offered by the School of Metaphysics. We teach people how thinking occurs, what the mind is, the energy and substances that it uses for creation, and the Universal Laws that govern any creation. When you mention that you and your husband sometimes wonder if your son has outsmarted you this is a question arising in your mind for a reason. It is a thought worthy of your investigation.

There are several articles at www.som.org that would be well worth your time reading. Parents of talented and gifted children, Indigo Children as they are being called nowadays, are challenged in their own beliefs and experience. When the parents are openly pursuing learning about self, consciousness, and our relationship to the Creator and humanity raising this type of soul is much more fulfilling and easier. Parents who are studying and applying principles such as those taught at SOM find what they are learning is a constant resource for guiding and teaching an intelligent willful child. The more you respect yourself the more the Indigo Child gives respect to you. It is most important to have a growing, living and breathing image of respect because stale, stagnant or polarizing concepts (like self respect is standing up for yourself, fighting for what you believe in, knowing your value, etc.) of respect tend to be unearthed in the presence of the Indigo Child. Love is essential as is respect in order to give and receive with these vital and spiritually advanced souls. You are most fortunate to have one in your presence.•

A Child's Empathy for His Parent

Now we share a recurring dream of the mother of a teenage boy. It is the boy, however, who writes to us. What he tells us reflects the sensitivity common in Indigo children. The ability to absorb what is in the environment, what is going on with others, and the need to know how to respond are common traits. This boy writing on behalf of his mother enables us to address how dreams can help Indigos to help others. Here is the value of learning to interpret your dreams.

CONCERNED FOR HIS MOM

I am 14 years old my mother keeps having a dream about her mother that died a year. she comes in her dreams every night i don't know what she is trying to tell her. Every night she has different dreams but her mother is always in it. she was very close to her mother and she is the baby of the family. My mother was really upset when she died. maybe she is coming in my mothers dream cause she knows my mother is not strong. my mother is depressed all the time.
my mother thinks that something is going to happened to her. i think my mother has a gift almost everyone who dies come in my mothers dream. can you find a way tell me why is this. write back

dreamschool response

You possess perceptive insight that you will want to keep alive and cultivate. Now is the time to learn about your consciousness, to learn a progressive form of meditation that will aid you to experience in the inner levels of consciousness. Now is the time to begin recording your own dreams and decoding them.

Your mother has earned her ability somewhere, sometime. If reincarnation makes any sense to you this could be an answer as to why she displays this ability for communication when others do not. I see reincarnation as a progressive, aggregate learning for the soul, a drawing to the self understandings that will give ever increasing abilities and awareness.

From what you describe this is exactly what is happening with your mother. She already has the intuitive connection to others which enables her to communicate telepathically and it makes good sense that she would do so with her own mother. It also makes sense her mother would sense your mom's need and continue to try to be there for her. Just because the body is left behind does not mean we lose this mental and emotional connections.•

Drawing on your Dreams for Conscious Parenting

I was the observer of the action in this dream. The action took place in a city with a foreign feel. Maybe Italy. The streets were stone or bricks. Very narrow and winding. Alongside were tenement type houses two to three stories high. It could have been "Little" something in any major US city.

There was a plot to assassinate the President. A parade was winding through the narrow streets, filling them from building to building like when they run the bulls in Madrid. A shot rang out. The President was hit. I knew instantly he was paralyzed, not so much the body as the throat. He couldn't talk. There were Secret Service men there, one died, the others whisked the President away.

The dream switched where I am now in the dream. I am with an Italian family. Laura Bush, the First Lady, is there. The television is playing. A report on the President comes on and I move between Mrs. Bush and the TV. My job is to keep her from knowing until we can get out safely.

These people are part of the plot, I learn. They all seemed friendly, preparing food for when the President will arrive, all the while knowing he is supposed to be dead. It's now my job to get the First Lady out of here.

I began learning the art and science of dream interpretation in 1975. Since then I have intepreted hundreds of thousands of dreams. I understand dreams as communications from the inner, subconscious mind to the waking, conscious mind. We are so busy when awake, even priding ourselves on thinking of three, four, five things at the same time, that our subconscious mind must wait until the conscious mind is pushed aside in sleep to communicate its message. What we remember as dreams are these messages.

Dream images are universal in structure, just like the lines that make up the letters on this page. You and I have learned these lines represent something. When arranged in particular ways these marks make up what we call words, and words have meaning. In this way I can write my thoughts for you to read and consider. Hopefully the process enhances both our lives. These principles hold true in any communication, including dreams. The subconscious mind gives, the conscious mind receives. When we understand the language of our dreams, we understand the message.

This was a very unusual dream for me. Rarely have I had the President of our country in a dream. Violence is also rare. Interpreting the symbols in my dream I learn that I am willing to explore a part of my consciousness that has to this point been unfamiliar to me. It is like deciding to sing solo in public for the first time or to cultivate sacred dance. This part of my consciousness is familiar enough to me that I recognize it as a place in mind, a group of related thoughts and attitudes, but I am as yet uncertain how it fits into my life.

I move on for more of the message.

The dream indicates my ideas of will are changing. This has been by design, by my own making, but I have been unconscious, unaware, of its progress. The aggressive quality of Superconscious mind expresses as will and there has been a change in this that I have felt powerless to stop. It has seemed out of my control. The change is in my ability to express the Superconscious Self.

Because this experience is unfamiliar and insecure, I am relying on the receptive Superconscious (First Lady) quality which is relative to love. In my imagination, there is always the need to protect this part of myself. To hold back until it is time, until I am secure, consciously knowing what to do. It is the root of self distrust or doubt. This affects how I receive information, how I interpret what happens around me.

Whatever I learn with this attitude is physical only. It is fake, not real.

This dream illustrates the value of subconscious mind to conscious mind communication for the Indigo parent. Remembering the previous day's experience, I begin to see how the dream fits into my life. I can see what I'm thinking and doing through my subconscious mind's eyes. I will share with you what I learned and how it helped me to be a better parent.

The day before this dream, my husband and I visited a health practitioner to receive energetic/chiropractic bodywork. We included Hezekiah (then six) in our visit. We had visited this doctor every other month since shortly after Ki was born, and it proved beneficial for all of us.

However, I had noticed as the months passed and after the initial bi-monthly vists the doctor's attitude seemed to change. It was not so much that he took us for granted - gratefulness is a big theme for him - rather I sensed an arrogance that pushed me away. I asked Daniel if he noticed anything and other than a tendency for Dr. M. to talk more than he listened, he hadn't seen much. I figured it was something inside me and decided to keep an open mind to see where it might lead.

During one visit, Dr. M.'s arrogance came through loud and clear. With a big smile and handshake, he asked how I'd been. Thinking he really wanted to know, I said, "Good" and proceeded to say a few things about what had transpired since last seeing him. I intuitively sensed his attention had moved. When I noted he's stopped listening I stopped talking, putting my mind on what we were there to do.

In previous visits, I'd explored the distance I felt existing between us. I'd used my interactions with and reactions to Dr. M. to update some old ideas about approval and acceptance. Sometimes his disinterest or briskness would provoke feelings of dis-ease and hurt by touching a place in me where "not being understood" ideas still lived. On this day I was going to a new place with my attitudes about authority.

At the end of the treatment, Dr. M. said, "You needed to come in today."

He might as well have slapped my face.

His words were a neutral statement of fact. It was afterall the reason I was there for a treatment. It was not the words that touched that sensitive place it was his *attitude* behind the words. He resonated with those males who I had felt had been in contol of my life at different times – my grandfather, my dad, a teacher. I felt like lifting my chin and walking out like a petulant thirteen year old. I hadn't felt like this in years. I was hurt and I felt it in the twinge of pain in my chest. This man was so intrusive in my world today. He resonated with a past I thought I had outgrown. That thought was descriptive of my current frame of mind.

Here was the root, the cause, that had spawned countless attitudes of rebellion, insecurity, fear of failure and the like. They all stemmed from allowing the idea that someone else knows better about me than me. In other words, I heard Dr. M.'s words - they were innocuous - *and I heard his attitude* which said, "You don't know as much as you think. I'm the doctor, I know better." I was able to separate the elements of the experience, in this case the words from the intent.

Now I understood the growing reaction I felt to Dr. M. The impression that he didn't really care what I had to say, that he didn't listen, that he just wanted me to agree with his ideas or accept them, all of these were true at one time or another. What I came to admit this day was how I felt about all that. I felt hurt. I felt rejected. I felt let down, because I had come to him for help and he was the needy one! He hadn't taken control with that paternal "I know better attitude", *I* was the one giving up the control. I was doing this to myself. When I realized this *at the time it was happening*, I moved out of the habitual emotional reaction and gained an entirely new perspective of me and him.

My old reaction pattern would have caused me to avoid Dr. M. in the future. I would not have wanted to go back to him and I would have denied my part by avoiding the physical stimulus in the form of Dr. M. This would have postponed my learning once again.

It had taken over ten years to draw this learning opportunity to me since both the grandfather and teacher had died within three weeks of each other thereby removing them as a stimulus for this learning. That's why I keep going back to Dr. M. With Self awareness, I know what our encounters bring to me in the form of learning are worth a great deal more than the $25 treatments. He'll probably never know his real value to me because he demonstrates in many ways a closed mind although he outwardly appears engaging, positive, and helpful.

This brings us to what brought on the assasination dream.

On this day, the entire family was visiting Dr. M. On the way into town, a thirty minute country drive, Kiah had made it known he wanted to stop at the Niangua River to catch minnows. We were running late and since he had fallen asleep in the backseat, I decided to wait to stop during the return trip when we would have an unlimited amount of time. About five minutes from the doctor's office Kiah suddenly sits up and says, "When are we going to get to the Niangua?" When we told him we'd already passed it he was disappointed and upset.

By the time we arrived at Dr. M.'s, Kiah was out of sorts. Of course, these discordant thoughts and emotions are part of what visiting Dr. M. helps alleviate.

Daniel went first, then me. Dr. M. and I were just about done when Ki decided he'd come see mommy. He came in and hugged me as I laid on the table, then proceeded to climb up on top of me. For a second, my attention moved from Kiah to Dr. M., and I could sense his disapproval. I also knew because of my self-evaluation work that his judgement came from his insecurity of knowing what to do.

Daniel coaxed Ki off, although it was not an easy task. Ki's will had set in. But it bought us the time we needed to finish, then it was Ki's turn. From Hezekiah's point of view, Dr. M. had kept him from mom and he didn't like that, or him.

He further didn't like Dr. M.'s, military, take control attitude when he said, "All right Hezekiah. *Now* it's your turn!"

Kiah wasn't buying it. And he didn't want to get up on that table. Daniel and I tried to influence him – "You'll feel better, remember last time, etc." and had succeeded when Dr. M. decided to tell Dan about a farmer's market in town. This was an incredible display of the bad timing that results from the attitude of "ignore the kid when you don't know what to do."

As a result the moment was gone, and Ki wanted out.

Then came the bribe, "Apple or orange?" Dr. M. asked hoping this would spark Ki's memory of previous visits when Dr. M. had given Kiah a piece of fruit for being "a good boy."

Ki wasn't buying it.

Rejected, Dr. M. didn't receive this well. He was going to give Ki what he'd come for, or what he had coming, and would have if Daniel hadn't put a stop to it all by simply saying, "No, he doesn't want to, he doesn't have to. We're not going to force him."

Dr. M. was flustered. Obviously not used to such parental intervention that differs from his own.

As we paid the bill and left, the room was heavy with Dr. M.'s disagreeable opinions toward our actions. The old idea of "spoiling children" found its expression in the veiled contempt his voice now reflected. In the first few month's of Kiah's birth I had learned that the only way you spoil anyone or anything is to leave it unattended. It is true of food, and certainly true of human beings. Daniel and I are both attentive parents, spiritually, mentally, and emotionally, as well as physically.

I projected love to Dr. M. as we went out the door.

As we walked down the street, I shared with Dan what I had seen and understood. What Daniel had done was so important in our child's life. For him, it was natural, the way he always is. For me, it was a revelation. Here was the experience lacking in my life of the loving parent who acts on what is right and as a result protects his child from psychic as well as physical harm.

Dr. M. was determined to give Kiah a treament even if it would have hurt him, as certainly it would in his frame of mind.

In simple terms, Ki's dad had stood up for him and that support would remain with Kiah all his days – I knew it in a way my spirit rejoiced.

Here was Ki's "I know better about you than you" with a totally different outcome than I had experienced at his age. I had learned to stuff it, endure, and call it control. Ki was learning to wield his will, not stuff emotion. He was being heard and would grow up free of feelings that no one will listen.

The next morning when I awoke with the assassination dream I realized how much this experience had transformed my sense of authority. My old ideas of authority included a great deal of forced change (assasination). I had learned to cope by looking for what I could learn in situations, enduring them, making the best of them, until they were over. Images of my own childhood came back to me. I remember just enduring the time until my parents would come pick me up from my summer visit with my dad's parents, or until our family could move into our own house, away from my other grandparents. Waiting until I would graduate and could leave the small town where I went to high school. The pattern of waiting for things to be over continued into adult years; ...*until* I graduate from college, ...*until* I get a job, ...*until* I move to New Orleans. It repeated over and over in my mind. Here "getting it done" paraded as accomplishments. Here were the attitudes that stole my happiness, the compulsion to "get things over with" that I could now see left me with a string of physical accomplishments where learning was in hindsight more than in the present moment.

In teaching, whether a child, an adult, or myself, awareness of the present is everything. Right here is the joy of creation. Now is the thrill of Being, the reality of entrainment.

All of this came into my awareness as I examined the dream and the experience that stimulated it. When dreams can stimulate this kind of Self revelation, just imagine what they reveal to us about our Indigo children!

T
H
E
G
O
L
D
E
N
R
U
L
E

Iris, with handpicked bouquet for her mum

This book started with a story about Ki having his heart set on being with Paul Blosser. If you'll remember Hezekiah had agreed to postpone playing with Paul for a half hour so Paul could complete some work.

There's more to that story.

Once Ki and Paul agreed to meet, Hezekiah settled down. We read another story and then Carrie, one of the students living at the College at the time, arrived. All seemed well.

Less than five minutes had passed when Hezekiah came into my room with an upset, sad look on his face. He literally fell into my lap declaring, "I don't want to play with Carrie."

Stunned, I wondered what had happen to cause the change of heart. This was not the first time, Ki had come to me declaring he didn't want to be with so-and-so. The first time I was in denial: "Hezekiah!" I said in shock, "You don't mean that!" Of course that was lost on a three year old and I quickly realized my own emotional reaction of feeling badly for the person he said it to. I also knew if I was going to teach my son how to open his heart, I'd have to do better than telling him he didn't mean something that he did mean.

So I began a period of learning how to teach the golden rule – "Do unto others as you would have them do unto you." This is a difficult concept for a three year old. It ranks up there with sharing. There is not yet sufficient experience and information for reasoning to stretch the mind to those places without considerable emotional or physical damage. I learned to be patient. I learned to observe, to study, to remember, to teach by planting seeds.

I had to be willing to move through my own ego reaction of "what do others think?" Honesty with myself helped a lot there. On this morning, the understanding I had been praying for, working for, would come to fruition.

With a still mind, I rubbed Ki's back. He rocked himself on my lap, and I said what entered into my mind, "Ki, Carrie's planned on being with you all morning."

"I don't want to," he replied. Whatever it was, he wasn't going to go into it now. I might not agree with that, or want that, but I had learned to give him respect, to allow him space. I made no verbal reply.

After a few moments he said, "I want to watch *Ouch!*"

Ouch! is a segment of the *National Geographic Explorer* television show we had recently taped. Videos were becoming a concentration tool as well as an imagination stimulator during this time in Ki's life. In the weeks to come,

I would learn how Ki would sometimes use a show to focus his mind so he could assimilate – not the show, but the experiences from his day.

When Carrie came, I looked up and motioned to her that everything was okay, so she would know she was free to go. She seemed reluctant and so before leaving she called, "Hezekiah, I'll be back." He did not reply. I could tell Carrie was a bit hurt by Ki's rejection and I noted that I wanted to give her counsel and instruction. Right now, though, Ki needed my attention more.

I had slowly been learning about Ki's ability to communicate. I knew his way with words combined with his considerable emotional delivery could hurt even the oldest adult's feelings. He did not yet understand his impact on others. Teaching him how what he says affects others was a constant effort. When he said "I don't want to play with Carrie" I knew he was trying to describe his displeasure that Paul hadn't joined the play yet. Ki needed to learn how to describe his thoughts better.

In the present moment, however, he didn't want to be with Carrie since he couldn't be with Paul. We sat there for a few minutes, just being together.

As we sat watching bees, I planted seed ideas: "Carrie cares about you, so she makes time to be with you." "How do you think it makes her feel when you run away? When you say you don't want to play with her?" "How would you feel if someone you wanted to be with said they didn't want to be with you?"

Ki heard every word but he didn't say anything.

I just added, "Think about it."

After a short time, Carrie returned and Hezekiah was ready to play with her. Just like nothing had happened.

Ki went off with Carrie and I went back to writing.

About half an hour later a deeper awareness came to me. It came into focus as if by magic. Ki's "I don't want to play with so-and-so" came from disappointment! If he couldn't have what he wanted, he'd have nothing at all! It dawned on me that this morning's experience for Hezekiah was a Taurean lesson. He was hurt because he believed Paul had come to be with him, not mommy. His disappointment in finding out differently quickly fell into hurt, then into self deprivation – if he couldn't play with Paul, he wouldn't play at all! It's the Taurean trap of "if you're not going to play the way I thought we were going to play then I'll take my ball and go home!"

It had been difficult for me to identify because it is one of my karmic lessons also. How many times had I fallen into that same self-effacing, punishing thought. For years I found it easier to give up, to erase a desire, rather than respond to the change at hand it required of me. This was something very familiar. I knew I was still figuring out its cause and effect in my own life. I also knew I had learned a great deal about these Taurean energies (my sun and rising are in the sign of Taurus, and Ki's moon is in Taurus) that I could pass on to him.

I discovered a commonality in Ki and me that day that would help us both as long as I could remain generous in what I know rather than protective of him or defensive of me. I promised myself to be more compassionate when Ki would go through these emotionally charged experiences. I knew working with him through these would help me synthesize my own understanding and give him outlooks and ways of responding it took me decades to cultivate. I knew the next time he would not want to play with someone it would be different for both of us. Having identified the pattern of the emotional energies, I was now free to imagine how I could convey, teach, what I know. This is one of the blessings children bring us.

This was a golden moment for me. I was so grateful to perceive the truth – to recognize it and know I can help. That's every parent's desire, to help. Sometimes it gets lost with the passing of time, or when answers are not forthcoming.

I began to list what I'd learned in these first few years that had proven very helpful to me and others. The list is not so much what to do with a child, rather it is what to do with yourself. I hope it will help you keep the energy flowing, in yourself and between you and the child you love.

Seven Things I've Learned in the First Seven Years

1 *Embrace new awareness.*

By remaining open as a parent you are free to learn, every moment, every day. The more you know about learning, the more you can contribute to your child's learning.

Having been raised by neat (as in tidy) parents, messes were something I learned to be an authority on early in life. It was the reason I didn't create exotic meals until I lived on my own in college. Mom said I'd just make a mess in the kitchen so she rarely let me. The first time Ki wanted to help make a cake, these were the first thoughts that flooded through my consciousness.

I could have said no, you'll make a mess. And I have been known to utter those words in spite of myself. I could have said, not now, when you're older. (I've also heard myself say these words.) I could have said, I'll do it, which I did at one point say.

This first time, at first I said no. Quickly assessed my own thoughts, and said yes, we can Kiah. He had the best time playing in the flour. We wasted little. Didn't make that big of a mess, and it was a great cake!

Being conscious of your childhood experiences frees you into your learning. Being conscious frees you to be the parent you can be.

2 *Be willing to become conscious of how you were treated as a child.*

I could have allowed the strong prejudice against making messes to rule me and therefore my son's life. Being aware gave me respect for my mom and dad and their viewpoints. It gave me freedom to respect my own and it has greatly expanded the learning opportunities Hezekiah has. From chalk designs on the floor to sandbox cities and mud dams, I am learning to appreciate the nature of the physical as change as I learn to appreciate boy energy.

Becoming conscious can reach beyond cleaning up and doing homework. Being conscious means frank, bold honesty. For instance, it took years for me to value being a singular child. I thought I'd been cheated because I never had a brother or sister. In time what I realized was having been taught the spiritual principle that we are all brothers and sisters gave me exactly what I was looking for. It was something I had had all along, but my attachment to the idea that I had lost out by not having physical brothers and sisters had blinded me. In fact I would be in my thirties before I would realize that all my adult life I have lived with ever increasing numbers of people, only one of which (Hezekiah) is blood related. This is quite a transformation of consciousness, that has served me well.

3 Meeting up to your ideals.

This is one of the surprises of parenting. About the fifth week after Kiah was born I looked down at his sleeping angelic face and wondered what on earth I had done. It was 3:30 a.m. and Ki had finally decided to slip into a peaceful slumber. I, on the other hand, was anything but peaceful. I was mentally, emotionally, and physically drained from too many nights of dream deprivation. My energies were imbalanced in ways I wasn't even sure of, but could feel. I remember thinking, "Why can't you be like this all the time?"

I knew the answer, of course, but it didn't change what I was feeling. The thought did however set off a chain reaction that would change quite a few of my thoughts.

My life had been very full in those first 41 years. Populated largely by adults desiring to understand the mind and consciousness. I had invested a small percentage of my time directly with children, most of experiences came through students who were parents, and I was very clear minded about the benefits for children in educating their parents. I knew I could influence the lives of many more children through teaching their parents than through having children born of my own flesh.

Well, that all changed when Daniel and I married. After almost three years of marriage, the Universe blessed us with the means to receive a soul, our son who Daniel named Hezekiah. I had not spent large amounts of time imagining being a mother or the type of child I might have. That morning, however, I came face to face with the televised image of sleeping babes I had seen throughout my life. Children were supposed to sleep. A lot. Mine wasn't. The image was conflicting with reality and my frayed emotions were caught in the middle. Ki wasn't fitting the mold I had made in my mind. What was I going to do?

It may sound funny to someone who has not experienced those first few years, but the challenge of trying to fit your child into your ideals is one every parent encounters. Those who meet the challenge, internalize it for understanding, become free to live their own ideals. These people teach their children to create and fulfill their own ideals, and this is heaven for an Indigo.

With few preconceived parent-child ideas in my consciousness, so much of my experience with Ki is fresh, new, sometimes disturbing and frightening, always an amazing, joyous journey of discovery. This has helped me considerably in the area of acceptance.

Acceptance is essential in raising a mystic child. They will continually surprise and delight you as long as you control your mind not theirs. They don't take well to others throwing their weight around. Respect is essential, and the parent's ability for respect determines in large part the destiny of their child. The old idea of respect is fear, the "do it or else" level of mentality. The newer idea of respect is bargaining, the "do this now so you can do this later." Neither of these "work" on an Indigo because both ask the Indigo to go against his/her innate understanding that respect is born from love.

Mystic children respond to honesty and truth. They want to know what you think and why. They are not interested in hearing how you think they should be. They will live their own life, and if you think otherwise they will straighten you out with very little premeditation.

So the key is to live your ideals. Trying to live through an Indigo will cause suffering for parent and child. They are not on the planet to fulfill your abandoned desires or to be your clone. They are connected with their mission and they are resistant to anyone or anything that works against that. These are children who respond to heart early, and they need lots of it. Loving completely, loving spiritually, gives an Indigo the Self trust they need for opening their reasoning abilities.

I learned at birth that Ki was going to surpass any expectation I had conceived. This was not a calm, quiet babe who slept often and was a constant source of joy and pleasure. This soul was his own person from birth, and the quicker I admitted that, the easier it was going to be for all of us.

I would have many opportunities early on to resolve the lingering attachment to wanting him to be something he wasn't. I learned quickly, and I am eternally grateful for my metaphysical background for that. At times I felt like I went through what so many people talk about with their teenagers. Countless times in counseling parents I have witnessed the anguish, fear, and worry of not knowing how to communicate with their kids, of guilt about the past. Learning to be present from the beginning, to accept the soul who is your child completely and unconditionally, frees you to make more correct decisions than incorrect.

Knowing the basics of how mind works, whether the messages in dreams or the mechanics of reasoning, allows you the freedom to teach your child the skills needed for fashioning a rewarding life, spiritually and physically.

4 *Respect other people's opinions.*

I first recognized this when Daniel, Ki, and I were at a restaurant and Hezekiah would not be consoled. Only a few months old, we were learning to interpret and respond to his signals. I knew he was dry and had eaten not long before. I tried holding him, rocking, and each movement had a short term response. Ki persisted in being distressed which was escalating my feelings of "I don't know what to do" inadequacy.

At one point I watched my thoughts move from concern about why Ki was crying to concern about bothering people around us. Within just a few seconds my mind was flooded with thoughts of disrespecting other's space and "children should be seen and not heard" ideas, and emotions of embarrassment, frustration and even fear. Gratefully when I would get stuck in these old patterns, Daniel, not sharing my limitations, would be there to help which gave Ki the calmness he needed and me the opportunity to clear my mind so I could think straight.

I learned early that Ki and I would feed off of each other's attention as well as our emotions. In time we would both have the ability to calm one another, and we would realize the significant mental influence upon one another we are. This helped me see the places where my thinking could be swayed or controlled by my thoughts of what other people think. My parents were probably the richest resource for this kind of self awareness.

5 *Face what has been unconscious.*

I remember in my 20's when I was studying the final series of lessons, I thought "I used to think it wasn't fair to bring a child into the world, then I learned about reincarnation. Now, I think it wouldn't be fair for me to bring a child into the world because I have all this unconscious stuff I'd be exposing him to." What I meant was I was becoming increasingly aware of just how many things I had yet to learn or even become conscious of. I felt like I was starting all over, a child again, who had tons to learn. What did I know about raising a child?

After teaching hundreds of adults how to use their minds more completely and productivity, and after marrying my dear Daniel, bringing a child into the world took on new meaning. Since Hezekiah entered our lives, I have found that when you are invested in becoming conscious, children help accelerate your journey of enlightenment.

One of the earliest and most profound recognitions of this came when Ki was four. About every other month, Daniel and I would participate in the Spiritual Focus Weekends at the Moon Valley Ranch. This necessitated both of us being gone for three or so hours. These were the first forays into Ki relying completely upon others for his care. Usually the transitions were smooth but one morning he decided it wasn't okay for both of us to leave.

I tried enticing. I tried reassuring. I tried explaining. I tried distraction. I tried everything I could think of, and he was stuck. As I sat holding him, the thought went through my mind, "Next time I'll not tell him we are leaving. It's too hard on him." I knew it was an option. I knew he would be fine, in good hands, and would probably not even know we were gone unless for some reason Dan or I came up. I could have stayed there so easily. After all, I wouldn't have to have my emotions stirred up before the Intuitive Reporting work I was to do.

As the thoughts came through I knew I would not lie to Ki. Perhaps others would not see leaving out something as a lie but I did. It would be a lie of omission. I wanted to teach Ki to value the truth and going through these experiences with him was all part of it.

But my lesson was far deeper.

As I sat there with these thoughts floating through my head, much deeper thoughts began to surface. I remember the times I heard my mother say, "Don't tell Barbara. She'll worry." I had heard it countless times through the lips of someone else. This had been her practice and it had separated us all the way to her death. I knew it would require vigilance and will power to keep connecting with Kiah. I could now understand just how easy it would be to slip away and over time lose communication with a child. Those difficulties we face with our parents, the lack of understanding we feel on both sides, start at the beginning. They are either healed early or the dis-ease grows.

6 *"Acting out" is multidimension experience.*

I had heard the term "acting out" a few times. Each time it held a negative context, like a label people place on something they don't understand and don't want to think about anymore. When I heard the words used in reference to Ki it became clearer what people meant and what they thought about children's natural evolvement. Acting out is the refined ability to experience learning. It is the means by which all senses can be engaged which opens the door to subconscious experiencing, and therefore greater understanding.

There is such a fear in our society because so little is known and taught about the nature of consciousness. It is as if humanity is afraid of its own shadow, of who it is and what it is to become.

I welcomed Ki's acting out. It has become a natural part of his processing what he experiences. Sometimes he'll draw pictures of what he experiences, a very effective communication tool for involving the subconscious mind. Sometimes he'll walk back and forth, retelling the story and using a prop (usually a just-the-right size raptor) for emphasis and rhythm. To the unaware, he can sometimes look self consumed, dramatic, and even fanatical. To those with eyes to see and the heart to know, they appreciate the depth of concentration characteristic of all genius.

7 *"I'm not going to tell you" is one dimensional.*

The first time Hezekiah said this I inwardly cringed. I value openness and honesty. They are traits that enable the ego to evolve. They are the gateway to harmonizing the inner and outer minds. To hear anyone say, "I'm not going to tell you" was not a statement of distrust, it was a slammed door that left me powerless to help.

I was already conscious of these feelings from interactions with adult students. I had accepted that my interpretation of these words as a personal rejection was my own karmic learning. Not knowing how to deal with being shut out, had motivated me to become aware of other levels of connectedness. It had made me work harder, become more disciplined, be unconditional in my love. These understandings were brought to bear the first time Ki told me he wasn't going to tell me something.

Without my teaching experiences I would have become paranoid, wondering what I had done wrong that he wasn't telling me. Or I would have worried about what he had done wrong that he didn't want me to know about. Or I would have thought, this is the start, just wait until he's a teenager. Or I would have resorted to bargaining (if you tell me then...), or fear (just wait til I tell your daddy...), or anger (tell me or else!), or any host of images from sitcoms and movies I've filled my brain with over the past 40+ years. Being a student of metaphysics taught me how to create a still mind. Being a teacher taught me how to use it.

I stilled my mind and asked, "Where did you hear that?"

"*The Land Before Time*," Ki replied. *The Land Before Time* is an animated movie with several sequels using characters from the original story in new plots. Ki loved the original and wanted the new videos whenever they became available. What I was about to learn taught me what I needed to know about the influence of media on the young mind.

I thought back over the videos. I'd watched each several times with Ki. Daniel and I made it a practice to be present whenever Ki watched anything new on television, so we could answer his questions, offer him guidance and even comfort, when needed. I didn't remember any of the characters saying "I'm not going to tell you."

Ki did. "Sarah," he responded.

"Oh," I thought. Sarah was the headstrong stegosaurus with the gruff, physically-minded dad. Her mom never appears in the stories so you don't know what happened to her. Sarah's stubbornness had gotten the kid dinosaurs in more than one predicament. "So you want to be like Sarah?" I asked Ki quite honestly, without implication or judgement.

"No."

"You will be if you imitate her."

Ki thought about this for a while in silence. After a while he said, "Do you know who I want to be?"

"No, who?"

"Petrie," the pterodactyl.

"Why?" This was a most curious choice.

"Because he is small and has two wings."

I learned a lot in this conversation. Certainly more than if I'd allowed my busy mind to take over. I learned the origin of the statement, that Ki did not think he was stubborn, and that he liked being loved and free. That was quite a lot for not being told something!

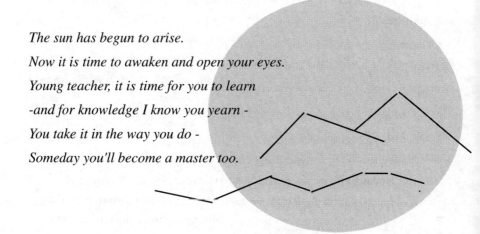

The sun has begun to arise.
Now it is time to awaken and open your eyes.
Young teacher, it is time for you to learn
-and for knowledge I know you yearn -
You take it in the way you do -
Someday you'll become a master too.

–Miranda Mobley, age 14

Respecting the Teacher in your Midst

So much of respecting a child is giving them space. I have learned just as much observing Hezekiah as I have interacting with him. He cherishes others' presence, while valuing his independent thought. Many times I have seen him get others involved in doing something – drawing a picture, building a toy, baking cookies, even cleaning a room – while he paces back and forth a short distance away telling one of his stories. Independent endeavors in shared space. You can feel the connectedness.

Much of the mystical child's experience is beneath the surface. It is emotionally tangible, and mentally rich. This is one of the reasons we have requested Intuitive Health Analyses on Hezekiah every six months since he was born. We wanted the objective, subconscious perspective available from these reports. As a result each has been affirming and illuminating for us as teachers/parents.

Your child is a soul that has come to earth. You have the privilege and responsibility of guiding that soul through the early, dependent years of infancy and adolescence. The reality that the little body contains a very wizened soul usually comes early. Kiah was telling me the quadruple syllable names of dinosaurs at the age of three. Five-year-old Iris teaches anyone and everyone about the complex world of Barbie. Eleven-year-old Ian teaches how to live peaceably through his poetry. Fourteen-year-old Briana creates and teaches a sacred dance for Camp Niangua. Listening to Indigo children tells you what they know.

Every individual is special, created equally and endowed by their Creator with certain inalienable rights. When we honor our divinity, we uplift all of humanity. As the inner wisdom is fostered, through encouragement and respect, from birth, we all reap the benefits many times over, every day of our lives.

May peace be with you all ways. I send you my circle of love.

10 Resources I Recommend

I have been most fortunate in drawing to me what I need when I need it. Seemingly out of the blue I began receiving Chinaberry and MindWare just at the time I was looking for books, puzzles, and good quality audio tapes. Here are the most valuable tools I have found thus far. If you know of more, please write me so I can share them in future publications.

1 Chinaberry...

What I appreciate about Chinaberry the most is the commentaries for each entry. These first person accounts tell me what I want to know: how the kids (and parents) respond to the book, tape, or game. This is where I found *Shiva's Fire* and all the Jim Weiss audio tapes. Jim's renditions of Hercules, Rip Van Winkle, and King Arthur have made traveling in the car with Ki a true pleasure. Contact them at 800-776-2242 or visit their website at www.Chinaberry.com. Other catalogues filled with ideas and products include: *MindWare* (where I first learned of the Multiple Intelligence concepts), *HearthSong, Young Explorers, Rosie's Hippos, Back to Basics.*

2 How to Multiply Your Child's Intelligence

and other books by Glenn Doman and Janet Doman
Institute for the Achievement of Human Potential 1-800-344-MOTHER
The message is simple, respect your child's intelligence from the moment of birth. These books reflect Doman's pioneering research into the field of child brain development. Subjects include how to read, math, encyclopedic knowledge, and physical development. Instructions in developing thinking and reasoning include simple daily programs. The words you see Ki and Dr. Dan reading on page 84 came from the Institute. Videos that support brain development include the *baby einstein, baby mozart,* and *baby bach.* These "video board books" fascinate children (and adults!) while stimulating brain pathway growth. 1-800-793-1454

3 Core Knowledge Series by E.D. Hirsch, Jr.

1-800-238-3233
What Your Kindergartner Needs to Know, ...Your First Grader, etc. books. Ki and I have already read through three of these books, several times, and are embarking on our fourth. It's the well-rounded approach (literature, world history, music, art, science, and math) in these books that I appreciate most. They make planting seeds of knowledge easy. Each book provides a progressive structure I can use as a springboard for subjects I want to explore with the youngsters. For example, Bri and I used the sixth grade book to round out her coursework between the ages of 11-13.

4 Anything from DK (Dorling Kindersley)

Hezekiah began watching *Eyewitness* videos at the age of two. Exquisitely executed, they cover a subject from many viewpoints in just 30 minutes. The how-we-did-it sections at the end of many of these shows is where Ki began to form his ideas for videography. The *Eyewitness* books are excellent companions, and a growing number of CD-ROM's are also available. DK products have a distinctive look, conveying their subjects with many pictures and interest-keeping words. For DK's complete line of knowledge products visit www.dk.com

5 Reader's Digest books often have the same attitude as DK books. The information is complete, expansive, and fully illustrated in color. Young ones "ooo" and "ahh" over the pictures while you "ooo" and "ahha!" with each idea. From *Big Book of Space* to *How Weather Works* these books are like subject encyclopedias. Barnes & Noble Booksellers are now producing some equally fine volumes.

6 Biographies of Famous People

Kids love stories, particularly about when you were their age. Reading bios that describe the young Lincoln or Disney or King is an excellent way to introduce youngsters to the values and virtues that lead to greatness. Our favorites are the *Childhood of Famous Americans* series published by Aladdin Paperbacks and widely available. Bri enjoyed The Princess Diaries a semi-autobiographical series of books for young adolescents.

7 Cricket Magazines

It started with Babybug, a board book Ki enjoys even now at 7. When he was a year old I read to him, now he is beginning to read to me. In the meantime he moved on to *Ladybug* (for 2-7) and *Spider* (6-10). Filled with stories, riddles, songs, crafts, games, and lots of color illustrations these magazines are worth keeping. This company also produces specialized magazines in science, history/art, and literature. 1-800-827-0227 or visit www.spidermag.com

8 Book of Virtues edited by William Bennett

The spinoff books are equally valuable. This eclectic array of stories and poems teach universal truths the inner Self resonates with. We have made plays from the stories, illustrated them, memorized poems, and written songs just with the stories in this volume. "The Legend of the Dipper" is a story Ki and I will probably be reading decades from now. Timeless is the appropriate word for this work. Another book of this caliber that Ki wants to hear again and again is *A World Treasury of Myths, Legends, and Folktales* told by Renata Bini.

9 Dover Publications

Dover is a godsend. With their $1 sticker books on everything from reptiles to space ships, these publications are easy on your pocketbook. From the diaries of da Vinci to books about mathematics, from Plato's *Republic* to *The Koran*, Dover offers every subject you need at an affordable price. Visit www.doverpublications.com.

10 Teach Your Child to Read in 100 Lessons by Siegfried Engelmann. This

book teaches/refreshes YOU on what you need to know to teach reading. That is its secret. So wonderfully simple, easy, quick (20 minute lessons) and fun.

Available from the School of Metaphysics

Intuitive Reports

Daniel and I requested the first Intuitive Health Analysis on Hezekiah when he was a month old. That story is described in the book *First Opinion.* Since then, every six months, Ki gets a check up, not so much for the physical exam as the insight given into his mental and emotional systems. To me a regular Intuitive Health Analysis is one of the resource requirements for being a conscious parent. For more information contact us at 1-417-345-8411.

Coursework

When you are ready to study we have School of Metaphysics branches throughout the Midwest. The first cycle of our course is available through correspondence for those not within driving distance of a school. Making time for this study will reward you, your spouse, and the children in your life many times over, afterall children learn what they live. When you record and interpret your dreams , practice concentration and listening, and meditate daily, your child has an example to follow that will serve him for years to come.

Spiritual Focus Weekends

The weekend Teresa and Ernie attended is especially designed for parents. The Conscious Parenting intuitive profile is an amazing tool for bringing out your best qualities as a teacher/parent and addressing those unconscious aspects that it is time to let go of. For information on this session contact us directly. Weekends to explore and strengthen your inner resolve center on becoming a healing presence, fulfilling your purpose in life, creating the life you desire, and learning/deepening your meditations. Call, write, or visit www.som.org for more.

Parenting

Parents are in every walk of life. Their relationships with those they love influence their attitudes away from home. The same Essential Life Skills discussed here can be applied in every life situation. We can show you how. Teachers are available to meet with your group, club, organization, class, or business. Call the School of Metaphysics nearest you to arrange for a representative to come to you.

To learn more

tapes and books for youngsters

PeaceMakers Songbook *& Cassette*   *$12.00*

Kanakam Meditation
set includes cassette tape, booklet, & wooden beads   *$12.00*

Radiance, *a millennium myth for all ages*   *$8.00*
Radiance, *a book on tape*   *$8.00*

Circle of Love, *an illustrated poem about connectedness*
$10.00

Together Videos
amazing videos to watch (and do) with the Indigos in your life

Essential Life Skills #6
Feeding Your Child's Imagination
the magic of drawing with your child
with artist Adam Campbell   *$20.00*

about youngsters

Interpreting Your Dreams for Self Discovery
by Dr. Laurel Clark & Paul Blosser   *$12.00*

Mystical Children: The Three New Races
a lecture by Dr. Barbara Condron
recorded at the College of Metaphysics   *$8.00*

Universal Peace Covenant

Peace is the breath of our spirit.
It wells up from within the depths of our being to refresh, to heal, to inspire.

Peace is our birthright. *Its eternal presence exists within us as a memory of where we have come from and as a vision of where we yearn to go.*

Our world is in the midst of change.
For millennia, we have contemplated, reasoned, and practiced the idea of peace. Yet the capacity to sustain peace eludes us. To transcend the limits of our own thinking we must acknowledge that peace is more than the cessation of conflict. For peace to move across the face of the Earth we must realize, as the great philosophers and leaders before us, that all people desire peace. We hereby acknowledge this truth that is universal. Now humanity must desire those things that make for peace.

We affirm that peace is an idea whose time has come.
We call upon humanity to stand united, responding to the need for peace. We call upon each individual to create and foster a personal vision for peace. We call upon each family to generate and nurture peace within the home. We call upon each nation to encourage and support peace between its citizens. We call upon each leader, be they in the home, place of worship or labor, to be a living example of peace for only in this way can we expect peace to move across the face of the Earth.

World peace begins within ourselves.
It arises from the spirit seeking expression through the mind, heart, and body of each individual. Government and laws cannot heal the heart. We must transcend whatever separates us. Through giving love and respect, dignity and comfort, we come to know peace. We learn to love our neighbors as we love ourselves bringing peace into the world. We hereby commit ourselves to this noble endeavor.

Peace is first a state of mind.
Living peaceably begins by thinking peacefully. Peace
affords the greatest opportunity for growth and learning
which leads to personal happiness. Self-direction promotes
inner peace and therefore leads to outer peace. We vow to
heal ourselves through forgiveness, gratitude, and prayer.
We commit to causing each and every day to be a fulfillment
of our potential, both human and divine.

**Peace is active, the motion of silence, of faith, of accord, of
service.**
It is not made in documents but in the minds and hearts of
men and women. Peace is built through communication.
The open exchange of ideas is necessary for discovery, for
well-being, for growth, for progress whether within one
person or among many. We vow to speak with sagacity,
listen with equanimity, both free of prejudice, thus we will
come to know that peace is liberty in tranquility.

**Peace is achieved by those who fulfill their part of a
greater plan.**
Peace and security are attained by those societies where the
individuals work closely to serve the common good of the
whole. Peaceful coexistence between nations is the reflection of man's inner tranquility magnified. Enlightened
service to our fellowman brings peace to the one serving,
and to the one receiving. We vow to live in peace by embracing truths that apply to us all.

We stand on the threshold of peace-filled understanding.
We come together, all of humanity, young and old of all
cultures from all nations. We vow to stand together as
citizens of the Earth knowing that every question has an
answer, every issue a resolution. As we stand, united in
common purpose, we hereby commit ourselves in thought
and action so we might know the power of peace in our
lifetimes.

May peace be with us all ways.
May Peace Prevail On Earth.

Additional titles available from SOM Publishing include:

PeaceMaking: 9 Lessons for Changing Yourself, Your Relationships, & Your World
by Dr. Barbara Condron ISBN: 0-944386-31-8 $12.00

The Tao Te Ching: Interpreted and Explained by Dr. Daniel Condron
ISBN 0944386-30-x $15.00

Atlantis: The History of the World Vol. 1 by Drs. Daniel & Barbara Condron
ISBN 0944386-28-8 $15.00

Interpreting Dreams for Self Discovery by Dr. Laurel Clark & Paul Blosser
ISBN: 0944386-25-3 $12

Karmic Healing by Dr. Laurel Clark ISBN: 0944386-26-1 $15

The Bible Interpreted in Dream Symbols by Drs. Condron, Condron, Matthes,
Rothermel ISBN: 0944386-23-7 $18

Spiritual Renaissance: Elevating Your Consciousness for the Common Good
by Dr. Barbara Condron ISBN: 0944386-22-9 $15

Superconscious Meditation: Kundalini & the Understanding of the Whole Mind
by Dr. Daniel R. Condron ISBN 0944386-21-0 $13

First Opinion: Wholistic Health Care in the 21st Century by Dr. Barbara Condron
ISBN 0944386-18-0 $15

The Dreamer's Dictionary by Dr. Barbara Condron ISBN 0944386-16-4 $15

The Work of the Soul by Dr. Barbara Condron, ed. ISBN 0944386-17-2 $13

Uncommon Knowledge Past Life & Health Readings by Dr. Barbara Condron, ed.
ISBN 0944386-19-9 $13

The Universal Language of Mind: The Book of Matthew Interpreted
by Dr. Daniel R. Condron ISBN 0944386-15-6 $13

Permanent Healing by Dr. Daniel R. Condron ISBN 0944386-12-1 $9.95

Dreams of the Soul - The Yogi Sutras of Patanjali by Dr. Daniel R. Condron
ISBN 0944386-11-3 $13

Kundalini Rising: Mastering Your Creative Energies by Dr. Barbara Condron
ISBN 0944386-13-X $13

To order write: School of Metaphysics
                  163 Moon Valley Road
                  Windyville, Missouri 65783   U.S.A.

Enclose a check or money order payable in U.S. funds to SOM with any order.
Please include $4.00 for postage and handling of books, $8 for international
orders. A complete catalogue of all book titles, audio lectures and courses,
and videos is available upon request.

Visit us on the Internet at *http://www.som.org*   e-mail: som@som.org